Preface and Acknowledgements |

CW01507358

This monograph represents the culmination of an ongoing personal and academic interest in the work of François Ozon. For the past decade, Ozon's unique position within French-language filmmaking has stimulated my enthusiasm for both cinema studies and theories of gender and sexuality. The present study provides an overview of François Ozon's career to date, highlighting his unrestrained, voracious cinephilia; his recurrent collaborations with women screenwriters (Marina de Van, Emmanuèle Bernheim) and actresses (Charlotte Rampling, Ludivine Sagnier, Valeria Bruni-Tedeschi); and the trademarks of his cinema. I also perform a detailed reading of nine feature films, organized thematically into three segments, in order to reveal the continuity of his cinematic endeavors. The introductory section discusses all of Ozon's available short films from 1988 to 1998, his work following his formal training at the Fémis film school (with special emphasis on *Une robe d'été* [1996]), his unique status within the French film industry, and the ways transgression and desire pervade his cinema. The second section, "Paternal Monsters," focuses on the ambiguous position of the father figure and on Ozon's inclination for genre b(l)ending and artificiality in *Sitcom* (1998), *Les amants criminels* (1999), and *8 femmes* (2002). In the third section, "Mourning Sickness," I examine how various forms of mourning (a returning obsession in Ozon's output) affect the lonesome, self-absorbed characters in the more naturalistic *Sous le sable* (2000), *Swimming Pool* (2003) and *Le temps qui reste* (2005). The final section, "Foreign Affairs," focuses on couples and the difficulties of conjugal life. It also underscores the director's taste for foreign actors and locations and his passion for adaptation—or, more accurately, reinterpretation—in *Gouttes d'eau sur pierres brûlantes* (2000), adapted from an early play by Rainer Werner Fassbinder; *5x2* (2004), inspired by two films from directors Ingmar Bergman and Jane Campion; and *Ricky* (2009), based on British writer Rose Tremain's short story "Moth."

Most short films and all feature films discussed in this study are available on DVD in the United States, except *Angel* (2007), an English-language film that has not yet been distributed in North America (except in French-speaking Canada) and that I chose not to treat in detail here. *Ricky* is still playing in American theaters as I write, but is soon to be available on DVD with IFC Films. When I met François Ozon in Paris for an interview in October 2009, he provided crucial insight on the short films that regularly appear in his filmography but have never been widely available to the public—notably, his only documentary, *Jospin s'éclaire* (1995), and the unreleased, Fémis-produced *Une goutte de sang* (1991) and *Peau contre peau* (1991). Ozon also spoke candidly about the recurring themes and obsessions in his cinema, the collaborative process of his craft, and his latest film, *Le refuge* (2009), which is scheduled for release in the United States in late 2010. I thank him for his kindness and am grateful for his flexibility and responsiveness in setting up our interview.

For their invaluable feedback and encouragement at various stages of the writing process, I thank Judith Mayne, Elena Past, Jumi Hayaki, Vinay Swamy, Julian Bourg, Caroline Yezer, Nathalie Dupont, and Philippe Dubois. I thank Joan Catapano and James Naremore of the University of Illinois Press for their support. I am grateful to the Department of Modern Languages and Literatures at the College of the Holy Cross, to Francisco Gago-Jover, Laurence Enjolras, the Holy Cross Grants Office and Committee on Faculty Scholarship, as well as Charles Weiss and Steve Vineberg for helping me fund both research trips to Paris that were needed for the completion of this book. I also thank the staff members at the Bibliothèque du film and at the Inathèque in Paris for assisting me in accessing printed and multimedia materials on Ozon's cinema. A special thanks to Michael Gott for his translation into English of my interview with François Ozon and, for their moral support, Sara May Plourde, Kathy Lanning, Heather Skowood, Jerome Anderson, Adele Parker, Will Edwards, Jessie Yamas, Kerri Galloway, Charles Gillilan, Dan Berglund, Andy Lang, and Randi Polk. Unless followed by a parenthetical reference, all information about the films' admissions and box office profits come from the Internet Movie Database website. Unless otherwise noted, all translations from the French are my own.

François Ozon

Contemporary Film Directors

Edited by James Naremore

The Contemporary Film Directors series provides concise, well-written introductions to directors from around the world and from every level of the film industry. Its chief aims are to broaden our awareness of important artists, to give serious critical attention to their work, and to illustrate the variety and vitality of contemporary cinema. Contributors to the series include an array of internationally respected critics and academics. Each volume contains an incisive critical commentary, an informative interview with the director, and a detailed filmography.

A list of books in the series appears at the end of this book.

François Ozon |

Thibaut Schilt

**UNIVERSITY
OF
ILLINOIS
PRESS**
URBANA
CHICAGO
SPRINGFIELD

Frontispiece: From the book 5 *Minutes*
by photographer Jennifer Gregori.

Library of Congress Cataloging-in-Publication Data
Schilt, Thibaut.
François Ozon / Thibaut Schilt.
p.   cm. — (Contemporary film directors)
Includes bibliographical references and index.
Includes filmography.
ISBN-13: 978-0-252-03600-2 (hardcover : alk. paper)
ISBN-10: 0-252-03600-x (hardcover : alk. paper)
ISBN-13: 978-0-252-07794-4 (pbk. : alk. paper)
ISBN-10: 0-252-07794-6 (pbk. : alk. paper) 1. Ozon, François, 1967—Criticism
and interpretation. 2. Ozon, François, 1967—Interviews. I. Title.
PN1998.3.O958S35   2011
791.4302'33092—dc22   2010028737
[B]

Contents |

The Fabric of Desire |

When François Ozon's full-length film *Sitcom* débuted in 1998, he had already earned a solid reputation as a talented and innovative short film director. In 1996 the fifteen-minute *Une robe d'été* (*A Summer Dress*) received awards at festivals in Brest, Grenoble, Pantin, Dublin, Geneva, Los Angeles, and Locarno; was shown at the Cannes film festival; and earned a nomination for a César (France's equivalent of the Oscar). That same year, one commentator wrote, speaking of Ozon and fellow filmmaker Laurent Cantet: "Any informed film festival organizer would bet his mother's life on the cinematic future of these two" (Malandrin 12). His predictions turned out to be accurate, for Ozon and Cantet alike. But Ozon was in no particular hurry to prove this journalist right. Before he made the jump into feature filmmaking, he enjoyed the frantic pace and freedom associated with the production of short films and experimented with multiple formats, lengths, and genres. Throughout the 1990s he collected festival prizes and caught the attention of more film critics: both *Cahiers du cinéma* and *Positif,* France's most well-known film magazines, wrote pieces on Ozon's shorts months before the release of *Sitcom*. Not yet thirty years of age, Ozon had become a force to be reckoned with. One of the most provocative aspects of Ozon's cinema, and one of the reasons for his early critical attention, concerns the audacious and candid ways in which his films tackle issues of gender, sexuality, and identity.

Consider the scene in *Une robe d'été* where we see a young man riding a bicycle clad in a blue, flowery woman's dress. The light fabric undulates gently in the wind, and a tracking shot records the cyclist's journey back to the vacation bungalow he shares with his boyfriend. Luc (Frédéric Mangenot) wears the garment out of necessity rather than choice—all of his possessions were stolen on the beach—yet a faint smile appears on his face, signaling that he is beginning to relish the cross-dressing episode. Luc is unsure of his sexuality. Although he and Sébastien (Sébastien Charles) are lovers, he willingly experiences heterosexual intercourse with Lucia (Lucia Sanchez), a Spanish tourist he meets on a deserted beach in the Landes region of southwestern France. It is Lucia's dress Luc wears on his way home, and the impromptu encounter with the uninhibited woman enables him to experience for the first time both opposite-sex lovemaking and opposite-gender impersonation. The tracking shot of Luc riding his bicycle is repeated toward the end of the film. This time, however, Luc is not wearing the dress (he is in fact meeting Lucia to return it), but has it wrapped around his neck. We see the fabric undulate more intensely now, suspended in midair, almost floating (fig. 1).

Fabrics in movement, like that undulating dress, occupy Ozon's cinema nearly as much as characters themselves, fluttering in a light summer breeze, twirling to the sound of music, or brushing against luxurious marble floors. The concept of fluidity, of which the dynamic movement of clothing in general and the airy summer dress in particular are powerful representations, is at the core of Ozon's cinema, from his early career as a short film director some twenty years ago to the present. The originality of this enfant terrible of French cinema, an expression used profusely in the French and international press to describe Ozon (Hain 277), lies in his filmmaking style. Drawing on familiar cinematic traditions—the crime thriller, the musical, the psychological drama, the comedy, the melodrama, the period piece—Ozon's cinema simul-

Figure 1. Luc and the dress in *Une robe d'été.* |

taneously defamiliarizes those traditions in the eyes of the spectator. His films consistently, even obsessively, venture into uncertain sexual territories, represent human interaction in unanticipated ways, and altogether defy generic categorization. As one scholar observed, Ozon's films contribute to several genres "without ever approximating to formulaic Hollywood-style 'genre cinema'" (Ince, "Cinema of Desire" 131). The iconoclastic director thus continually evinces a reticence to fit inside the boundaries of mainstream cinema, engaging in a cat-and-mouse game with critics and often wrong-footing the spectator. The rapidity with which he releases his films—at least one a year—is enough to make him noteworthy. His ability to go from burlesque ensemble-cast farces to intimate, heartrending tragedies bedazzles some and perplexes others. And despite the occasional critical tendency (Gallic or otherwise) to discount his work, Ozon's inventiveness has made him one of the most recognizable French directors outside his motherland: *Sous le sable* (*Under the Sand,* 2000), *8 femmes* (*8 Women,* 2002) and *Swimming Pool* (2003) were significant popular successes both in France and abroad, and the latter film (shot partially in English) grossed an impressive ten million dollars in the United States in 2003.

"The Fabric of Desire" is the overarching title I have chosen to describe my commentary on Ozon's entire film career to date. This reference to *fabric* and its close link to *desire* refer both to textiles in movement in my discussion of *Une robe d'été* and, more generally, to the importance of clothing choices in Ozon's cinema. Although I will occasionally make references to the director's choice of costumes throughout this book, the term *fabric of desire* also functions on a figurative level, pointing to the complex renegotiation of desire present in all of Ozon's films. In the latter case, *fabric* becomes synonymous with *structure* or *framework*. It is now time to ponder the unique relationship between fashion, gender, sexual identity, and cinema.

In *Undressing Cinema: Clothing and Identity in the Movies,* Stella Bruzzi declares that on the screen "clothing exists as a discourse not wholly dependent on the structures of the narrative and character for signification" (xvi), suggesting that the significance of clothes goes well beyond their function as props. In François Ozon's case, clothes, flowing fabrics in particular, weave their way into his films, connecting dots and providing metaphorical seams between what some may see as perplexingly eclectic cinematic endeavors. According to his longtime collaborator, costume designer Pascaline Chavanne, Ozon participates in the selection of the color, fabric, texture, and shape of all costumes that appear on camera (main roles, supporting roles, but also extras), making clothing choices an essential part of his aesthetic preoccupations (Wild Bunch 33). Naturally, the dynamic movement of clothing often occurs during the musical interludes that Ozon incorporates, in true camp fashion, into most of his projects. Thus we witness, in close-up, the suede, burgundy-colored miniskirt of transsexual Véra (Anna Thomson) in *Gouttes d'eau sur pierres brûlantes* (*Water Drops on Burning Rocks,* 2000) as she jiggles to the German sound of Tony Holiday's "Tanze Samba mit mir." In *8 femmes* there are many opportunities to see dresses dance, but particularly memorable is the twirling frock worn by Virginie Ledoyen's character in the first musical number sung by the younger daughter Catherine (Ludivine Sagnier). In *Swimming Pool* it is Julie/Sagnier's turn to sway in a tight-fitting brown dress as she tries to seduce both the man and the woman present in the room. There is an instance in *5x2*'s (*Five Times Two,* 2004) wedding scene when the bride, Marion (Valeria Bruni-Tedeschi), swings the bottom part of her wedding gown as if she were dancing the cancan. A culminating scene in *Angel,* a lavish costume drama released in 2007, involves the gliding of a dramatic, vermilion-red ball gown. In addition to capturing the vivacious beauty of Ozon's cinema, these seemingly unrelated moments share something crucial in that they create narrative junctures that enable moving garments and the characters who wear them to flourish (in all senses of the term) in front of the spectator's eyes.

I want to propose that despite tremendous diversity in terms of cinematic choices (on generic, formal, and thematic levels), Ozon's oeuvre is decidedly consistent in its desire to blur the traditional frontiers between the masculine and the feminine, gay and straight, reality and fantasy, auteur and commercial cinema. The moving fabrics mentioned above are a leitmotif that visually represents the permeability of those frontiers. Before examining Ozon's early cinematic career, the shorts leading up to his feature-film début, *Sitcom*, let us return to *Une robe d'été* and follow the trajectory of the blue dress, which, as the title indicates, is the true heroine of the story. Despite its fifteen-minute running time and outwardly uncomplicated narrative, this impressive, understudied tour de force contains many elements that will be found in Ozon's later films.

Une robe d'été opens to a close-up shot of a Speedo-wearing young man's crotch, revealing Ozon's firm desire to present the male body and male sexuality straightforwardly in contemporary French cinema. The film recounts the adventures of bored eighteen-year-old Luc, on vacation with his boyfriend, Sébastien, who decides to go to the beach alone one afternoon. Luc's escapade, which leads to the young man's first sexual encounter with a woman, is triggered by a musical number featuring French gay/pop icon Sheila's "Bang Bang," a French-language version of Cher's 1966 song of the same title. Using the bungalow's terrace as a stage, Sébastien sings and dances to the tune, which comes out of a small tape player behind him, as he looks not in Luc's direction but straight into the camera, violating the invisible fourth wall between characters and spectators in genuine musical fashion. The French version of the song, similar in content to its original English-language counterpart, though with some variations for the sake of poetics, describes the bittersweet memories of a woman who recalls her early teens and first love with a boy her age (ten years old). The "Bang Bang" onomatopoeia repeated in the chorus and preferred over the French equivalent "Pan Pan," represents both their "boyish" childhood games, which involved fake shooting and playing dead, and the narrator's broken heart when, years later, the now grown man left her for another woman.

When asked about the profusion of musical numbers scattered in his films, François Ozon responds that songs are precious time savers: "A single song summarizes four pages of dialogue, conveys feelings, and instantaneously reveals something about the characters' psychology. It's extremely convenient. In my short *Une robe d'été,* two guys are having a fight, I play Sheila's 'Bang Bang,' and everyone knows what will happen next" (Murat, "Femmes égales"). Sheila's simple, unpretentious lyrics indeed foreshadow Luc's "adulterous" affair with Lucia, yet they introduce a hint of violence that remains relatively unseen in the film, from which feelings of treason and pain caused by love are ultimately absent—much unlike, as we shall see, most of Ozon's violence- and crime-ridden oeuvre. Beyond the film's universe, Sébastien's number also foreshadows Ozon's later attempts at experimentation, particularly with regard to genre blending and the intrusion of ostensibly incongruous, unannounced musical interludes, such as the campy four-person dance sequence in the melodrama *Gouttes d'eau sur pierres brûlantes* and the eight musical numbers in the whodunit *8 femmes.* Finally, looking back on French film history, the number clearly winks at Jacques Demy's earlier musical films, especially his most popular 1960s achievements such as *Les demoiselles de Rochefort* (*The Young Girls of Rochefort*), which was released in 1967, a year after Sheila's song featured here. The evocation of the cinema of Demy, the unchallenged master of French musicals and whose cinema has aptly been called "*follement gaie*" (Boursier 39)—literally, "crazily gay," though *folle* also means "fairy" or "fag"—may well cause pleasure for the viewer, queer or otherwise. Luc, on the other hand, is less impressed. Clearly embarrassed, he precipitously leaves the premises after worrying what the neighbors will think of Sébastien's "fag music" (*musique de folle*).

What follows is an uncommon variant of the typical gay coming-of-age narrative, as Luc's pleasurable heterosexual encounter with Lucia comes *after* multiple (unseen) same-sex lovemaking sessions with Sébastien. Another play with traditional gender roles occurs as the experienced female character Lucia initiates the encounter with the less-experienced Luc. The young man originally downplays his relative experience by claiming to be a virgin, but later confesses that he has in fact been sexually active, just not with a woman. Lucia candidly asks if he is gay, and he responds in vague, elusive terms, "No, no, but I'm on vacation with a (male) friend,

and sometimes . . . ," obliquely indicating that he has had sex with Sébastien but is nonetheless unsure of (or wishes not to have to choose) his
sexual orientation. The next sequences further complicate Luc's identity
construction. Back on the beach from the woods, Luc realizes that his
clothes have vanished: he is forced to wear the Spanish woman's dress
home (fig. 2). Upset at first, he gets used to the idea, and even comes to
enjoy it. Wearing the dress eventually enables Luc, whose name clearly
establishes him as Lucia's male counterpart, to embrace both his feminine
side and his relationship with Sébastien. Luc fancies the cross-dressing
episode so much that he does not take off the garment when he arrives
home, which also arouses his boyfriend sexually. In the end, after he is
shown sewing the dress, which has been ripped in the heat of the action
(with Sébastien), his one-afternoon stand, Lucia, tells him that she does
not want the dress back: "It's yours; you might want to wear it again." The
film ends with a close-up shot of Luc staring at the ocean offscreen with
the dress wrapped prominently around his neck and the non-diegetic
strains of Sheila's "Bang Bang" lilting in the background.

Luc's appropriation of the dress recalls Judith Butler's well-known
comments on drag as a powerful and parodic imitation of gender that
in fact exposes the imitative structure of gender itself (137). Luc's in-
voluntary act of transvestism may well begin as a *comedic* transgression

Figure 2. Lucia and Luc in *Une robe d'été*. |

of traditional gender roles: Lucia's lucid and perfectly delivered remark "your choice: you either go home in a dress or you go home stark-naked" coupled with the initial image of Luc uncomfortably stomping down a sand-covered hill in the dress are both intentionally humorous moments. However, the initial shock of Luc's new persona quickly subsides, for the young man as well as the spectator, opening up a space for a pluralistic, unlabeled view of gender, sexuality, and identity. Bruzzi distinguishes only two ways in which transvestism has been approached on film so far: "Whereas comedies of cross-dressing [such as *Mrs. Doubtfire*, Chris Columbus, 1993] seek to affirm the inflexibility of sexual difference and so leave gender binaries unchallenged, the androgynous image [contained in films such as *The Adventures of Priscilla, Queen of the Desert*, Stephan Elliott, 1994] strives to break such oppositions down" (xx). In the second category of films, to which we may add *Une robe d'été* and the gender-blending *Ma vie en rose* (*My Life in Pink*, Alain Berliner, 1997), released just a few months after Ozon's short, the discrepancy between anatomical sex and constructed gender is, according to Bruzzi, "celebrated not hysterically dismissed" (xx).

Une robe d'été is nothing if not celebratory, contrasting sharply with earlier, guilt-ridden French films about homosexuality such as Patrice Chéreau's *L'homme blessé* (*The Wounded Man*, 1983). Despite the increased presence of queer characters in contemporary filmmaking, an altogether guilt-free film about gender b(l)ending and sexual freedom is a rare occurrence in French cinema, as Thierry Jousse of *Cahiers du cinéma* reminds us: "[*Une robe d'été* is] a summery, sexual comedy about the circulation of adolescent desire, presented with boldness, humor, lightness, frankness, elegance, poetry, a combination which is extremely rare in French cinema . . . It is . . . the cinema of [Jacques] Rozier coupled with that of [Pedro] Almodóvar; in short, something utterly new" ("Ozon!" 12). The "circulation of desire" Jousse mentions here is enabled, as we have seen, by the physical transit of a blue summer dress between a woman and two men. The main character is given a chance to vacillate between anonymous (yet safe) sex with a woman to sex with a steadier male partner, thus presenting a surprising alternative to a more well-known adulterous scenario, that of married "heterosexual" men who seek anonymous sex with other male partners. In fact, the film goes as far as suggesting that the young man's opposite-sex affair and subsequent cross-dressing help him better accept himself and his fluctuating sexuality. The transformation is flagrant: in the opening scene, he leaves the bungalow because he dislikes Sébastien's musical tastes and prancing ways. Upon returning from his tryst in the woods, Luc starts humming the very Sheila song he denigrated in the first scene. When Sébastien asks him if the neighbors saw him wearing the dress, Luc retorts: "Who cares about the neighbors?" The dress seems bestowed with talismanic powers that liberate its wearer from the confines of fixed identity.

The film's last image of Luc with the dress dramatically wrapped around his neck—a vision Ozon insists on by showing us two consecutive shots of it, from the back and the front of the young man's head—resembles a modern, airier version of a regal lace ruff. This unisex fashion accessory for the neck was worn most notably by both Elizabeth I and Louis XIII in the sixteenth and seventeenth centuries. So we as spectators, in addition to having, like Luc before us, fallen victim to the dress's charms, have gone from an image of a black Speedo (the film's opening shot), the anti-dress par excellence and a rigidly masculine garment, to a wind-flapping, androgynous, rufflike item of clothing, thus representing a trajectory from the form-fitting to the free-flowing. Of course, not all the accoutrements in Ozon's cinema display the same ability as our summer dress to open up a third space of gendered and sexual identities for anyone who puts it on. They may, however, occasionally inform us about Ozon's unwavering determination to fashion a panoply of protean, unbound characters who scarcely ever choose a predictable path.

Before examining the colorful cast of characters in the short films Ozon wrote and directed between 1988 and 1998, a ten-year period upon which I will concentrate in this section, let us pause briefly to explore the director's own path to filmmaking. François Ozon was born in Paris on November 15, 1967, and grew up in the heart of the French capital. The oldest child of a large middle-class family (he has four siblings), his parents both worked as teachers and encouraged their children's access to literature and the arts (Martin). According to Ozon, the couple "did not exercise any kind of censorship; my brother, my sisters and I were allowed to read and watch anything we wanted" (Murat, "Femmes égales"). Little François was a precocious film enthusiast. As a young child, he devoured Disney and Tarzan movies and was equally fond of *Sissi,* a 1950s film trilogy about a nineteenth-century Austrian empress starring a young Romy Schneider. Describing his early filmic tastes, Ozon declares: "I already loved melodramas, lavish costume dramas . . . However, I quickly became attracted to films that were not meant to be watched by children: while my parents thought I was watching a John Ford movie on channel three, I remember watching, at ten years old, [Alain] Resnais's *Providence,* which (it may sound pretentious) I completely understood. I remember the state of shock [Roberto Rossellini's] *Germania anno zero* [*Germany Year Zero*] put me in, the story of a kid my age who commits suicide in Berlin's ruins" (Murat, "Femmes égales"). If Ozon's parents did not restrict their children's enjoyment of the arts, they were well aware of their elder son's ardent, if not obsessive, cinephilia. Occasionally they would use it against him. As punishment for being naughty, the boy was prohibited from watching films on television or going to the movies. Ozon later admitted that this association between cinema and the forbidden excited him and made film even more desirable (Ozon, "Entretiens *Amants*").

Although Ozon has never directly discussed it in interviews, his fascination for film may have emerged from his parents' own interest in the medium. His mother, Anne-Marie, regularly bought *L'avant-scène cinema,* a specialized, semimonthly film periodical that includes a complete post-montage film script of a particular motion picture, whether classic or recently released. Ozon would read the issues avidly and remembers that of Claude Chabrol's lesbian-portraying *Les biches* (*Bad Girls,* 1968) particularly fondly. He also recalls feeling an intense frustration when, after seeing the film for the first time a few years later, the sexual tension between the characters played by Stéphane Audran and Jacqueline Sassard was only alluded to and did not turn into an on-screen sexual act (Murat, "François Ozon"). His father, René, an amateur videographer equipped with a Super 8 camera, shot numerous family vacation films throughout the boy's childhood. Ozon reminisces: "One day, I decided [that my father's Super 8 camera] was mine, and I became responsible for shooting those vacation films" (Ozon, "Entretiens *Amants*"). Ozon's more serious directorial ambitions developed somewhere during that time period (his mid to late teens). After doing some modeling as a child and participating in school plays as an actor in his early teens, the adolescent Ozon realized that he disliked being in the spotlight but preferred, in his own words, "pulling the strings."

He also came to the conclusion that directors, unlike actors, were the ones with the "true power." As a director he could tell stories and could reveal many things about himself while hiding comfortably behind the camera (Ozon, "Entretiens *Sitcom*"). Despite a solid desire to become a filmmaker, Ozon was uncomfortable admitting it to people around him, confirming the aforementioned association between filmmaking and prohibited acts and desires: "At sixteen years old, I was very ashamed to admit that I wanted to make films; it was something I knew I wanted, but that I couldn't reveal. Whenever I did reveal it, I would blush, I felt ill at ease, as if the idea of wanting to make films was linked to something profoundly intimate; as if such a 'confession' exposed me" (Ozon, "Entretiens *Amants*"). This feeling of discomfort, this lack of connection with the world around him, did not simply concern his professional aspirations but also made him "a rather violent and agitated teen, very averse to authority in general and paternal authority in particular . . . Although the oldest, I was not a good example to follow, nor did I wish to be. I got written up for setting my middle-school's bathroom on fire; I ran away from home several times and often had to deal with the police regarding various petty crimes" (Murat, "François Ozon").

After this rebellious adolescent phase and upon completing high school, our director-to-be followed a fairly conventional itinerary in terms of education and training. Ozon majored in fine arts (*arts plastiques*) before specializing in cinema at the Université de Paris I, where he obtained a master's degree in the late 1980s. One of his university professors was Joseph Morder, an independent underground director whose filmography includes countless works shot in Super 8, Morder's preferred format. The professor encouraged his students to create as many short-length pieces as they could. Ozon complied enthusiastically and became, as he calls it himself, a "bulimic" filmmaker (Goudet, "Court métrage" 94). In three years he made approximately thirty Super 8 films at the rate of one film a month, sometimes two a week. The shorts were usually written in two or three hours and shot in one weekend, using nonprofessional actors composed of family and friends. Although never officially released at the time of their production, three of those silent Super 8 shorts are now available to the public. They appear as special features of the "Collection François Ozon," the simultaneous (French) release of five DVDs in early 2002. The comprehensive DVD collection came out astonishingly early in Ozon's career, barely three years after *Sitcom* appeared in theaters, and features his first four full-length films made between 1998 and 2000—*Sitcom, Les amants criminels (Criminal Lovers*, 1999), *Gouttes d'eau sur pierres brûlantes*, and *Sous le sable*—as well as most of his 35mm short films from the 1990s. Ozon himself selected the three early Super 8 shorts he wanted people to see and paired them with thematically similar feature films: *Photo de famille* (Family Portrait) is a special DVD feature of the dark comedy *Sitcom*, while *Les doigts dans le ventre* (Fingers in the Stomach) and *Mes parents un jour d'été* (My Parents on a Summer Day) appear in tandem with the psychological drama *Sous le sable*. Many Super 8s from the same period were ruled out, including one in which Ozon plays a cross-dresser and others the director judged "too intimate" (Ozon, "Entretiens Collection").

In 1988 Ozon convinced his parents to appear in a short film in which one of their own children would brutally assassinate them. According to the director, they gave their unhesitating assent, arguing that "it is very good therapy. That way, you won't have to do it in real life" (Ozon, "Entretiens *Sitcom*"). The seven-minute film, titled *Photo de famille*, was shot in December 1988 in the Paris apartment of the Ozon family and stars, in addition to René and Anne-Marie Ozon, their son Guillaume and daughter Julie (François remains behind the camera). What is immediately striking upon first viewing is the film's level of formal complexity on the one hand and its thematic similarities with Ozon's subsequent work on the other, particularly such murderous family dramas as the short 35mm film *Victor* and the features *Sitcom* and *8 femmes*. *Photo de famille* opens with a moving shot of the face of Donissan, a dying priest played by Gérard Depardieu in Maurice Pialat's *Sous le soleil de Satan* (*Under the Sun of Satan*, 1987). The next shot shows a mother, father, and daughter captivated by the image of the agonizing clergyman before the word *Fin* (The end) appears on the television screen (cinephilic homages such as this one will become, as we shall see, one of Ozon's trademarks). Like the priest, they, too, are about to die, at the hands of the son of the family, who makes his entrance in the following dinner scene.

The film, then, starts as an innocuous family home movie: the editing is simple, and the camera records everyday occurrences such as watching television, setting the table, and sharing a meal. But *Photo de famille* quickly becomes a tragicomic story of death and murder. The ominous change from quotidian routine to acts of irreversible violence is announced cinematically via a fast-paced montage of the future victims' relaxed, smiling faces as they enjoy what will be their last supper. One by one, the son murders his parents and sibling, now each in a different room, using various methods: he poisons his mother's coffee, stabs his sister in the back with a pair of scissors, and suffocates his father to death with a pillow. Ozon uses the medium playfully, experimenting with such techniques as extreme high and low angles, backlighting, and play with shadow, all reminiscent of cinematic representatives of the crime thriller and horror genres. Despite such stylistic sophistication, the film still feels artisanal, and the spectator may find the murder scenes more amusing than terrifying. The last scene, nevertheless, is as unexpected as it is morbid, for the family portrait of the title becomes quite literal: Guillaume drags every dead family member across the apartment, lines them up on the sofa, and, after setting the timer on a picture camera, joins them (all smiles) for a macabre group photograph. One critic saw this scene as Ozon's "own protest against treating photography as a mass social practice for integrating and protecting the family" (Cavitch 318). More generally, Ozon's very first film questions the authenticity of familial bonds, a theme that reappears notably in *Sitcom, 8 femmes, 5x2,* and *Le temps qui reste* (*Time to Leave,* 2005).

Also in 1988, Ozon directed the jarring Super 8 *Les doigts dans le ventre.* The twelve-minute film recounts the daily plight of a young bulimic woman, and the title (Fingers in the Stomach) refers to the process of self-induced vomiting (or "purging") that usually follows a binge-eating session. Given Ozon's repeated use of the word *bulimic* to refer to himself as a director, the film may be read as a metaphor for his own insatiable appetite to direct. The camera trails the unnamed woman (played by Ozon's friend Judith Cahen) for an afternoon as she wanders the streets of Paris's fifth arrondissement (the Lycée Henri IV, rue Soufflot, and Luxembourg Gardens are clearly identifiable landmarks) and inhales any food she can find: croissants, hamburgers and fries from a fast-food restaurant, cold cassoulet right out of a tin can, granola bars from a grocery store, and cookies once she arrives home. The film alternates between sequences representing motion (the search for food) and stasis (its insatiable consumption). The woman's solitary roaming about the streets of the capital coupled with occasional point-of-view shots of her surroundings are reminiscent of Agnès Varda's 1961 New Wave classic *Cléo de 5 à 7* (*Cleo from 5 to 7*), which features another itinerant, anguished Parisian woman. The binging in *Les doigts dans le ventre* culminates with the woman's drinking an entire bottle of vegetable oil, a common lubricating method that precedes purging. A trip to the bathroom, where she makes herself vomit all she has ingurgitated, follows while a high-angle shot of the toilet bowl provides an unobstructed view of the episode. Her stomach empty, she is now ready to share a family meal with her mother and brother in the final scene.

Although the film is silent, the French-speaking, lip-reading spectator may easily understand the woman's last words (*J'ai faim*/I'm hungry) seconds before its homophone *Fin* flashes on the screen. The former phrase is uttered twice earlier in the film. In a scene that is "queer" in both senses of the term, a red-haired female acquaintance encounters the bulimic woman on a park bench. In an unanticipated, homoerotic attempt to soothe the suffering woman's pain, the redhead gently lifts her friend's shirt and begins to caress her bare stomach before moving on to her face and lips. Presumably upon realizing that for the bulimic woman, human contact cannot replace the comfort of eating—her repeated *J'ai faim* during the caressing session implies that food matters more than anything else at that moment—she provides the hungry woman with two cans of food and leaves after a gentle kiss on her cheek. Stylistically speaking, the outdoor, on-location shooting of *Les doigts dans le ventre* allows for a variety of camera movements, such as the tracking and panorama shots not present in *Photo de famille,* and a repeated motif: recurring images of the heroine shot behind bars, fences, and palisades that underscore her entrapment and the inescapable character of her food addiction. Even the white shirt with blue horizontal stripes she wears throughout the film—a uniform of sorts, especially reminiscent of prison inmate garb—reinforces for the keen spectator that sense of self-imprisonment.

Two years later Ozon requested the acting talents of his parents once again in the impressive, action-packed *Mes parents un jour d'été.* The title (My Parents on a Summer Day) acknowledges a direct familial or autobiographical link between the filmmaker and the subjects on screen:

"my parents" are clearly Ozon's parents. Yet that link is deceptive. The film, like *Photo de famille,* is an elaborately constructed work of *fiction* that may well contain autobiographical elements, but it is certainly not an improvised or semi-improvised family home movie. Shot in August 1990 in and around the villages of Clamecy and Armes in France's Burgundy region, this eleven-minute treat is, like most of Ozon's concoctions, a story with a twist. Throughout the narrative, the characters played by René and Anne-Marie Ozon—here credited as Anne-Marie Godard, her maiden name and/or a wink at the rebellious Franco-Swiss director Jean-Luc Godard—are shown as leading at once separate and connected lives with, the film seems to insist, a fairly conventional distribution of gender roles: René rides his bicycle while Anne-Marie eats breakfast alone; he drinks wine, she goes shopping for groceries; she cooks, he smokes a pipe; he goes out for a swim in the nearby river, she stays out on their summer home's back patio to read fashion magazines. When they *are* shown together—for example, as Anne-Marie tends to her husband's knee wound after he crashes into a haystack with his bicycle, or as they share a meal together on the terrace—they seem to alternate between enjoying each other's company and getting on each other's nerves.

About halfway through the film, the tone changes and the story takes an unforeseen turn. While on a hike together, Anne-Marie stands behind her husband and extends her hand with the evident intent to push him off a cliff to a probable death. She resists the temptation and appears shaken by her murderous instincts, but her husband fails to notice anything and they walk back down the hill, arm in arm. Back at the house, a game of Scrabble ensues in which the words *couple, cuckolds, fight, lovers,* and *bicycle* are displayed on the board. René's attempt at cheating (at Scrabble) triggers another argument: he is out of vowels, an ironic metaphor for the near peril he unwittingly just narrowly escaped, and steals some from the bag of letters. Anne-Marie catches him red-handed and immediately stops playing. In the final scene they meet up in a nearby cemetery and embrace amorously, seemingly reconciled, next to an unnamed child's grave with which they both seem familiar—the graveyard setting reappears notably in *Regarde la mer* (*See the Sea,* 1997), *Sitcom,* and *Sous le sable.* In this ambiguous ending, the spectator is left to wonder what triggered Anne-Marie's desire to kill, or at the very least harm, her husband. The film appears to suggest that multiple causes such as the daily grind of living together, a possible past or present adulterous relationship, and the painful story of a lost child are precisely, however paradoxically, what simultaneously keeps them together and tears them apart.

These three Super 8 films—*Photo de famille, Les doigts dans le ventre,* and *Mes parents un jour d'été*—were directed when Ozon was between the ages of twenty and twenty-two, with very limited budgets and no film crew to speak of. Despite that, they contain many of the elements that would become Ozon's cinematic signatures: candid, unfiltered portrayals of human behavior; a taste for (preferably patricidal) murder; a fascination for the gruesome; a postmodern tendency to toy with generic conventions; and, in the case of *Les doigts dans le ventre,* an ephemeral yet clearly queer intrusion.

In 1990 Ozon entered the Fémis (Ecole Nationale Supérieure des Métiers de l'Image et du Son), the Paris-based national film school that in 1986 replaced the equally reputable IDHEC (Institut des Hautes Etudes Cinématographiques). The prestigious school provides technical and artistic training for various film and audiovisual trades, including directing, screenwriting, editing, and distribution. Ozon specialized in film direction, relinquished his Super 8 camera, and began shooting in 16mm and 35mm, with much higher budgets and valuable collaborators. In a school famous for molding directors with personal visions—that is, young inheritors of the still influential, auteur-centric French New Wave of the late 1950s and early 1960s—Ozon studied under the tutelage of former New Wave directors Eric Rohmer and Jacques Rivette, and film critic, actor, and director Jean Douchet, among others. Although Ozon generally speaks of his Fémis training in positive terms, he admits that his eclectic filmic tastes put him at odds with his fellow students: "[I loved film] unconditionally, from 1950s Hollywood to Pialat. Seeing *Passe ton bac d'abord* [*Graduate First,* a 1979 film by Pialat about a group of youth in northern France] was like a slap in the face for me: a carbon copy of what I was living at the time . . . When I was a Fémis student, this refusal to choose between two apparently contradictory cinemas put me in an uncomfortable situation vis-à-vis my colleagues" (Murat, "Femmes égales"). Here, Ozon explains his disinclination to choose between France's well-known and persistent attachment to the notion of "auteur cinema," which originates in postwar French film criticism, and commercial filmmaking (Hollywood, French, and otherwise), whose box-office aspirations are often seen, in the French critical context, as incompatible with quality. Although Ozon ultimately chose Maurice Pialat as the subject of his master's thesis—his topic was "the ways in which the social act of shooting a film affects the end-product in Pialat's cinema"—he was reticent to decide between the cinemas of Jean Renoir, Jean-Marie Straub, Martin Scorsese, and other masters. Unlike many of his Fémis peers, he strongly believed there was nothing antithetical about liking all of them equally (Frodon).

During the four years when Ozon was a student at the Fémis, he directed seven short films. *Une goutte de sang* (A Drop of Blood), *Peau contre peau* (Skin against Skin), *Le trou madame* (Madame's Hole), *Deux plus un* (Two Plus One), all made in 1991, and *Thomas reconstitué* (Thomas Reconstituted, 1992) were never released or shown at festivals and remain unavailable to the public. Also made during that time are Ozon's first 35mm films, *Victor* (1993) and *Une rose entre nous* (*A Rose between Us*, 1994). Like all of his shorts from 1993 onward, with the notable exception of the 1995 documentary *Jospin s'éclaire* (Jospin Lights Up), these two films have been released on DVD in both Europe and North America. They mark the beginning of the filmmaker's ongoing collaboration with cinematographer Yorick Le Saux, with whom Ozon has worked regularly since the Fémis years. The fourteen-minute *Victor* revisits the theme of parricide present in *Photo de famille* and gives it a surrealistic twist. Reminiscent of Buñuelian satirical farces like *Le charme discret de la bourgeoisie* (*The Discreet Charm of the Bourgeoisie,* 1972), this *huis clos* follows Victor (François Genty), a twenty-something awkward and suicidal man who lives with his parents in an opulent country mansion. Determined to end his life, this only child writes a farewell letter, heard in voice-over against the backdrop of sepia-tinted family photos, to apologize to his parents for what he is about to do. We see Victor, who feels "unworthy of living," insert a gun into his mouth, but we realize in the next sequence that he has decided to shoot his parents as well before killing himself. The maid arrives in the parents' bedroom too late to save her masters, but just in time to prevent Victor from committing suicide.

There ensues an outlandish story in which Victor goes on with his life as if the couple were still alive (a prelude to Marie's delusion in *Sous le sable*). He dresses them, combs his mother's hair, and sits the two at the dinner table; he places them on a swing in the property's park, he lies down on the bed with them, polishes his father's shoes, and so forth. The maid is aware of the situation but finds it quite amusing and terribly convenient: she begins to wear the jewelry and clothes of the late lady of the house and encourages her lover to steal from her (now former) employers. The elderly gardener, from whom Victor seeks advice on what to do next, is equally unaffected by the tragedy and insists upon reciting platitudes about the joys of gardening and the beauty of nature. Left to his own devices, Victor breaks away from an upbringing most likely filled with bourgeois restrictions. For example, we see him slurping his soup loudly at the dinner table, eventually abandoning his spoon and lapping up the beverage straight from the plate, like a dog. Later, Victor sniffs his father's crotch before slobbering on the dead man's man face and barking at him. While the two corpses are dangling from the swing, he masturbates naked on the grass and ejaculates on his chest and face (the camera shows a medium close-up of Victor from the waist up). The young man's sexual awakening climaxes in a threesome lovemaking session with the maid and her male lover, followed by a scene where Victor buries his parents in the park under the indifferent eyes of the gardener. Now liberated from the chains of an allegedly repressive past, the young man is ready to go out into the world, and the film's last shot presents a smiling Victor as he is about to board a train away from his provincial, rural life.

Like *Victor*, the screenplay of *Une rose entre nous* was cowritten by Ozon and fellow Fémis student Nicolas Mercier; it also marks Ozon's final project at the school before graduating in 1994. Echoing *Victor*, the twenty-seven-minute film concerns the sexual awakening of a young male *ingénu*. The story follows shy and inexperienced Paul (Rodolphe Lesage) as he goes to sexual extremes to please his new love interest, Rose (played by Ozon's friend Sasha Hails). In the first scene, Paul meets and is instantly smitten by an eccentric, carefree British woman who walks in for a hair coloring at the salon where he works as an apprentice. After a champagne-filled night at Le Palace, a gay-friendly Parisian nightclub patronized by wealthy businessmen in three-piece suits and eccentric drag queens alike, Rose forces Paul into prostituting himself with an older man so that they can both earn some extra cash. Paul complies quite hesitantly—in his words, he doesn't "feel like getting fucked in the ass"—and it is suggested that this first (safe) sexual experience with a man may well be his first sexual experience tout court. Paul's complaisance ends upon discovering that Rose lied to him about the amount of money made from the trick: she cashed three thousand francs from Paul's john, gave one-third to Paul, and kept the rest. The two quarrel, make up, and eventually have sex in Rose's apartment; from the start, Rose had promised her body as a reward to Paul's willingness to engage in prostitution. By the end, it is clear that they have developed feelings for each other, despite Rose's manipulative ways. Paul's loss of virginity, however, comes with a loss of naïveté. In the last scenes, Paul leaves Rose's studio apartment to buy breakfast and promises to return immediately. Instead, he goes to work at the hair salon, croissants in hand, with a confidence and defiance he lacked in the film's introductory scene. Whether he will elect to see Rose again is up to the spectator to decide.

There are evident thematic similarities between *Une rose entre nous,* in which Ozon briefly cameos as the boyfriend of Paul's coworker Rémy (Christophe Hémon), and *Une robe d'été,* made two years apart from each other. The two films chronicle erotic encounters between summer-dress-wearing, strong-willed, sexually adventurous non-French women and virginal, malleable, sexually ambivalent younger men. *Une rose entre nous* is also the first of many Ozon films to include a musical interlude: Rose/Hails's piano-accompanied performance of Charlotte Julian's maudlin yet playful "Fleur de province" (originally released in 1972) about a provincial woman, or "flower," determined to find success in the French capital and meet a handsome Prince Charming. Like *Une robe d'été*'s "Bang Bang," "Fleur de province" functions as a narrative shortcut that provides information without recourse to lengthy dialogue and, in the case of *Une rose entre nous,* justifies the Englishwoman's flowery first name. The song also informs us of Rose's past as an ambitious country girl who longed for the big city as well as her present as a woman with greedy, rather than romantic, aspirations. Significantly, Ozon changed the original lyrics to Julian's chorus from "I came to find . . . a little Prince Charming who will give me lots of children" to a more fitting "Prince Charming who will give me lots of money." Partly because of those modified lyrics, the woman's developing feelings for Paul at the film's conclusion appear all the more genuine in that they are out of character. The thorny, covetous Rose has, in Ozon's words, "fallen into her own trap" by falling for a man from whom she initially intended to obtain nothing but money (Ozon, "Entretiens Courts").

In 1994 Ozon graduated from the Fémis school and began his ongoing, faithful relationship with Fidélité Productions' Olivier Delbosc (whom Ozon met at the Fémis) and Marc Missonnier, who financed or cofinanced the majority of his fiction films, short and full-length, from 1994 to 2007. "Bulimic" as ever, Ozon manufactured more short-length films at the steady pace of two or three a year. Most of the pieces made during that period were presented at national and international film festivals, amassed countless prizes, and some were shown on French television. Nineteen ninety-four saw the release of *Action vérité* (*Truth or Dare*), awarded best short film by the French Syndicate of Cinema Critics. Two films followed in 1995, *La petite mort* (*Little Death*) and *Jospin s'éclaire,* a fifty-two-minute documentary about the presidential campaign of left-wing politician Lionel Jospin. *Une robe d'été,* nominated for a César and awarded the Leopard of Tomorrow at the Locarno film festival, came out in 1996 and is perhaps Ozon's best-known, most critically acclaimed short film to date. It was followed by the medium-length, fifty-two-minute *Regarde la mer* and two additional shorts released the same year as *Sitcom* (1998): *Scènes de lit* (*Bed Scenes,* Prix Panavision at the Avignon film festival) and *X2000,* rewarded at festivals in Seattle, Oberhausen (Germany) and Ourense (Spain). When questioned in 1997 about the frenzied pace with which he wrote and directed films, Ozon replied by quoting Jean-Luc Godard and named other directors whom he admired: "The short-length format allows you to 'practice your scales' [*faire ses gammes*], as Godard says, to train [*s'entraîner*], to take risks. I love bulimic filmmakers, who make films that are not always great achievements, but . . . [who] have built a phenomenal career, like Fassbinder, or Chabrol, who alternates between third-rate flops and magnificent films" (Goudet, "Court métrage" 94). Fassbinder and Chabrol are, not coincidentally, directors to whom Ozon will often be compared later on in his career.

Four-minute *Action vérité* is the director's first post-Fémis work and has been described as the short film that "best summarizes Ozon's cinema, a curious mélange of rules and transgressions" (Nicouleaud 10). The film, shot exclusively in close-up, starts rather innocently as a truth-or-dare game between four adolescents, two girls (Hélène and Rose) and two boys (Paul and Rémy). The youngsters sit in a circle, question one another about past romantic and sexual relationships, and perform various predictable acts, well within the context of the game, including same-sex and opposite-sex kissing and fondling. The result of the last dare brings the jolly party to a halt, and the film ends in uncomfortable and complete silence: Rose is asked to reach into Hélène's panties to "find out how it smells." When Rose pulls out her hand from her friend's underwear, it comes out covered in menstrual blood. Here, Ozon's stylistic choices reveal a bold inclination to show what many filmmakers would consider wanton and uncinematic (the bloody hand) while maintaining strict rules—those of the game, but also formal rules, such as the exclusive, oppressive use of the close-up shot. The coexistence of rules—be they generic, cinematic, or narrative—and transgressions is indeed a format found in many other films, "as if the filmmaker liked nothing more than to choose a genre, a frame [*cadre*] only to better test its boundaries and overstep them" (Nicouleaud 10).

The longer, more complex *La petite mort* came out the following year, in 1995, and immediately precedes the release of *Une robe d'été*. Ozon pointed out a strong connection between the two films: "Free from the Law, the Father, and the adult world, [*Une robe d'été*] was made against *La petite mort*. But also thanks to it: I needed to make a film completely rooted in transgression and guilt before making this liberating film" (Ozon, "Entretiens Courts"). *La petite mort* follows a taciturn, emotionally unavailable young gay photographer named (yet again) Paul (François Delaive) who is forced to interrupt his latest artistic project and confront his painful past. Encouraged by his sister, Camille (Camille Japy), who runs the family business, he reluctantly agrees to visit his estranged, dying father at the hospital. When the father fails to recognize him, Paul runs away from the room and begins a journey of self-discovery that will ultimately improve his relationship with both his sister and his loving partner, Martial (Martial Jacques). The father, whose homophobia toward his son is strongly implied, dies before the two can reconcile. But after Camille gives her brother a baby picture of him sitting on his dad's lap, the ending insinuates that Paul will finally allow himself to leave his torments behind and move on with his life.

The film opens with a black-and-white picture of Paul as an infant.

The voice-over of a now grown-up Paul recollects: "The day I was born, my father was abroad on a business trip." After seeing the picture of his newborn son, the father allegedly exclaimed, "This monster cannot possibly be my son: he is way too ugly." As an adult, Paul has been trying to (re-)create his own interpretation of photographic beauty. His current project involves taking photographs of various men, including himself and his lover, at the exact moment of orgasm, in an attempt to visually capture this ephemeral "little death." One commentator sees a direct correlation between the baby picture and the young man's artistic endeavor: "What [Paul] is doing, then, is attempting to erase photographic pain with photographic pleasure, as well as in some sense . . . evading and ultimately trying to control reality—his reality. The central sequence of the film (structurally and thematically) has Paul sneak into the hospital where his dad lies on his deathbed and take pictures of his naked body as he sleeps" (Bingham). But Paul and the spectator are in for a big surprise. Back in the darkroom of his own apartment, he realizes that his father has his eyes wide open in one of the nude photographs he took at the hospital. Paul cuts out his father's eyes from the photo and then holds the photo to his face as he looks at his (and his father's) reflection in the mirror. The gesture may well signify that Paul cannot escape his biological origins; it has also been read as a "symbolic castration of his father" as well as something that "evokes the common association of photograph and death mask: an imprint of the real aligned with mortality" (Cavitch 321, 319; see Cavitch's article for a rare, extended reading of the film). It is only after he decides to accept the bonds he shares with both Camille and his father that he can look forward to the future; the mother is mentioned in the opening sequence but remains inexplicably absent from the rest of the narrative. Sometime after the chilling death mask scene, a phone call from Camille announces their father's death, triggering Paul's reconciliation with his sister and his ability to accept Martial's affection: the two of them have passionate sex immediately after he hears the news, which contrasts with Paul's earlier refusal of the sexual act. This reaction confirms Cavitch's contention that "pleasure [is] at the core of the experience of mourning" (313).

Ozon's mise-en-scène highlights the stages of Paul's cathartic voyage into becoming a (self-) loving individual, especially in the way his spatial movements, and initial lack thereof, are represented. Paul's character evolves from a state of complete stasis at the beginning (he mostly stays indoors and is reluctant to leave the apartment), to one of relative mobility midway through the narrative (he is driven by his sister to the hospital; he takes the train home, but his journey is abruptly interrupted when the ticket taker asks him to get off at the next station), to spatial freedom in the end. In the second-to-last scene, Camille reveals to Paul at a café that her childhood and her relationship with her father have been difficult as well and, in an attempt to help her brother overcome his familial anxieties, gives him a tin box of old pictures she claims his dad wanted him to have. The following scene is in contradistinction to Paul's earlier inertia or interrupted movements—the motionlessness of the photos with which Paul surrounds himself echoes his own initial spatial stillness. As he leaves Camille to catch the métro, Paul is seen riding up an escalator in a high-angle shot, a literal upward movement toward the platform and symbolic ascension toward a life free of demons (it is significant that Ozon chose to shoot the scene in an elevated, outdoor portion of the Parisian métro rather than in a more common underground station). It is on this very platform that Paul opens the box full of pictures and discovers, in an envelope labeled *Paul,* the picture of him and his father. The film ends in a close shot of his face, which is eventually obstructed by the arrival of a train, a fast-paced lateral movement again signifying, much like the ending of *Victor,* a progression through space, an evolution to come.

As the credits roll, Paul is unaware of the fact that Camille (*not* his father) placed his baby picture and envelope in the tin box, a detail the spectator may or may not catch upon first viewing. Although the exact way Paul will cope with this postmortem reconciliation with his father remains unclear, Camille's stratagem has clearly provided closure and presumably given Paul the freedom to live his life as a gay man. Martial's devotion to Paul is evident, and their impassioned lovemaking in the latter part of the film suggests that their relationship has become, if not blissful, more harmonious. If Paul is not yet fully aware of that fact, Camille reminds him in the café scene that, unlike herself, he has found someone who truly loves him: "Martial . . . loves you; my relationships with guys, on the other hand, have been nothing but fiascos."

The comparably dark and unsettling featurette *Regarde la mer* is Ozon's first attempt at expanding the duration of his films, although at fifty-two minutes it is still technically considered a short film, or *moyen métrage,* because of a running time less than sixty minutes. This is Ozon's first creation to get an official theatrical release in France, but also in Europe, North America, and Hong Kong, where it was shown in conjunction with *Une robe d'été* and subsequently released on video and DVD together with the equally summery yet far more lighthearted fifteen-minute short. *Regarde la mer* was shot in two weeks on a very limited budget (two hundred thousand francs), with a minimal crew and no screenplay, only a "framework" (*une trame*), as Ozon explains on the director's commentary track of the DVD: dialogues and scenes were usually written in collaboration with the two actresses the night before shooting. In addition, Ozon had deliberately failed to reveal the ending to actress Sasha Hails, who thought the vague possibility of a sexual encounter between her character and Tatiana (which actually does not happen in the film) was the extent of the story (Ozon, Le Saux, and de Van).

Regarde la mer also touched off, arguably because of one single controversial shot, the notorious love/hate relationship between film critics and Ozon's art. The film stars *Une rose entre nous*'s Hails in the role of Sasha; the actress's real-life ten-month-old daughter, Samantha (Sioffra); and Marina de Van (Tatiana), whom Ozon had approached after seeing the Fémis-made 1996 short *Bien sous tous rapports* (Perfect in Every Way), which she directed and starred in. The setting is Ile d'Yeu, a small island reachable only by ferry off the Atlantic coast of western France. Such isolation from the mainland suits this thriller perfectly, as the two women, oceans apart from each other both physically and socially, have plenty of uninterrupted time to get acquainted, with fatal consequences for Sasha: Tatiana kills her, steals her baby and possibly her identity, as indicated by her wearing the young mother's red summer dress in the last scene on the ferry boat (Tatiana's desire to steal the baby arguably stems from a previous interrupted pregnancy that left her childless).

Although peculiarly reminiscent of Ozon's Super 8 short *Mes parents un jour d'été* for its quiet, isolated vacation setting, its mise-en-scène, as well as the murderous impulses of its female characters (Anne-Marie there, Tatiana here), *Regarde la mer* may also be seen as the first opus in what I have called elsewhere Ozon's "trilogy on female desire," alongside *Sous le sable* and *Swimming Pool.* Made three years apart from one another, the three films share many characteristics. Slow in pace, almost (falsely) dormant at times, the three works grant the lead role to a British-born woman (Hails in the first one, Rampling in the last two), and take place in an aquatic, outlying vacation setting. In all three cases, the women have to deal with the absence of a male figure, a spouse or a lover, and the intrusion of a more or less welcome visitor (Tatiana, Vincent, and Julie, respectively). In all three cases their sexual urges are made explicit, either through masturbation scenes or actual lovemaking with strangers or flings. In all three cases someone dies (Schilt).

Frédéric Bonnaud recognizes a connection between the first two films, as he calls *Regarde la mer* a "rough draft" of *Sous le sable*, but, like others, he is much less impressed with the former than the latter film. The reason? "A single shot," Bonnaud argues: "This damned shot in *See the Sea* shows a young woman [Sasha] brushing her teeth. So? What's the problem? It's that her toothbrush had been dipped in a toilet bowl full of excrement a few shots previously by the creepy drifter [Tatiana] whom she has taken in . . . This shot unforgivably diminishes the sense of mystery that the film has painstakingly constructed" (53). If some critics have been equally bothered by this scatological reference in *Regarde la mer* (see Gorin, "Regarde"), a proof that cinema can still be genuinely shocking more than a hundred years after its invention, others have either seen it as part of the logic of the narrative or rejected its provocative value and read it as a Bataillan reference (Goudet, "Projections scandaleuses" 58). All in all, if one looks at the big picture and notes that this film has allowed Ozon to be compared to such thriller masters as Roman Polanski (Jousse, "Sans toit ni loi" 67), Claude Chabrol (Maslin, "Mother"), Henri-Georges Clouzot, and Alfred Hitchcock (Enjolras 54), as well as Ingmar Bergman (Goudet, "Court métrage" 59), this critical dismissal becomes all but relative.

Scènes de lit can be regarded as the culmination of Ozon's short film career: it came out in 1998, the year that marks the beginning of the director's feature film career and, with the exception of *X2000* (also released in 1998) and *Un lever de rideau* (*A Curtain Raiser,* 2006), the end of his contribution to the short-length format. It also features a significant number of actors and actresses whom he had previously cast: *Victor*'s François Genty, *La petite mort*'s Camille Japy and François Delaive (the latter actor also starred in Ozon's never-released 1992 *Thomas reconstitué*), and *Une robe d'été*'s Lucia Sanchez and Sébastien Charles.

This twenty-five-minute family reunion of sorts, filmed principally in shot/countershot with few camera movements, contains seven brief bed scenes between a variety of couples and explores their idiosyncrasies and the changes of heart that can occur during sexual encounters. Most couples have never been in bed together before. Each new vignette is announced by a bell ring and a title and is radically different in tone. A one-of-a-kind prostitute and her john ("Le trou noir" [Black Hole]); a fifty-two-year-old widow and a nineteen-year-old man who is sexually attracted to her ("Madame"); a soap-allergic man and his turned-off date ("Monsieur Propre" [Mr. Clean]); a Spanish-speaking woman and a Frenchman engaged in an erotic, bilingual countdown to the number sixty-nine ("Tête bêche" [Heads or Tails]); a lesbian and her female object of desire ("L'homme idéal" [Ideal Man]); two young men ("Les puceaux" [The Virgins]); and a man who prefers sex in the dark and his frustrated would-be lover ("Love in the Dark") make for a colorful, tragicomic parade of characters who often manage to take the spectator by surprise.

With humor and boldness, *Scènes de lit* portrays characters of all ages, backgrounds, and sexual preferences. Ozon calls this project, shot in two weekends in a hotel in Montmartre, a "recreational film" he made to fight boredom and "to have a good time" with the actors (Ozon, "Entretiens Courts"). Although Ozon asserts he had no particular desire to "prove anything" in making the film, Kate Ince sees in *Scènes de lit* a "preoccupation with permutations and permutability latent in all Ozon's dramas about couples" as well as a "space of mutable sexuality [already] established in *Une robe d'été* two years earlier" ("Cinema of Desire" 116). Only two of the seven couples share the same gender (in the segments "L'homme idéal" and "Les puceaux"), and only one person in each of these two pairings has had previous same-sex experiences. Yet, unlike the other scenes, which mostly narrate aborted attempts at sexual intercourse, both of these encounters end with a passionate, reciprocated kiss.

X2000 is an unusual film in Ozon's corpus. In 1998 television channel Canal Plus contacted the director to ask him to make a short science-fiction film around the theme of the year 2000 that would air alongside other shorts by different directors. He was reluctant at first: "[S]cience fiction is not at all my thing, but I became interested in proposing an image of the year 2000 that would be something other than science fiction" (Ozon, "Entretiens Courts"). Instead of playing on a futuristic vision of "Y2K," Ozon opted for a more naturalistic approach: all the characters in the film are in the nude. The filmmaker justified their nakedness threefold: first, he did not know what fashion would be like at the turn of the new millennium, so depicting them without clothes avoided the problem of a possible retrospective fashion faux pas; second, he wanted his characters to be like "Adam and Eve of the year 2000"; and, third, he likes to film naked bodies in general, finding it "rather pleasant" (Ozon, "Entretiens Courts").

In this quasi-silent, visually stunning film, an unnamed man (Bruno Slagmulder, who appeared in *Scènes de lit* as the photophobic lover, Frank) awakes with a serious hangover on January first, 2000, in an apartment that was clearly the site of a New Year's Eve party. We follow this groggy, unclad individual as he wanders into the kitchen, where he prepares a cocktail of aspirin in the hopes of eliminating his pounding headache, and the living room, where he discovers, astonished, a set of identical male twins (Lionel and Olivier Le Guevellou) sharing a sleeping bag. He then turns into a shameless voyeur as his attention switches to a couple making love (Lucia Sanchez again and Flavien Coupeau) in the high-rise building opposite his (*X2000* was shot in one of the immense housing towers in a Parisian *banlieue*). The film changes perspectives as the man's partner (Denise Aron-Schropfer) awakes, silently glances at the man (who is ogling his copulating neighbors), walks down the hallway, and runs a bath for herself. The remainder of the film alternates between shots of the woman bathing quietly in the tub (the camera shows us various parts of her body in close-up, including her feet, pubis, breasts, and relaxed face staring up at the ceiling) and shots of the man in the position of the observer; after falling from the window ledge he has climbed upon for a better view of his neighbors, he gazes tenderly at the twins, who now have their eyes open, and later peers at a colony of ants living under the kitchen trash can. The film ends melodramatically as the man, visibly anguished, announces to the woman that "ants are attacking." In eight short minutes, *X2000* highlights both intra-diegetic and spectatorial scopophilia (pleasure in looking) inherent to the cinematic medium and articulated most famously by feminist film criticism (see Mulvey) while also arguably pointing to the cinematic past by referencing another (silent) classic featuring a nameless couple and a close encounter of a male character (Pierre Batcheff) with a swarm of ants, Luis Buñuel and Salvador Dalí's *Un chien andalou* (*An Andalusian Dog*, 1929).

This cinema of reference continued into Ozon's full-length film career, where the director maintained his customary velocity: *Sitcom* was released in 1998, *Les amants criminels* in 1999, followed by two films in 2000, *Gouttes d'eau sur pierres brûlantes* and *Sous le sable*, and exactly one a year from 2002 to 2005: *8 femmes*, *Swimming Pool*, *5x2*, and *Le temps qui reste*. In the (relative) two-year hiatus between *Le temps qui reste* and *Angel*, he managed to release his first short film in eight years: *Un lever de rideau*, a thirty-minute adaptation of the play *Un incompris* (1943) by queer author Henri de Montherlant. Ozon's short stars prominent French actors with whom the director had never worked before (Mathieu Amalric, Louis Garrel, and Vahina Giocante) and recounts the story of a young man determined to end his passionate relationship with his girlfriend on the sole basis of her consistent tardiness. *Ricky* (inspired by English writer Rose Tremain's contemporary short story "Moth") followed in 2009, two years after *Angel* (a filmic rendition of the 1957 novel by English author Elizabeth Taylor).

As we have seen, the complexity and variety of Ozon's cinema has provoked diverse reactions from commentators, who have striven to find thematic trends that unify the iconoclast's many projects. To this end, French critic Benjamin Delmotte offered the metaphor of "the same and the other" as a way to understand Ozon's filmography. Delmotte argues that beyond the director's recurring obsessions with homosexuality, death, and the family, the duality between sameness and otherness is "at the core of this cinema, which describes the stubborn return of the same in the other's desire; it is an imprisonment in the same because of the difficulty, if not impossibility to be other, to be the other or to be elsewhere" ("Le même et l'autre" 83). Ince recognizes the threat posed by the other in Ozon's films and proposes the "dirty and clean" dialectic, observing that in films such as *Regarde la mer*, *Action vérité*, and *X2000*, "dirt, vermin and abjected body contents (faeces and menstrual blood) signal danger, decline, and fear or disgust in those who view them" ("Cinema of Desire" 130). In an interview with the director and his muse Ludivine Sagnier (who dubbed into French *Angel*'s main character played by British actress Romola Garai), the television host Daphné Roulier of Canal Plus's show *L'hebdo cinéma* describes Ozon's cinema as oscillating between pureness (*l'épure*) and profusion (Ozon and Sagnier). Ozon himself has used the former noun (*l'épure*) and the verb *épurer* (to purge/to purify) to characterize the cinema of "economy" and simplicity epitomized by *Sous le sable* (see Roy; Ozon, "Entretiens Collection"). These suggestions of thematic and stylistic similarities between often diverse projects directed by the same filmmaker are a reminder of the everlasting importance of the auteur, particularly in France, and invite us to ponder Ozon's position within auteurist cinema.

For the past sixty years, the figure of auteur has been of primordial importance in French film criticism. While critics like Alexandre Astruc and André Bazin had already articulated notions of cinematic authorship in the late 1940s and early 1950s, the *politique des auteurs*—literally, "auteur politics/policy," but coined "auteur theory" by American critic Andrew Sarris—became a coherent form of criticism after a series of immensely influential articles, most of them published in *Cahiers du cinéma* in the mid to late 1950s. These writings insisted that the film director, much like a novelist or a painter, should maintain the ultimate authority over his or her artistic product (see Truffaut, "Une certaine tendance du cinéma français"). Young critic François Truffaut was the forerunner of this trend, but other *Cahiers* critics, such as Jean-Luc Godard, Eric Rohmer, and Jacques Rivette, soon followed. Dissatisfied with what they perceived as a lack of quality in French films made in the 1950s (a cinematic era known as the *Tradition de qualité* or *Qualité française*), they resolved to put their own theory into practice in the latter part of the same decade. Their unique style of filmmaking came to be known nationally and internationally as the *Nouvelle Vague* (New Wave). Despite later accusations of nostalgia and objections to auteurism as an unnecessary and inaccurate fetishization of the director, the ongoing influence of this cinematic and critical period on film production and film criticism, French or otherwise, cannot be overemphasized. As filmmaker Jean-Claude Guiguet clearly stated in 1998, "The New Wave . . . is now engraved in the genes of cinema" (qtd. in Vasse 29).

If François Ozon was born roughly around the time when the French New Wave period ended (in the year 1967), the beginning of his film career coincides with the well-documented revival of the auteur in 1990s

French cinema. Film scholar Phil Powrie attributes this return partly to the influential 1994 television series "Tous les garçons et les filles de leur âge" (All the Boys and Girls of Their Age), produced by Franco-German channel Arte (*French Cinema 1990s* 1). The series was composed of nine one-hour episodes directed by five female and four male French-speaking filmmakers, each recounting more or less autobiographical stories of adolescent life in France and Belgium (in the case of Chantal Akerman) from the late 1960s to the late 1980s. Powrie comments on the ambiguous status of auteurism in contemporary French cinema: "In terms of the simplistic binarism centre/periphery, auteur cinema is complex, since arguably, for historical reasons, it is central to French film production and its sense of cultural worth (a marketing issue), while also being peripheral, since much auteur work defines itself in opposition to mainstream cinema (more of a stylistic or narrative specific issue)" (2).

Chris Darke confirms the ambivalent position of auteur cinema vis-à-vis the French film industry, noting that "throughout the 1990s a genera-tion of French film-makers has been stubbornly reassessing the myth of the auteur and revitalising its place within an industry and film culture that alternately supports and looks askance at such film-making" (154). The author cites François Ozon alongside Arnaud Desplechin, Cédric Kahn, Catherine Corsini, Pascale Ferran, and Gaël Morel as examples of a group commonly referred to as the *jeune cinéma français* (young French cinema) and sometimes *Nouvelle Nouvelle Vague* (New New Wave), a generally youthful, somewhat homogeneous congregation of independent filmmakers who started directing in the late 1980s or early 1990s (for more information on contemporary French auteurist cinema, see Prédal; Vasse). These individuals often graduated from the Fémis school, which Darke equates to an institutionalized version of the auteur spirit of the original *Nouvelle Vague* (157). The fundamental difference, however, between the New Wave from the early 1960s and the so-called rebirth of the auteur in the 1990s is the fact that the preoccupations of the former were mostly male-centric and heteronormative; in contrast, the latter trend has facilitated the arrival of a new, more diverse genera-tion of auteurs, including a significant number of women, *beur* (French citizens of North African origin), and queer filmmakers (see Tarr with Rollet; Tarr; Rees-Roberts).

The generically and stylistically hybrid cinema of François Ozon particularly exemplifies the paradox of contemporary auteurism and reveals that the boundary between auteur cinema and its so-called mainstream counterpart is more porous than one might think. Given the director's inclination to alternate between small-budget independent films (*Sous le sable, 5x2*) and more ambitious commercial undertakings (*8 femmes, Angel*), critics have had a particularly difficult time categorizing his cinema within the contemporary context (see, for example, Bingham). One French critic managed to capture this paradox by stating Ozon's ability to successfully release "commercial auteur films" (Murat, "Femmes égales"). Indeed, while most of his ventures may be seen as (subversive) representatives of genre cinema, a term typically associated with mainstream filmmaking, these are also marked by a strong personal style and a bold iconoclasm, both of which are usually linked to auteur cinema. Like the independent directors of the French New Wave, his projects are inundated with intertextual references (cinematic mostly, but also literary). Like them, his filmmaking is both "personal" and, this is another conundrum of film authorship, "collective." Ozon writes his own original or adapted scripts and dialogues, sometimes alone, but often with the recurring assistance of fellow Fémis graduate Marina de Van and novelist and screenwriter Emmanuèle Bernheim. Throughout his career, Ozon has solicited the help of other (often female) artists and technicians: Pascaline Chavanne has been the costume designer on nine of his films between 1998 and 2009, while cinematographers Jeanne Lapoirie and Yorick Le Saux have operated the camera on four and nine films, respectively, from 1994 to 2009. Ozon also regularly collaborates with musician Philippe Rombi, editor Monica Coleman, and choreographer Sébastien Charles (who appears as an actor in two shorts, *Une robe d'été* and *Scènes de lit,* and in *Sitcom*). In front of the camera, actresses Lucia Sanchez, Sasha Hails, Marina de Van, Ludivine Sagnier, Charlotte Rampling, and Valeria Bruni-Tedeschi have worked with Ozon on multiple projects—contrary to male actors, who, with the exception of a few early shorts, do not tend to reappear after one film.

Like other filmmakers of his generation, Ozon has an ambivalent relationship with New Wave cinema. He once cited Chabrol, Rohmer, and Truffaut as the three directors who "taught [him] the trade of filmmaking" (Murat, "Femmes égales") and regularly refers to Godard in interviews as an influence and a model; like Godard, Ozon has described his films as *tentatives* (attempts, essays) rather than finished products (Ozon, "Entretiens *Sitcom*"). Conversely, when asked whether he felt part of the *politique des auteurs*, he declared: "Whereas the generation before mine placed the New Wave and a certain conception of auteur cinema on a pedestal, my inspirations include Hollywood B movies, European auteur filmmaking, television series and Japanese films . . . I do not feel the weight [*lourdeur*] of a cinephilic heritage, nor do I feel the need to 'kill the father'" (Rouyer and Vassé, "Danger" 24; also see Frodon). The desire to "kill the father" refers to the New Wave's oedipal determination to move away from the thematic and formal constraints of what Truffaut and others called *cinéma de papa* (daddy's cinema) and start a radically new style of filmmaking. In the context of Ozon's cinema, where the theme of patricide is a quasi idée fixe, the remark is amusing. Ozon, however, maintains in the same interview that if fathers are killed on a regular basis in his films, such obsession is "unintentional" ("Ce n'est pas volontaire") (Rouyer and Vassé, "Danger" 24).

Given Ozon's much discussed propensity to oscillate between film projects that are either "exuberant and satirical" or "contrastingly sober" (Ince, "Cinema of Desire" 112), critics have generally struggled with his status as auteur. One such struggle concerns the apparent incompatibility between a cinema that provokes controversy (Ozon as enfant terrible) and one that is worthy of the auteur label. James Quandt deplores the "shock tactics" and the "willfully transgressive" nature of a recent cinematic trend he calls "New French Extremity" (127), also known as "extreme cinema," "cinema of evil," and "cinema of the abject" (Beugnet 15). Quandt calls Ozon "an outrider of French extremity" (128) and cites *Regarde la mer* and *Les amants criminels* as undeniable proof of his provocateur status. The critic, however, welcomes *Sous le sable* (2000) as evidence that Ozon has "since matured" (128). Film scholar Mark Hain also cites *Sous le sable* as the critical period after which "Ozon has largely shed his label of enfant terrible and has been hailed as an up and coming auteur," despite what the writer calls "the relatively conservative nature of French film criticism" (277; also see Asibong, "Meat" 203).

The information is accurate: before Quandt's 2004 article in *Artforum*, French critic Frédéric Bonnaud titled a 2001 article published in the American magazine *Film Comment* "François Ozon: Wannabe Auteur Makes Good." Here, the journalist admits to "having switched sides" after the release of *Sous le sable* from being a "detractor" of Ozon's "easy provocation and a certain symbolic heaviness" to being a "champion" who sees in the director "evidence of great audacity and talent" (53). After noting *Sous le sable*'s enormous success in France— six hundred thousand admissions and four million dollars gross, "a huge number for such an uncompromising *film d'auteur*" (53)—Bonnaud summarizes: "Ozon has risen from the status of an 'over-eager young show-off' to that of a 'definite asset to French cinema, a bankable auteur.' Such a trajectory is rare in France, where the critical tradition, in thrall to auteurism, is all too frequently to embrace or dismiss filmmakers for good on the basis of one film" (53). The even more accurate truth, if one counts Ozon's early career as a short film director (a period that should evidently not be dismissed, given its richness), is that for critics he has gone from genius filmmaker (*Une robe d'été* and other 1990s shorts) to recalcitrant, wanton provocateur (*Regarde la mer, Sitcom,* and *Les amants criminels*) to "bankable auteur," if not *enfant prodigue* (*Sous le sable* onward). This trajectory reveals the challenges commentators have had describing a career as unconventional and multifarious as Ozon's.

Given Ozon's penchant for showcasing a pluralistic or, as Eve Sedgwick calls it, "universalizing" view of (homo)sexuality (1), it is significant to remark that it is with *Sous le sable* that the director gained massive critical acclaim from the public as well as the critical establishment. The film, although sexually explicit at times, is also Ozon's first feature to remain firmly within the realm of the heterosexual. One cannot help but think that the dismissal or hasty categorization of Ozon's early oeuvre (I am referring to his pre–*Sous le sable* career, particularly his first two or three features) has something to do with the candid on-screen portrayal, not of sexuality per se, but of homosexual and bisexual desire. For example, one has to wonder whether *Télérama* critic Jacques Morice would have described Ozon in 1998 as a lover of "deviance" (43) had *Sitcom* and previous shorts not contested the supremacy of heterosexual love. *Sitcom* was marketed in the French media as an example of an allegedly new Gallic trend labeled *humour trash* (trash humor), and a young François Ozon, then virtually unknown to the general public, appeared on the set of the popular talk-show *Tout va bien* (on French channel Canal Plus) to promote the film. Much of the "trashy" qualities of the film evoked by the show's two male interviewers revolved around its unapologetic engagement with nonnormative lifestyles: the coming out of the family son, the revealed bisexuality of the maid's husband, the daughter's espousal of sadomasochism, and so forth. This is not an isolated case, and the English word *trash* has been used repeatedly by French commentators to describe the work of Ozon as well as that of some of his contemporaries, one other notable example being bisexual writer Virginie Despentes. It would of course be preposterous to claim that the fluidity of sexuality that is frequently invoked in Ozon's projects is the only reason for what has to be read as a critical disallowance (*trash* rarely being used positively). But as Ince, who prefers the less extreme term "cinema of desire" to describe Ozon's filmography, asserts: "[T]he condemnation of Ozon's 'immaturity' typified by Bonnaud's criticism has served to mask the depth and brilliance of [his] exploration of sexuality, and his originality as France's first mainstream queer *auteur*" ("Cinema of Desire" 113).

The phrase "first mainstream queer *auteur*" is provocative, to say the least. First, it once again juxtaposes the seemingly antithetical terms *mainstream* and *auteur*, thus demonstrating that in Ozon's case, they are no longer at odds with each other. Secondly and perhaps more importantly, *mainstream* and *queer* are generally not used concurrently. As Harry Benshoff and Sean Griffin remind us, "Queer can be used to describe any sexuality not defined as heterosexual procreative monogamy (usually the presumed goal of most classic Hollywood couplings); queers are people (including heterosexuals) who do not organize their sexuality according to that rubric" (1). The term *queer*, as it is understood in the Anglo-American context of "New Queer Cinema" (also significantly called "Queer New Wave"), points to a cinematic phenomenon from the 1990s famously identified by B. Ruby Rich whereby "a flock of films . . . were doing something new, renegotiating subjectivities, annexing whole genres, revising histories in their [queer] image" (15). In short, queer may have become "hot," as Rich remarks, but it was hardly "mainstream," especially since those films, which include the works of independent gay filmmakers Christopher Münch, Gregg Araki, Tom Kalin, and Laurie Lynd, emerged out of the independent film festival circuit rather than the Hollywood film industry.

Although not included in this exclusively North American trend (the above-mentioned directors are all from the United States and Canada), French cinema, too, has seen an increased on-screen visibility of sexual minorities around the same period, in popular as well as more independent cinema. It has been argued that the genre known as "the AIDS film," anticipated in Leos Carax's *Mauvais sang* (*Bad Blood/The Night Is Young*, 1986) and fully developed in Paul Vecchiali's *Encore* (1988) and César award-winning Cyril Collard's *Les nuits fauves* (*Savage Nights*, 1992), contributed to the development of this tendency (Ince, "Queering the Family" 90). Since then, queer or otherwise sexually ambivalent characters have seeped into more commercial cinema, such as Josiane Balasko's *Gazon maudit* (*French Twist*, 1995), Gabriel Aghion's *Pédale douce* (1996), Berliner's *Ma vie en rose*, Benoît Jacquot's *L'école de la chair* (*The School of Flesh*, 1998), Valérie Lemercier's *Le derrière* (*From Behind*, 1999), Francis Veber's *Le placard* (*The Closet*, 2001), and Marzak Allouache's *Chouchou* (2003). Cristina Johnston sees a direct correlation between these films and the French social context of the mid to late 1990s: "Alongside contemporary political debates on gay rights, antidiscrimination laws and the PaCS [*Pacte Civil de Solidarité*, a civil union that has recognized both straight and gay couples in France since 1999], on-screen visibility of the gay community in France has developed from an apparent concentration on sexuality and sexual activity to a wider, more accessible consideration and depiction of gay issues within mainstream French culture and society" (23; also see Reeser 36). Examples of other successful directors whose films consistently avoid the confinements of heteronormativity and arguably encourage antihomophobic responses include André Téchiné, Patrice Chéreau, Catherine Corsini, Sébastien Lifshitz, Christophe Honoré, Gaël Morel, codirectors Olivier Ducastel and Jacques Martineau, and, of course, François Ozon.

The phrase "queer cinema," however, is one that is used almost exclusively by Anglophone critics and LGBTQ festival organizers to describe the French cinematic projects of Ozon and other above-mentioned directors (see Rees-Roberts; Griffiths). In contrast, their status as "queer filmmakers" and accompanying penchant for depicting queer desire on screen are largely downplayed in the French context, France being notoriously averse to identity politics in the name of republican universalism. Let us cite the anecdotal yet telling example of *Cahiers du cinéma* critic Jean-Marc Lalanne, who, while discussing *8 femmes* and the famous passionate kiss between the characters played by Catherine Deneuve and Fanny Ardant, shrugs off the lesbian nature of the embrace and posits that what we see is not two women kissing, but rather two icons of François Truffaut's cinema, two "images" that come together for an instant ("Les actrices" 83). Another such downplay occurred in February 2001 on the set of Bernard Pivot's famous television show, *Bouillon de culture,* where Ozon and Charlotte Rampling appeared together to promote the release of *Sous le sable.* In an exchange between Pivot and Rampling, the interviewer expressed his surprise at a comment the British actress had previously made regarding her film career: Rampling had claimed in a published interview that the best roles she had ever been offered were in films directed by homosexual filmmakers. Pivot proceeded to cite such names as Patrice Chéreau and Luchino Visconti, whom Rampling herself had mentioned in the interview, before asking her if she maintained the statement. A smiling Rampling timidly confirmed that she indeed still felt that way, and neither she nor Pivot proposed to add Ozon, who was sitting next to them, to that list (Ozon himself remained silent). The interview moved on to another topic after another guest of the show exclaimed rather angrily that Rampling's remark was hardly flattering for (heterosexual) director François Truffaut (with whom, for the record, Rampling has never worked) (Ozon and Rampling).

One must briefly revisit the concept of auteurism to comprehend, if only partially, such reticence to identify a film or an artist as "queer" or "gay" in the French context; these two English terms exist and are used in the French language, especially the second one, but rarely to refer to a cinematic trend or a filmmaker. Carrie Tarr articulates it best in a discussion of contemporary women's filmmaking in France: "The figure of the auteur/artist, as it has been constructed and valued in the French universalist discourses, is understood to transcend the particularities of gender, sexual orientation and ethnicity, thus obviating debates on the lack of access to representation on the part of women, gays and lesbians, and ethnic minorities. In this context, it is not surprising that French women directors routinely reject the label of 'woman director' . . . since claiming a supposedly gender-neutral auteur status is often the best way to gain legitimacy and recognition within the film industry" (Tarr with Rollet 10). As it turns out, Ozon is much less reluctant about the relationship between gender, sexuality, and authorship than some of his contemporaries. In a 2004 interview in the magazine *Positif,* he was asked to define the change in the representation of desire in contemporary film. He mentioned two categories of French filmmakers who, in his opinion, contributed to that change: women directors, who "have an audacity [*frontalité*] absent from many male filmmakers" and "have succeeded in rendering feminine desire more complex," and homosexual filmmakers, who "have allowed a return to the eroticization of the male body that was missing in French cinema" (Ozon mentions Catherine Breillat, Claire Denis, and Noémie Lvovsky in the first category of filmmakers, but no names in the second) (Rouyer and Vassé, "Danger" 45).

When asked in the same interview whether he himself ever feared, because of his persistent tendency to depict homosexual desire on screen, being "trapped in an image" (of a "gay filmmaker," the question implied), Ozon replied rather forwardly: "I have no problem with the risk of being 'labeled' [*catalogué*], especially when one knows that Stephen Frears or Pedro Almodóvar had this label at the beginning of their career and managed to escape from it. I never saw myself as making militant films, but when I realized that *Une robe d'été* had been reappropriated [*récupéré*] for militant purposes, I was pretty happy about it [*ça m'a fait plutôt plaisir*]" (Rouyer and Vassé, "Vérité" 41). Ozon is also fully aware of the fact that his cinema differs from that of the previous generation of gay filmmakers in that his belongs to the so-called post-AIDS era. After insisting upon the "bisexual" rather than "homosexual" character of *Une robe d'été,* Ozon declares: "I was providing a vision a bit different from what Cyril Collard [born 1957, died of AIDS-related illness in 1993] or Patrick Mimouni [born 1954] did in their shorts, where homosexuality is part of a much more socially anchored framework. In my shorts, homosexuality is shown just as it is [*telle quelle*], it is not problematized" (Rouyer and Vassé, "Vérité" 41). Ozon's cinema may not be militant in the traditional, out-on-the-street sense of the term, but there is a desire to "undo" a certain image of gay representation that may have prevailed until recently. Ozon has notably used two words with the prefix "dé" ("de" or "un" in English) to describe his way of portraying homosexuality on screen: *dédramatisation* (Delmotte, "Entretien" 90), which refers to the process of rendering something less frightening, and *déculpabilisante* (Rouyer and Vassé, "Vérité" 45), or an attempt to reduce one's guilty feelings (here, about gay desire).

As we have seen and shall continue to see in more detail, what *is* problematized in Ozon's oeuvre is the fixity of things and people on the one hand and of the cinematic art on the other. Like the dress that gets exchanged between the characters of *Une robe d'été* and *Regarde la mer*, like the water that flows in and out of most of his projects, the films of François Ozon are undeniably mutable. Playing on the well-known French homophones *mer* (sea) and *mère* (mother) in her article "Toujours tu chériras la mer" (You will always cherish the sea/the mother), Cécile Nicouleaud sees the liquid and the maternal/the feminine as binding elements within Ozon's cinematic output: "Water is never far away; or rather the liquid element, impossible to define [*cerner*], fluid and opaque, be it sea, river, blood, sperm or just a water drop" (11). As the ensuing discussion will show, privileging the liquid and the maternal comes at the expense of father figures throughout much of Ozon's cinema, particularly in the three films discussed in the next section.

Paternal Monsters: *Sitcom, Les amants criminels,* and *8 femmes*

Looking back on the director's feature film career in a 2002 review of *8 femmes,* Jean-Marc Lalanne asserted that Ozon's creations had told only two kinds of stories thus far: one dominated by abusive fathers, the other pervaded with madness and chaos precisely because of the absence of the father ("Les actrices" 83). The three works discussed in this section—Ozon's first, second, and fifth full-length films (released in 1998, 1999, and 2002, respectively)—feature three middle-aged paternal figures who could all, for different reasons, be considered "monstrous" (the label also applies to the protagonist played by Bernard Giraudeau in Ozon's third feature, *Gouttes d'eau sur pierres brûlantes,* which will be discussed in another context later on). At first glance these monstrous father figures might seem to comprise a critique of the role of the patriarch within the Ozonian family. In *Sitcom* Jean witnesses the disintegration of his family with indifference and literally turns into a giant, hideous rat. The unnamed, authoritative forest hermit in *Les amants criminels* viciously sequesters two runaway lovers, eventually abusing one of them sexually. Marcel, the unseen paterfamilias in *8 femmes*, though first assumed to be a victim of one of the eight women's murderous scheme, is later revealed to be a sadistic manipulator and possibly an incestuous father. All three father figures are clearly "removed" both physically and emotionally from the world around them, whether it is their immediate family circle or society at large. All of them get punished in the end for their behavior: two will die, and one is arrested by police. Yet with a filmmaker like Ozon, any seemingly straightforward chastisement of the patriarchal system becomes, upon closer analysis, a much more ambiguous depiction that redefines the boundaries between normalcy and monstrosity, between the familiar and the queer.

Like most of Ozon's early work, *Sitcom* was made on a tight budget (2.5 million francs, the cost of an average short), a Super 16 camera, and a two-page synopsis; there was no formal script, and dialogues were written immediately prior to shooting. The film was shot quickly in four weeks, recycles a number of actors from previous projects, and introduces new ones—notably Stéphane Rideau, whom Ozon noticed when he played the part of sexually confused Serge in André Téchiné's *Les roseaux sauvages* (*Wild Reeds*, 1994). The very production of the film occurred because Ozon's original first feature, *Les amants criminels*, which he later released as his second feature, failed to convince potential producers. Fidélité Productions was on board, but the Centre National de la Cinématographie (CNC), the state-funded organization that financially supports numerous national filmmaking projects, deemed the script of this crime thriller/fairy-tale hybrid "too violent" and refused to offer financial assistance. According to Ozon, funding for *Sitcom* proved easier to secure because it was a comedy, the most popular genre with audiences in France, as opposed to a drama (Ozon, Delbosc, and Le Saux). The title *Sitcom* is a direct reference to both American and French television situation comedies, two notable examples of which are the popular 1980s *Maguy,* a Gallic remake of the American *All in the Family* spinoff *Maud,* and the mawkish 1990s teenage sitcom *Hélène et les garçons* (Hélène and the Boys), whose main heroine shares a first name with the lady of the house in *Sitcom.* French-produced sitcoms usually take place in bourgeois settings and are often laden with conservative family values. In contrast, *Sitcom*'s intentions are clearly to subvert and transgress the norms of upper-middle-class *bonne société,* as the film explicitly presents or implicitly suggests every perversion and taboo in the book: homosexuality, interracial adultery, sadomasochism, incest, pedophilia, group sex, and even bestiality. A laboratory rat recently brought to the home by the father turns out to be directly responsible for the chaos (its "negative vibrations" are blamed), and after the death of the rat *and* of the father, order is reestablished in the end.

Sitcom's first image is that of a red curtain being drawn, accompanied by the *trois coups* typical of French theatrical performances. In addition to being evocative of Jean Renoir's filmic homages to the theater such as *La chienne* (*The Bitch,* 1931), which also opens with the parting of a curtain and ends with murder, this opening insists upon the fact that we are about to see a staged drama, a story we should perhaps not take too seriously. But this warning can scarcely prepare us for what is about to unfold. In the first scene a man returns from work to his cozy home, where his family eagerly awaits to wish him a happy birthday. Their jubilant singing is abruptly interrupted by a round of eight gunshots, heard but not seen by the spectator, who must continue to stare at the house's splendid façade. The shots are prefaced by a female voice, later identified as the mother's, asking, "Jean, why?" and followed by hysterical screaming and, eventually, complete silence. The ensuing intertitle, "Several months earlier," deceivingly leads us to believe that the film will be an elucidation of the reasons behind the paterfamilias' impetuous murderous act. But it is revealed later that *Sitcom*'s first scene was "only a dream," a ploy to which television series occasionally resort, one memorable example being the so-called dream season on the American nighttime hit show *Dallas.* In *Sitcom*'s diegetically "real" final murder scene, it is the wife and children (more specifically, the daughter) who kill the father, who has transformed into a colossal rat after eating the small one.

The first flashback sequence, which is the film's second scene, introduces the eclectic clan: the extravagant new Spanish maid, Maria (Lucia Sanchez); the slightly uptight, diet and exercise addict, stay-at-home wife, and mother of two, Hélène (Evelyne Dandry); the nerdy, conservatively dressed son, Nicolas (Adrien de Van); and handsome and affectionate David (Stéphane Rideau), who is the boyfriend of the sprightly, ponytailed daughter, Sophie (Marina de Van, real-life sister of Adrien). Finally, daddy/Jean (François Marthouret) comes home . . . with a gift. The sight of the albino rat enchants the children but frightens the mother. From here on, each person—with the notable exception of the father—who comes into contact with the rodent acts upon previously repressed sexual desires. Needless to say, the unity of this seemingly blissful family becomes seriously threatened as a result. The introduction of an intruder who destabilizes the familial nucleus is a well-known narrative strategy, cinematic and otherwise. To remain within possible Renoirian inspirations, one can think of the French master's *Boudu sauvé des eaux* (*Boudu Saved from Drowning*, 1932), starring Michel Simon in the main role of a street hobo who moves in with a Parisian bourgeois couple and ends up seducing the housewife. But there is something both disturbing and Kafkaesque about the replacement of a human version of otherness with an animal, especially a rat, a creature that is often viewed as repulsive, including for Ozon himself, who vehemently refused to touch the rodent during shooting. Ozon justifies his choice and mentions an oft-cited inspiration for *Sitcom*, a 1968 film by controversial Italian writer/filmmaker Pier Paolo Pasolini: "The rat is a strong symbol and is indeed used to unveil [the characters' true desires]. The rat interested me in that it is an animal used for laboratory experimentation; it is a guinea pig. Here, I reversed the situation: others become guinea pigs after the rat is set free. It is a zoophile version of *Teorema* [*Theorem*]: the intrusion of an outside character destabilizing a group" (Ozon, "Entretiens *Sitcom*").

After referencing, like Ozon, Pasolini's initially banned film as an example of "a recipe for family discord," Jonathan Romney pertinently notes that the rat is not the only perturbing element in *Sitcom:* "But to make matters more complex there are three intruders, each an exaggerated version of Otherness as it might appear to the French bourgeoisie: an African man and a Spanish woman, both of them sexually up for anything, and the laboratory rat, which . . . seems to be the narrative genius experimenting on the humans" ("*Sitcom*" 56). The African man in question is Maria's Cameroonian-born husband, Abdu (Jules-Emmanuel Eyoum Deido), who becomes acquainted with the family at a dinner party that takes place early in the narrative (fig. 3). The couple, clearly identified as "foreign" from their first appearance on screen and sub-

Figure 3. Nicolas, Maria, Abdu, Hélène, Jean,
Sophie, and David in *Sitcom.*

sequent conversations with the family—Hélène knows nothing about Africa, and the dinner scene both highlights and mocks her ignorance—certainly contributes more actively than the rat to the dismantlement of the household.

After coming into contact with the rodent, Abdu seduces young Nicolas, who has just come out to his family, while Maria performs "typically Spanish" sexual favors on David once Sophie, turned suicidal dominatrix, rejects him. Another consequence of the rat's presence is the mother's decision to seduce her son in order to "cure" him (her phrase) of his recently revealed homosexuality, despite Nicolas's protests that he is "not at all unhappy." Completely at ease with his new sexuality, thanks in part to Abdu's gentle initiation, Nicolas has started organizing same-sex orgies in his bedroom. In this enclosed space, an array of eccentric characters, among whom a young boy scout, a fake doctor, and a handsome playboy (played by Sébastien Charles), take part in a series of erotic role-playing games involving an absurd amount of uncooked zucchini. The spectator, however, never sees those acts and is even led to believe that the enraptured clique may merely be playing a miniature version of casino roulette.

To declare that critics, Anglophone as well as Francophone, have not been kind to *Sitcom* would be an understatement. Although a rare positive review came out of the Québécois film magazine *Séquences,* in which Maurice Elia judges *Sitcom* to be a film that "embraces and seduces" the spectator (48), an overwhelming majority of commentators have merely dismissed it as a failed, tasteless comedic (and cinematic) attempt. Most criticism is geared toward the film's presumably gratuitous intentions to shock as well as the absence of a clear message or motivation behind the perversions. Janet Maslin of the *New York Times* compares it to Ozon's earlier, middle-length *Regarde la mer,* which she found "exquisitely unsettling," opining, "Mr. Ozon pushed the limits of shock value much more effectively with the carefully measured violence of *See the Sea* than he does with this frontal assault" ("*Sitcom:* Erotic Encounter"). After bemoaning that transgressive cinema "ain't what it used to be," *Sight and Sound's* Richard Falcon deplores, "*Sitcom* plays every sexual combination it can with its characters," and ponders: "[A]re we meant merely to be congratulating ourselves on recognizing the kitsch-camp sensibility of a European John Waters fan? Or is Ozon, deep down, really expecting us to be shocked?" ("Reality Is Too Shocking" 10). The film reminds Falcon of another cinematic period. He writes, not without sarcasm: "If the shots survive intact we may look back on these films as the pre-millennial equivalent of the European art films of the late 50s and early 60s which drew audiences partly through their introduction of screen nudity and relative sexual candour" (11). Falcon does not mention directors' names or countries, and it is difficult to determine whether he is referencing the French New Wave, which was indeed criticized for showing people "always in bed," or other national cinemas. Romney suggests that Ozon's inspirations are not to be found in hexagonal cinema and sees other influences besides John Waters, such as Luis Buñuel, Joe Orton, and Pedro Almodóvar. He recognizes, however, Ozon's originality in his tackling of gay themes: "The film belongs in the by now altogether cosy cinematic tradition of *épater les bourgeois,* although Ozon is perhaps the first to 'out' the tradition, taking it to queer territory" ("*Sitcom*" 56). The reference to Buñuel is appropriate, given that Ozon and his crew watched *Le charme discret de la bourgeoisie* prior to shooting *Sitcom,* and the director saw in Dandry/Hélène a counterpart to the character played by Stéphane Audran in Buñuel's surrealist opus (Ozon, Delbosc, and Le Saux). In the end, Romney does not find the queering of the plot enough to salvage the film and writes toward the end of his review: "It's hard to know quite what Ozon is offering beyond the standard lampooning of repression. It's hardly that taboo-busting to reveal that under the squeaky-clean appearance everyone's up for a romp with the domestics and a fistful of courgettes" (*"Sitcom"* 56).

On the French side, *Positif*'s Jean-Pierre Jeancolas equates *Sitcom* with a sterilized experimentation in which Ozon "lost himself by deliberately hiding his talent" (44). Pierre Murat writes in *Télérama* that attacking in 1998 the social and moral order that the family represents is comparable to "shooting a mosquito with a machine gun" and concludes that "by being so maladroit, Ozon himself might just explode" ("Potache"). Jean-Marc Lalanne's *Cahiers du cinéma* critique describes the film as a "UFO in the generally tamer young French auteur cinema," an "off-balance, disorganized, completely kamikaze" endeavor ("Place du père" 108). Although in agreement with most reviewers who argue that the characters' sudden appetite for transgressive deportments is unjustified, Lalanne nevertheless finds redeeming qualities to the latter part of the film: "Much like its characters, [*Sitcom*] engages in a frantic race to transgression and can hardly keep up the pace. But it eventually manages to be convincing after breaking free from its generically narrow framework (the *trash* pastiche of sitcoms)" (107). He, too, compares it to Almodóvar's early features, but notices a distinction: "There is a difference, though: here, despite the escalation of sexual fantasies, no one is able to reach orgasm . . . This important lack tormenting each character comes from the fact that someone is missing: the father figure (symptomatically absent from the film poster)" (107). Though the father does not get killed until the very end and physically lives under the same roof as his wife and children, he is indeed relatively absent, at least emotionally, in that he appears indifferent to the various changes that have occurred since the arrival of the rat: Nicolas's newfound sexual orientation, Sophie's multiple suicide attempts—the first of which leads to the paralysis of her lower body—the maid's unrestrained libido, his wife's incestuous tendencies. When the mother's psychotherapist (played by Jean Douchet) recommends group therapy, he refuses to participate, excluding himself from the family circle and arguing, "[I]t's a very good idea for you three to do it." In addition, his rare verbal interventions appear meaningless (with some exception, as we shall see), because they are almost exclusively composed of timeworn proverbs and aphorisms.

François Ozon declared in 2001 that he took great pleasure in rewatching *Regarde la mer* and *Gouttes d'eau sur pierres brûlantes* during the recording of the director's commentary tracks for his comprehensive DVD collection. He admitted, however, that viewing *Sitcom* was instead a painful experience: "I stopped commenting after half an hour. I couldn't go on. I made that decision because I didn't want the experience to turn into a masochistic exercise" (Ozon, "Entretiens Collection"). It has become almost clichéd to suggest that audiences and critics respond to films in radically different, if not opposite, ways, and *Sitcom* certainly reinforces this assumption. Despite the general dismissal of *Sitcom* by the French and international critical establishment and later, arguably, its own author, the film fared quite well at the box office. Approximately 220,000 French spectators saw it in theaters the year of its release, a respectable number for a French-language film, and a number almost ten times as high as Ozon's next full-length film, *Les amants criminels,* which sold a meager 25,000 tickets. Of course, one may argue that Ozon's first film benefited from the author's well-established notoriety as a creator of short films. But after being shown as part of the "Semaine de la critique" at the Cannes film festival that same year, *Sitcom* amassed six million francs in foreign sales from distributors who were certainly less familiar, if familiar at all, with his previous work. Still, in 1998 Evelyne Dandry, a TV and theater actress whom Ozon chose for the part of Hélène after having seen her on a Parisian stage in *Harold and Maude,* where she played Adrien de Van/Nicolas's mother (Ozon, Delbosc, and Le Saux), collected two Best Actress awards at festivals in Belgium and Spain for her performance in *Sitcom.*

I must confess my own initial disappointment as a first-time viewer of *Sitcom,* which I saw one evening in May 1998, in a French movie house the week of its first release. I was then completely unfamiliar with Ozon's cinema. But unlike its catchy, genuinely amusing trailer, which I had enjoyed watching the week before and which had prompted me to hasten back to the cinema, I found the film's sitcom framework perplexing, its comedic values dubious. Later on, I acquired more knowledge of Ozon's work. Like the director himself, I recognized a continuum, particularly with regard to sexual fluidity, between the 1990s short films and *Sitcom* (Ozon, "Entretiens *Sitcom*"). Yet I have suggested elsewhere that in marked contrast to Ozon's previous output, treating same-sexuality in *Sitcom* as one "perversion" among a plethora of others, including pedophilia, group sex, incest, and sadomasochism, risked reinforcing the firmly established homophobic stereotype that gay men have loose morals and tend to be sexually aroused by young boys (Schilt). As much as one may argue that this is all part of Ozon's "dedramatization" agenda, it nevertheless still seemed problematic to me.

My reading of the film has since changed, for two reasons. The first stems from a desire expressed by a number of queer theorists to move away from the confines of the "good queer, bad queer" binarism, a perilous and potentially unproductive enterprise, given that *any* sexual behavior outside heteronormative codes runs the risk of being interpreted as deviant. As film scholar Ellis Hanson angrily exclaims in the introduction to *Out Takes: Essays on Queer Theory and Film,* "We [in lesbian and gay film criticism] are still in the throes of a lesbian and gay campaign for so-called positive images, representations of sexual minorities as normal, happy, intelligent, kind, sexually well-adjusted, professionally adept, politically correct ladies and gentlemen who have no doubt earned all those elusive civil rights for which we have all been clamoring" (7). Once queer scholars, activists, and spectators relinquish the idea that positive or "accurate" depictions of queer subjects is the only possible cinematic route to follow, so-called homophobic portrayals of queer villains such as vampires or serial killers (8–9) and unabashed, oversexed "flamers" such as Nicolas in *Sitcom* become terribly entertaining again.

Secondly, I find that upon closer analysis, the treatment of (homo) sexuality in *Sitcom* is in fact much in line with Ozon's previous shorts, particularly in its tolerance with regard to sexual freedom. One must remember that the film was released the year before the French parliament officially recognized the civil union of same-sex (and opposite-sex) couples in the form of the PaCS, voted in November 1999. One brief but significant sequence in the first half of *Sitcom* stands out both stylistically and thematically as it frankly addresses the contemporary situation of gay and lesbian citizens in Western Europe: It is dinnertime. Nicolas has abruptly come out to his family and withdraws to his bedroom.

Maria's partner, Abdu, whom the family hardly knows at this point, is summoned to go talk to him, as "he knows how to talk to adolescents" because of his job as a high school gym teacher. Abdu complies and we follow him into Nicolas's quarters. There, Abdu is bitten by the rat, which drives him to seduce Nicolas, and the two soon kiss and fondle each other. A traditional form of parallel editing allows the spectator to travel back and forth between the bedroom, where Nicolas's initiation occurs, and the dining room, where conversations attest to the family's various reactions to the young man's coming out. One such cross-cutting is far less traditional than the others. Appearing to address the camera and the spectator directly in medium close-up shots, three characters, each with a cigarette in hand, make their best effort to "dedramatize" the situation, not without humor.

David appears first and recalls: "While in high school, one of my gym teachers was a homosexual. He was very manly, not at all effeminate. Thanks to him, I received a good grade on my *baccalauréat* exams" (fig. 4). We then cut to Maria's soliloquy, which extends the subject to her native land: "There are lots of homosexuals, even in Spain. In my family, we have a very friendly aunt who for the past ten years has been living happily with a woman a bit masculine but very nice nonethe-

Figure 4. David addresses the camera in *Sitcom*. |

less." Sophie's declaration is shorter and more general: "Nowadays, living one's homosexuality has become very easy, especially in bigger cities." Although a countershot of a devastated Hélène creates the illusion that the three interlocutors were attempting to convince the mother that her son's life was far from doomed, Ozon's choice of mise-en-scène—close shots on the characters and, more importantly, direct gazes at the spectator—suggests that in the late 1990s Hélène is certainly not the only person in need of convincing.

Hélène's outright rejection of Nicolas's sexuality contrasts with the father's wholehearted, albeit mechanical, acceptance of it, thereby challenging the stereotypical "accepting mother, rejecting father" coming-out scenario. Within the context of the film in general and its treatment of same-sexuality in particular, these opposed reactions also question, at least initially, the "loving mother, monstrous father" dichotomy to which the film eventually wants us to adhere; in fact, Sophie reminds Hélène throughout the narrative that her motherly love has been exclusively directed at Nicolas, thus explaining her suicidal tendencies as a desperate call for attention. The father first voices his opinion on homosexuality in a section that precedes by a few minutes the testimonial sequence described above. In a long monologue, Jean compares today's perception of same-sex love with that of ancient Greece, arguing that the Greeks did not distinguish between homosexuality and heterosexuality, were naturally bisexual, and engaged in "pederasty" guiltlessly. Despite the shopworn character of the "Homosexuality and Ancient Greece" tale, it is nevertheless the father's discourse of tolerance that arguably triggers the other three testimonials, paving the way for acceptance among other family members. This idea is reinforced cinematically by the framing of the father in a four-shot, occupying the center of the frame and surrounded by three characters who seem genuinely interested in what he has to say (particularly Hélène and Maria). In a later, one-on-one conversation with Nicolas, who fears that his father may be ashamed of and disappointed in him because of his recently revealed sexuality, Jean answers positively to his son's query "Daddy, do you love me?" and states that he accepts Nicolas "in all [his] difference . . . with no value judgment." Although delivered in his proverbial monotone voice, the father's response, which brings a smile to Nicolas's face, is more positive, face-to-face affirmation than Nicolas will personally get on the subject from any other family member, including his mother.

How, then, does *Sitcom* transition from the present figure of a non-effusive yet relatively accepting father to that of a veritable paternal monster who must be eliminated in order to preserve the unity of the family? The answer lies not in his relationship with his son, but in his monstrosity toward women. In a conversation with his daughter, Sophie, who intends to seduce him just as Hélène had seduced her brother, Jean confesses without scruples that he finds Sophie to be utterly unattractive. Furthermore, Jean's relationship with his wife appears stolid, loveless, and altogether lacking any meaningful form of communication. Hélène's frustration at her spouse's impassivity eventually prompts the dejected woman to call him a "rat" after a failed attempt at bringing to his attention the increasingly less conventional (in her view) sexual practices of their children. This conversation, a turning point in the narrative that forces Hélène to take matters into her own hands, occurs after a symbolic castration of the father: the zucchini that were once (possibly) used as sex toys have been finely cut up by Sophie, steam-cooked by Hélène, and avidly consumed for dinner by the entire family (only Jean finds the taste of these vegetables "passable"). Now that the uselessness of the father has been established and confirmed, an alternative family structure may be fashioned.

In her Freudian reading of *Sitcom,* Michelle Chilcoat argues that the rat may be understood as the fetish signifying the penis and sees the film as a "restaging or queering of Freud's Oedipal drama, which turns on the recognition of a multiplicity of sexual desires, as opposed to masculine desire alone, the only one Freud would legitimate in his theories of human sexuality" (23). She claims that this essential distinction gives women access to their own sexual urges: "Whereas Freud breaks off treatment when faced with the idea of woman's desire, *Sitcom* imagines another scenario: the woman as fetishist (i.e., as one who desires, both sexually and intellectually)" (27). The mother's own enactment of the "woman as fetishist" lies in her open transgression of the incest taboo. Chilcoat interprets Hélène's decision to sleep with her son as "a deflating and disabling of the Oedipal drama that served to regulate a family order resting primarily on the non-recognition of woman's desire" (28–29). Although

Hélène's attempt to change her son's sexuality ultimately fails, it enables her to free herself from preconceptions and act upon her own sexual urges. Not only does she end up endorsing Nicolas's same-sex relationship with Abdu after the latter comes out as gay and divorces Maria, but also the last scene at the cemetery (a recurring shooting location of Ozon's) suggests that Hélène and Maria have become lesbian lovers.

Jean's complete inability to adapt to the fluid environment around him leads to his failure as a patriarch. Jean opts out of a group therapy session during which the mother and two children serenely soak in a womb-like swimming pool, an exercise reminiscent of "rebirthing therapy" that brings the fatherless family to realize that the rat is to blame for the recent chaos. In the end, it is the father's immutability, his failure to actively defend the patriarchal regime—except in the wish fulfillment of his dreams, and even then only by force—and refusal to integrate the newly queered family (he complies with Hélène's request to kill the rat but consumes it instead of discarding it) that causes his demise. As if to reinforce such inflexibility, Jean is the only member of the household who does not receive a head-to-toe, clothing and hairdo makeover: Nicolas goes from rigidly conventional to Gaultier chic, Sophie from schoolgirl to S&M queen, while an unfettered Hélène dons an animal-print coat, and Maria is seen with dreadlocks and in sexier variants of the traditional African *boubou*. But when the father is successfully disposed of, the six remaining characters' rebellious tendencies and need to affirm their sexual and cultural identity subside. The depatriarchalized vision of society presented in the final graveyard scene, where two newly formed couples (Nicolas/Abdu and Hélène/Maria) and one recently reunited (Sophie and David) gather to visit Jean's grave briefly and rather indifferently, contrasts with the opening sequence, where family members are presented as hopeless victims of the father's (fantasized) murder rampage. The cemetery sequence presents an image of love, peacefulness, and interracial as well as intercultural unity: they smile, hold hands, are all dressed in sober black ensembles and get along beautifully. They have also gotten away with murder. But as is often the case with Ozon, this is not the end of the story. Our rebels have not altogether managed to get rid of the penis/father, and the utopian character of the film's conclusion is exposed as the white, red-eyed rodent triumphantly reappears on its master's grave immediately after the family leaves the premises. Patriarchy is tough to kill, and male monsters are too crucial in Ozon's cinematic realm to be done away with permanently. In the director's next feature, this archetype takes the form of a taciturn, sadistic ogre-like figure. As if to link the two films together even further, the ogre's cellar is infested with rats.

Aside from these two elements, at first glance the neo-noir *Les amants criminels* appears to stand in sharp contrast to *Sitcom* in terms of genre, tone, and narrative. Yet like Ozon's first opus, a large part of this feature is confined to a *huis clos* (*Sitcom's* single setting in a bourgeois mansion becomes a shabby cabin in the woods) and confirms the director's obsession not only with inadequate fathers but also with the relationship between sex, violence, and death. Like its predecessor, *Les amants criminels* features a gruesome murder scene with a mise-en-scène reminiscent of the horror/gore genre, a stylistic choice that has led commentators to dismiss Ozon's early output as part of an essentially Gallic trend of films aimed at "pushing the extreme [as] a time-honoured method of attracting attention in these harsh, commerce-driven times for young European directors" (Falcon, "Reality" 10; also see Quandt 126). An inventive take on the seemingly incompatible crime drama and fairy-tale genres, the film begins with the intrusion of a "foreign" element that challenges the status quo, produces chaos, and triggers the murderous instincts of its main protagonists. *Sitcom's* fantastical figure of the rat is replaced here in Ozon's second film by a human version of otherness, the character of Saïd, a classmate of the two adolescent heroes, who serves as a "conduit for the transgressive desires of the protagonists" (Asibong, "Meat" 211).

Les amants criminels takes place in and around an unnamed town in the French provinces. The title's criminal lovers are Luc (Jérémie Renier) and Alice (Natacha Régnier), a teenage couple who, although manifestly enamored of each other, are unable to have sex because of Luc's inability to produce an erection in Alice's presence. Upon Alice's insistence, the two resolve to assassinate one of their high school classmates, a handsome, sexually uninhibited kickboxing jock named Saïd (Salim Kechiouche). After Luc stabs the young *beur* multiple times in the gym's shower, the adolescents clean up the mess, rob a jewelry store, and drive to a remote forest to bury the corpse. It is at this point that the narrative turns into a queer variation of a Hansel and Gretel–like fairy tale. Unable to trace their steps back to the car after interring Saïd's body, they spend the night cruising down a river in a rowboat. The next day they stumble upon a lodge, where an evil middle-aged man (Miki Manojlovic) who speaks with a foreign accent (fairy-tale villains often tend to be extraneous beings) captures them and locks them in his cellar.

As basement roommates the youngsters discover a colony of rats and Saïd's disinterred body. The brute, who has found out about their criminal activities by witnessing the burial of Saïd and by reading Alice's personal diary, takes a special liking to Luc. He releases the naïve, inexperienced teen from the locked space, feeds him rabbit and—as is strongly suggested—part of Saïd's leg, caresses various erogenous parts of his body, and eventually penetrates him anally. Out of what appears to be genuine affection for Luc, he allows the couple to escape. The woodsman's sexual initiation enables Luc to finally make love to Alice, but they are interrupted by the arrival of the police, who shoot Alice dead and arrest both Luc and the ogre. In the final scene Luc implores the gendarmes to release his former captor, who, according to Luc, "has done nothing wrong." The film ends inside a police wagon, where an extremely distressed Luc gazes lengthily and quite disapprovingly at the camera.

Although *Les amants criminels* received three prizes on the international film festival circuit, including a Grand Jury Award at the 2000 Los Angeles Outfest, it was a veritable box office and critical flop. Ozon attributed the film's poor reception to its complex (and admittedly frustrating) nonsequential narrative, which drove him to reedit it and propose an alternate, more chronological version for its 2001 DVD release. In the theatrical cut from 1999, the version I focus on here precisely because of its complexity, the murder occurs early in the story (in the third scene), and its exact circumstances and motives are articulated much later by way of five distinct flashbacks. The spectator is made to travel back and forth between the ogre's remote dwelling and the lovers' familiar surroundings—the high school, the gym, Alice's bedroom—during the days that lead to Saïd's slaying. In the 2001 version the first half hour is significantly altered in order to present the main characters more thoroughly, delaying the murder and thus potentially softening the shocking effect that Saïd's graphic, blood-flying stabbing may have on the viewer (fig. 5). This later version, in which four flashbacks are still present but shorter in length, is more faithful to the original screenplay, where the

Figure 5. Luc, Alice, and a slain Saïd in
Les amants criminels.

story unfolds chronologically (Ozon, "Entretiens Collection"). On the downside, the 2001 cut is ten minutes shorter than the version originally shown in theaters—some key scenes were shortened, others altogether omitted—making this alternate version an arguably less powerful work, despite its potentially improved narrative clarity.

Les amants criminels can be seen, in the same fashion as *Sitcom* and the later *Gouttes d'eau sur pierres brûlantes* and *8 femmes,* as both a reworking or queering of genre and an homage to various cinematic pasts. Ozon has acknowledged multiple sources of inspiration in addition to Hansel and Gretel, his "favorite fairy tale," and Charles Laughton's thriller classic *The Night of the Hunter* (1955), which *Les amants criminels* quotes rather unabashedly: real accounts of adolescent crimes in Europe and the United States, including the wanton murder of a homeless man at the hands of two affluent teenagers in New York's Central Park; the American cinematic tradition of young outlaws on the run, such as Nicholas Ray's *They Live by Night* (1948), Arthur Penn's *Bonnie and Clyde* (1967), and Leonard Kastle's *The Honeymoon Killers* (1970); and Disney's rendition of *Snow White and the Seven Dwarfs* (1937) for the idyllic love scene between Luc and Alice by the waterfall near the film's conclusion, where, in Ozon's account, "little forest animals huddle around like voyeuristic spectators" ("Interviews *Criminal Lovers*"). Nick Rees-Roberts mentions previous fairy-tale films by queer directors such as Jean Cocteau's *La belle et la bête* (*Beauty and the Beast*, 1946) and Jacques Demy's *Peau d'âne* (*Donkey Skin*, 1970), a French legacy Ozon updates here "by taking the male body as the primary source of pleasure" (Rees-Roberts 31). Andrew Asibong sees a correlation between this film and "a series of modern French literary texts dominated by seductive, sadistic, and paedophiliac 'ogres,'" two examples of which are Michel Tournier's *Le roi des aulnes* (*The Erl-King*, 1970) and Sylvie Germain's *L'enfant méduse* (*The Child Medusa*, 1991) ("Meat" 211). One may add to the list of filmic antecedents France's own lovers-on-the-lam classics, Jean-Luc Godard's *Pierrot le fou* (1965) and François Truffaut's *La sirène du Mississippi* (*Mississippi Mermaid*, 1969), and an earlier thriller also recounting a murder contrived by a woman and elucidated via a flashback sequence, Henri Decoin's *La vérité sur Bébé Donge* (*The Truth about Bebe Donge*, 1952). As we shall see, Ozon cites the same films by Decoin and Truffaut more explicitly in *8 femmes*.

It is out of a wish to marry the contrasting components of the film—the *fait divers* and the *conte de fée*—that Ozon opted for the use of flashbacks. The idea was to remind the viewer repeatedly of the couple's past criminal deeds in order to avoid seeing Luc and Alice as mere victims of the ogre's cruelty in the second half of the film. Thus the murder scene, filmed in a medium-long, continuous shot, is shown twice, once in "real time" with matching sound track, the other in slow motion with Alice's voice-over in the background as she recalls the events retrospectively from the lodge's basement. Ozon explains: "I was afraid that the spectator would forget the murder. The second time, the shot is in slow motion, as if to make it unreal. There is no more audible violence of the stabbing, the cries, the heavy breathing. We're in Alice's head. It was necessary to feel again the pleasure of killing that Alice experienced. At the same time, I was curious to see if using the same shot could produce completely different sensations" ("Interviews *Criminal Lovers*"). This and other flashbacks reinforce Alice's femme fatale attributes as the main instigator of the couple's crime while simultaneously suggesting that she, like Lewis Carroll's famed character after whom she was probably named, might not be able to distinguish fully between reality and make-believe. Alice's bedroom reflects this complexity; it is an ambivalent space that elicits both childlike innocence—an illuminated dollhouse prominently stands next to her bed—and predatory tendencies—the color red is omnipresent, and a crimson carpet with spider web–like patterns covers the floor. In a 2001 interview filmed for the French DVD release of the film, Natacha Régnier described her wardrobe as "offbeat" (*décalé*), arguing that Alice's tormented personality is evident in her choice of pairing an airy, feminine skirt with heavy, bulky shoes, a combination the actress sees as a peculiar mélange of "childhood, violence and masculinity" (Régnier and Renier).

Flashback sequences uncover two additional, essential pieces of information. First, it transpires that Alice's apparent principal motive for the assassination—a heinous gangbang orchestrated by Saïd where photos of Alice and her assailants have been taken and used as blackmail—turns out to have been completely fabricated by the young woman in order to convince Luc to execute her macabre plan. Secondly, it becomes quite clear, as more events leading up to the murder are shown, that Saïd was an object of sexual fascination for both Alice and Luc. Alice's obsession with her classmate's body is made increasingly more explicit with every flashback, in the words she speaks as well as the looks she casts: we first see her read out loud a carnal poem she has penned about Saïd's sensual "brown" and "purple" lips and wet tongue; in literature class, she observes him from behind and draws the nape of his neck (a body part traditionally eroticized on women, in Japan as well as other cultures) before reciting with great fervor Arthur Rimbaud's "Nuit de l'enfer," a poem about a man who poisons himself and is thirsty for crime. A close-up reverse shot of a smiling Saïd returning Alice's gaze demonstrates that her lusty attraction is reciprocated. Two conversations, one between Saïd and his best friend, Karim (Yasmine Belmadi), in an early scene (cut out in the reedited version), the other between Saïd and Alice, further confirm the young man's determination to consummate his attraction for her. In fact, it seems to be *Saïd's* confessed desire for Alice that triggers her wayward anger and murderous plans, perhaps more so than her own desire toward him: "I'll be the one fucking you, asshole," she once utters to herself, reminiscing about a conversation at the conclusion of which the illicit couple decide to meet in the gym's locker room. This idea is reiterated when Luc asks Alice why she lied about the rape. Her simple reply—"[H]e wanted to fuck me, he got what he deserved"—reveals both her detachment from reality and her inability to tolerate the reciprocity of her lust for Saïd.

Luc's desire for the confident boxer is presented as a more clandestine though equally unequivocal affinity. The revelatory scene occurs as Luc visits the boxing area with the intent to steal Saïd's pocket knife, the future murder weapon, from his gym bag. Instead of hurrying to the empty locker room, Luc runs the risk of being discovered and lingers inside the roomful of athletes in practice. He pauses to observe Saïd boxing in the ring, and the camera zooms in on Luc's captivated face while theatrical music crescendos in the background. Later in the story, Luc catches sight of Alice and Saïd kissing passionately in the high school's playground. Another close shot on Luc's face, filmed from a similar angle, suggests that the tears he sheds upon discovering the embracing duo may betray his unfulfilled desire for Saïd more than (or at least as much as) sorrow caused by Alice's infidelity.

The presence of *beur* characters is an exception rather than a norm in Ozon's output, which, if one puts aside *Sitcom*'s Abdu, is generally more preoccupied with cultural differences between white European subjects than with the racial contours of French society. By the time Kechiouche and Belmadi appeared in *Les amants criminels,* they had already performed in films by two other gay (white) directors, the first in Gaël Morel's *A toute vitesse* (*Full Speed,* 1996) and the second in Sébastien Lifshitz's short *Les corps ouverts* (*Open Bodies,* 1998). Both actors, whom Ozon presumably noticed in the above-mentioned films, continued to collaborate with Morel and Lifshitz, often playing sexually ambivalent characters, but did not work again with Ozon.

The original cut of *Les amants criminels* alludes to a homoerotic attraction between Saïd and his best friend, Karim, foreshadowing the narrative's "shift from a heterosexual to a homosexual orientation" that occurs through the figure of Luc (Ince, "Cinema of Desire" 116). The opening sequence—that which immediately precedes the murder—crosscuts between the criminal lovers and the two kickboxing friends. While Alice desperately attempts to arouse a blindfolded Luc by verbally staging her own striptease (Luc's penis remains flaccid throughout the exercise), a topless Saïd, in contrast, expresses intense arousal for Alice as he primps in front of his bedroom's mirror, anticipating a sexual encounter with her later that night. Queer tension develops as Saïd relates to Karim a verbal and physical exchange he has had with Alice. Using Karim's body as a substitute for his own, Saïd assumes Alice's role and sensually runs his hand down his friend's chest, eventually grabbing Karim's penis through his workout pants. The scene ends as Karim bursts into laughter and accuses Saïd of wanting to sleep with *Luc* rather than Alice. This episode, which remains equivocal, has received opposing readings: one commentator saw it as evidence of Saïd's homosexual tendencies (Hain 287), while another opined that its abrupt, laughter-filled conclusion altogether erases the possibility of same-sex desire between the two men by returning to a "properly homosocial friendship based on a shared rejection of an abject queerness" (Rees-Roberts 32). The truth probably lies somewhere in a more sexually uncertain middle. Saïd and Karim's physical interaction, although unrepeated, is replicated visually by a strikingly similar shot of the woodsman stroking Luc's chest (which eventually leads to Luc's first orgasm) in the film's second half, arguably asserting that for Ozon, queer possibilities, whether seen on screen or cut short, are never entirely inconceivable (figs. 6 and 7).

While the (often negative) reviews of the film generally acknowledge both Luc's and Alice's uncontrollable sexual attraction for Saïd, they surprisingly fail to mention that his murder, for which neither adolescent expresses any remorse, is an act motivated at least partially by racial fear (see Bruyn, *"Les amants criminels"*; Larcher; Gilbey, *"Criminal Lovers"*; Knecht). Some scholars, however, have commented on the implications of Ozon's casting choice for the role of Saïd (Kechiouche was born in

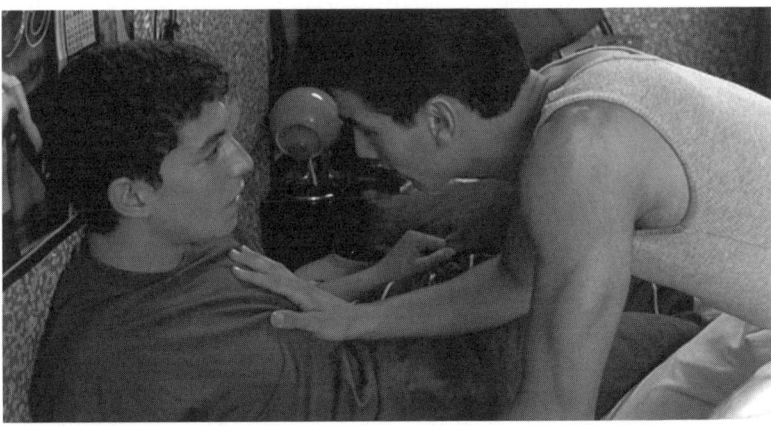

Figure 6. Karim and Saïd in *Les amants criminels.*

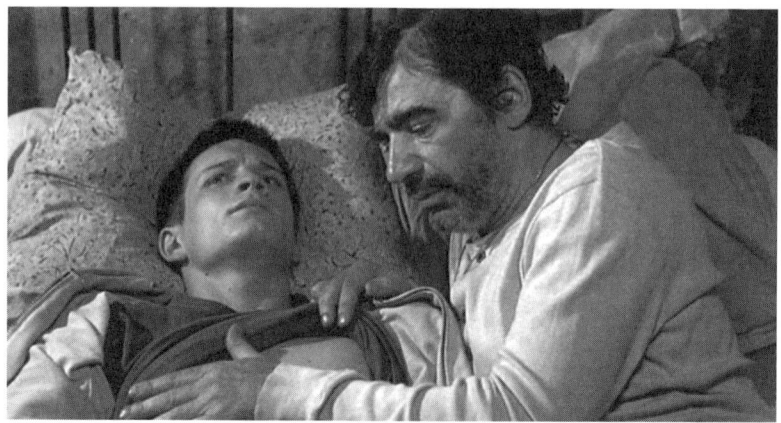

Figure 7. Luc and the ogre in
Les amants criminels.

France of Algerian parents) as well as the stereotypical, potentially problematic and unproblematized ways in which this character is depicted.
Echoing Benjamin Delmotte's contention that the cinema of Ozon is fix-
ated on the duality between sameness and otherness, Mark Hain affirms
that "Alice's hatred of her own desire, in this case, desire for the racial
Other, is displaced onto the object of desire. The film thus evokes the
fear of desiring the Other (another race) as much as desiring the same
(homosexuality), as it's clear that both Alice and Luc are attracted to Saïd
and dangerously conflicted at how this complicates their conception of
normative desire" (286). Asibong notes that the intrusive figure of the
rat in *Sitcom* has been replaced by "the more plausibly fetishized and
dehumanized body of a person, Saïd—a feared, hated, eroticized object
of study that needs to be endlessly watched, described and mastered"
("Meat" 211). In his chapter on *beur* masculinity and queer fantasy in
contemporary French cinema, Rees-Roberts analyzes the figure of the
beur man in films made by gay white directors. Contrasting *Les amants
criminels* with Morel's films starring Kechiouche—*A toute vitesse* and *Le
clan* (*Three Dancing Slaves*, 2004)—he opines that Ozon's "critical stance
is one of apparent postcolonial unawareness," deploring Kechiouche/
Saïd's double objectification by both the camera and the homicidal lovers
and affirming that "[t]he *beur* boy is here denied any sense of subjectiv-
ity, existing purely as a figure of the lovers' distorted imaginations" (31).

These comments are pertinent and impossible to contest. Luc's subsequent fetishization by an accented ogre (Manojlovic is Belgrade-born) who literally feeds Saïd's flesh to the adolescent confronts us, in Asibong's terms, "with the possibility of actually becoming the 'foreign body' we always thought of as somebody—or something—else and through which we have hitherto channeled our unchecked desires" ("Meat" 34). It is difficult to determine whether this gruesome twist in the narrative suffices to countervail the racially imbalanced power relations at play in the film's first half, especially given the generic and geographical distance that separates the realist, contemporary (sub)urban setting where the murder occurs from the fantastic, rural world that the ogre inhabits.

The sequestration of the lovers inside this fantasy world, with Alice confined underground and Luc generally admitted into the main living space, facilitates what may well be the film's principal preoccupation, the sexual awakening of its young male protagonist. The very framing of *Les amants criminels,* with its first close-up shot of Luc with a blindfold and its concluding image of the same teen staring at us with authority, indicates a trajectory from sightlessness to acute awareness, from an inability to "see" queer desire to its acceptance (see Reeser 38–39)—Luc's queer tendencies are reinforced inter-filmically in the first name he shares with the sexually fluid vacationer in *Une robe d'été.* It is the woodsman who assumes the role of sexual facilitator in what becomes a bizarre coming-of-age narrative, turning this paternal monster into a multifaceted figure that is simultaneously good and evil, father and lover, savior and executioner. Ozon unsurprisingly cherished this ambivalence and hoped the spectator would question the man's animality by wondering who was most monstrous, him or the felonious couple (Ozon, "Entretiens *Amants*"). Luc's passivity in his rapport with Alice, sexual or otherwise, persists in his interactions with the woodsman. Frustrated at his inability to take initiative after the pair gets lost in the wilderness and runs out of food, Alice begs him for the first time to "be the man, for once," relinquishing her status as main decision maker. Once in the cabin, the grisly owner takes over Alice's commanding ways.

Initially presented as an unexpectedly moral authority who knows, according to him, "what is good and what is evil," the ogre wishes that Luc and his girlfriend would "pay for all [their] nasty deeds [*saloperies*]." But his intentions become more redemptive as his attention turns exclusively to his male prisoner, who undergoes an "initiation" that attempts to make him comprehend the gravity of his murderous act and transfers his unruly, unfulfilled desire for Saïd to a controllable and potentially more enjoyable form of sexual pleasure. For Todd Reeser, Luc's self-realization is closely tied to what he calls a "domesticated homosexuality" whereby "a kind of fantasmatic domesticity puts the coming-out process in motion, appearing inseparable from it" (38). Luc is thus forced to serve his host in various ways and engage in domestic tasks such as hunting, cooking, and dishwashing, preserving, with increasing pleasure for the young man, an obsequious role in this master-and-slave relationship and deferring his ability to "be the man, for once." In fact, the brute encourages Luc to do exactly the opposite. He infantilizes his protégé by recommending that he "be a good boy" and by calling him "*mon lapin*" (my little rabbit), a common term of endearment in French and an omnipresent animal figure in the film—whether live, trapped, cooked, or stuffed—evoking both children's tales and adult sexuality. As he becomes more emotionally attached to his houseboy, he claims to have dug up Saïd's body to "help [Luc]," a decision that leads to the forced act of anthropophagy—Luc first believes he has eaten rabbit stew, until Alice, who notices Saïd's missing leg, suggests the ghastly truth that causes Luc to regurgitate his dinner. Ozon deemed it necessary to confront Luc with his victim in such a radical fashion and make him "eat his own shit in a way, eat the very object of his guilt," adding that "in fairy tales, the idea of 'eating each other' is very important" (Ozon, "Entretiens *Amants*"). The film, then, toys with the conventions of the fairy tale in order to activate the discovery of Luc's primary sexual preference, a process that cannot occur without the utter subservience of the discoverer on the one hand and the "purging" of his past sins on the other.

Belgian (and unrelated) actors Jérémie Renier and Natacha Régnier have declared in interviews that the sadistic manipulation of the burly beast onto their characters extended to the movie set and their rapport with Ozon, particularly during the shooting of the scenes inside the forest hut. Renier/Luc, who notably appeared in Jean-Pierre and Luc Dardenne's *La promesse* (1996) before contributing to this project, described having to deal with two monsters while filming: "François himself would turn into an ogre; I was to submit to both of them. I had to deal with two ogres, one behind the camera and one walking me around on a leash. And sometimes they would switch roles on me." As for Régnier/ Alice, acclaimed for her powerful performance as Marie in Eric Zoncka's *La vie rêvée des anges* (*The Dreamlife of Angels*, 1998), she described the spatial configuration of the movie set as identical to the ogre's fictional space, with the one-room living area situated upstairs and the cellar below. The actress was to stay alone in the basement, with nothing to do but think about her solitude, while all the scenes between Renier and Miki Manojlovic (Emir Kusturica's preferred actor) were being shot above her head. She confessed feeling a sense of complete abandonment before adding that the scheme was "deliberate" and devised by Ozon himself (Régnier and Renier). Ozon does not deny occasionally extreme shooting conditions and has commented on Kechiouche's genuine state of fear during the murder scene. Filmed through a doorframe, from relatively far away in an uninterrupted sequence, there was no possibility for the actors to take breaks during Saïd's stabbing; Ozon originally intended to shoot a much edited version with multiple shots and various angles, but at the last minute opted for a more detached, newsreel type of filming. Ozon reminisces: "[Shooting in real time] meant that actors had to really reflect on how to kill someone, how to pin the body down so it wouldn't move. We realized how violent it all was when the young guy playing Saïd almost fainted. He is a strong, virile kickboxing champion, but he practically passed out. He said: 'I thought that was it, I thought I was going to die for real.' To make matters worse, Jérémie had to hit him in earnest, so [Kechiouche] had to contract his entire body while at the same time screaming and trying to fight back with his arms" (Ozon, "Entretiens *Amants*").

Sometimes the manipulation took a less violent, more seductive turn. When Renier learned that he was to wear nothing but a pair of briefs for the entire three-day shoot in the ogre's cellar (which happened to be a real, cold one), he initially refused. According to the actor, it is only after Ozon complimented him on how good he looked in his underwear that Renier "accepted his compliments" and agreed to undress (Régnier and Renier). These seduction games match those unfolding within the fictional content of the film, from Alice's "innocent" blindfold game in the opening sequence to the dangerous stratagems that lead to Saïd's tragic demise. Now imprisoned in the cellar, Alice is no longer able to "play," except in her memory-filled mind, and has no other choice but to forsake her seductive powers. Desperately eager to find a way out of her situation, the blonde woman uses Luc as a surrogate player and advises her boyfriend to "seduce [the ogre], just like [they did] with Saïd." Luc complies by becoming more of a "good boy" and showing no resistance when his captor lays him on the bed facedown for full intercourse. The maneuver, for which Luc probably did not need Alice's advice, functions beautifully, so much so that the ravishment of Luc's virginity coincides with that of the older man's heart, as indicated in his feigning sleep to allow the couple to escape, and confirmed by a shot/countershot where Luc and the ogre exchange a tender glance as Luc exits the shack for the last time.

As we have seen, the development of the homosexual plot coincides with the evacuation of the film's only female character. Alice's physical removal from the action in all but a few cabin scenes compels Luc to become, for the first time and despite his utter submission to his host, the dominant agent inside the teenage partnership. Luc retains his sovereignty during their escape as he commands Alice not to kill the ogre and, later still, as he makes love to her, in top sex position, by the waterfall. Nevertheless, the artificiality of the latter scene—from the maudlin orchestra music, to the blinding radiance of the light, to the overly cute wild animals marveling at the two lovers in action—although audacious on Ozon's part, makes this reinstatement of heterosexual desire both preposterous and contrived. The lovers' newfound carnal symbiosis appears all the more dubious when their mechanical copulation is cut short by the arrival of policemen and their barking dogs before either is able to reach orgasm. The police chase through the woods, which signals an abrupt return to reality, results in Alice's death by gunfire and Luc's arrest, and aborts any possible heterosexual resolution to the plot.

The object of the criminal lovers' "last gaze," a mental image for Alice and a real sight for Luc, further discredits the authenticity of their bond beyond platonic friendship. As the bullets enter Alice's body, her ultimate thought goes to Saïd, and an overexposed image of the young boxer appears to the spectator after her final collapse. While the police escort Luc to the patrol wagon, his cries for Alice suddenly stop upon witnessing the ogre being violently, and somewhat inexplicably, kicked in the stomach by the authorities. The teen's enraged and persistent affirmation of the hermit's innocence ("please let him go, he has done nothing wrong") and his subsequent, tear-filled glare at the camera have been convincingly read as "Luc's assumption of his sexuality" and an "end to the ironic tone and fairy-tale ambiance of the film" (Reeser 39), a tone most strikingly illustrated in the aforementioned bucolic love scene. Ozon proves more elusive in his interpretation of Luc's demeanor—inevitably reminiscent of Antoine Doinel's famous look at the camera at the conclusion of Truffaut's New Wave classic *Les 400 coups* (*The 400 Blows*, 1959)—and sees it as "Luc's last tears of childhood . . . [Alice] refused to become an adult. Luc, with his expression, becomes a man." When asked specifically about the stare, which lasts a monumental fifteen seconds, the answer becomes more interesting: "I filmed that on instinct. During the shot, I abruptly asked actor Jérémie Renier to look at me. I needed that" ("Interviews *Criminal Lovers*"). Although the filmmaker does not confess the reason for his "need" to be looked at from behind the camera (Ozon's usual position while filming), this choice invites the possibility for Luc to connect again with another (queer) male figure. This new connection relays, beyond the film's universe and thus perhaps more powerfully, the ultimate, broken exchange of looks between Luc and the handcuffed, beaten-up ogre that occurs in the shots immediately preceding the young man's final angry gaze.

After the box office failure of *Les amants criminels*, François Ozon followed up quickly with two feature films, both released in the year 2000, that brought about significantly more critical acclaim than his first two features and established solid foundations for his career as a director of full-length films. The queer melodrama *Gouttes d'eau sur pierres brûlantes* marks Ozon's first literary adaptation; it is also an explicit homage to the cinema of German filmmakers Rainer Werner Fassbinder and Douglas Sirk, which, in the same vein as *Sitcom* and *Les amants criminels*, "makes an important contribution to current debates in contemporary French film-making concerning the role of genre" in cinema (Handyside 207). But it is perhaps thanks to the star power of Charlotte Rampling and the much discussed "subdued" filmmaking style of *Sous le sable* that Ozon was finally able to conquer the mainstream, export his films internationally, and gain legitimacy among the French critical establishment. Echoing *Les amants criminels* on a thematic level, these two films recount the agonizing attachment of a protagonist—a young male student in the first, a fifty-something woman in the second—

to a middle-aged man, a recalcitrant obsession that ends in suicide in *Gouttes d'eau sur pierres brûlantes* and possible lunacy in *Sous le sable*. Further acclaim came in 2002 with Ozon's most marketed, most popular, and most well-known film to date (rivaled only by his later, immensely successful *Swimming Pool*), the star-studded, multiple-award-winning *8 femmes*, which narrates yet again the impassioned, treacherous attachment of eight women for an older man.

Loosely adapted from an eponymous 1960s French *boulevard* play by the now forgotten dramatist Robert Thomas, *8 femmes* is, like *Les amants criminels*, a generically diverse tale of dark secrets and murder. The static framing of characters in long shots, the use of vivid, Technicolor-like hues, and studio shooting in a limited number of sets maintain the theatricality of *8 femmes*'s stage inspiration. But unlike Thomas's relatively formulaic, Agatha Christie–inspired murder intrigue involving an internal, detective-free investigation, Ozon's filmic interpretation clearly refuses to fit inside the boundaries of the *polar* or murder mystery genre: it is at once a burlesque comedy, a melodrama, and a whodunit, seasoned with a pinch of the musical. The death of the father that occurs at the conclusion of *Sitcom* is now at the center of the narrative, as in *8 femmes* he is found assassinated ten minutes into the film. *8 femmes* takes place in 1950s France and opens as Suzon (Virginie Ledoyen), a student in an English boarding school, returns home for Christmas break on a snowy winter morning. The remote country mansion belongs to her parents, Marcel (Dominique Lamure, a mere shadow) and Gaby (Catherine Deneuve), and also houses her younger sister, Catherine (Ludivine Sagnier); her spinster aunt, Augustine (Isabelle Huppert); her grandmother, Mamy (Danielle Darrieux); and two servants, Madame Chanel, the long-term cook and governess (Firmine Richard), and Louise, the recently hired chambermaid (Emmanuelle Béart). The discovery of Marcel with a dagger in his back triggers an investigation led by Suzon, a younger, better-dressed, but equally tenacious stand-in for Christie's Miss Marple. A violent snowstorm traps the dynasty inside the house. The phone line and family's only car have been sabotaged. As Suzon probes into everyone's lives, including that of Marcel's sister, Pierrette (Fanny Ardant), who later joins the overwrought clan, secrets are revealed about all of them, making each and every one a plausible murder suspect. The film's final twist, however, undoes the patriarch's status as "victim" and exposes an unforeseen subterfuge.

François Ozon's resolution to make a film with a woman-only cast originated in his admiration for two films: Fassbinder's *Die bitteren Tränen der Petra von Kant* (*The Bitter Tears of Petra von Kant*, 1972), the tragic story of a lesbian affair "where Fassbinder recounts one of his own love stories" (Rouyer and Vassé, "Danger" 19), and George Cukor's *The Women* (1939), a prewar, all-star Hollywood classic featuring Joan Crawford, Rosalind Russell, Joan Fontaine, and Paulette Goddard. Based on a 1936 play by Clare Boothe, Cukor's lavish MGM comedy chronicles the lives of high-society Manhattan women who lead an existence of leisure that includes a copious dose of gossip and catfights, visits to beauty salons and fashion shows, and even a trip to an out-of-the-way dude ranch in Nevada. Ozon initially intended to direct a French remake of Cukor's picture, but quickly learned that the rights had already been sold to Julia Roberts and Meg Ryan (Ozon, *8 femmes* 21). Because of this technical hurdle, Ozon's project was temporarily put on hold until his agent, Dominique Besnehard, proposed Thomas's play, a man-free whodunit performed in Paris between 1961 and 1962 starring most notably veteran film and stage actresses Jane Marken and Denise Grey. Like Cukor's work, Thomas's play abounds with adulterous intrigues and other scandals, making it a perfect substitute for Ozon's remake project. One year before the play's first performance in Paris, Robert Thomas had become an acclaimed playwright almost overnight after the success of his police comedy, *Piège pour un seul homme* (1960).

Huit femmes, with the number eight spelled out, unlike Ozon's film, was Thomas's next theatrical undertaking. Although successful at the time of its running and into the following decade, thanks to its appearance in the popular French television program *Au théâtre ce soir,* the play had fallen into oblivion until Ozon decided to adapt it. The film's published screenplay describes Ozon's design to keep the framework of the original story but ultimately transform it into something else: "Of [Thomas's play], François Ozon kept the letter, that is to say, the police intrigue and the characters. What he adjusted was the psychology, the rapports between the women, their family secrets and the historical context. In order to pay tribute to Hollywood cinema made by great European exiles, the film takes place in the 1950s; the characters thus interact in décors and costumes directly inspired by the Technicolor movies of that era. This choice also justifies the film's musical dimension created by the songs that the director chose to reveal each character's personality, in the same fashion as a monologue" (Ozon, *8 femmes: Scénario* 5).

I have already pointed out that Ozon's ardent cinephilia comes through rather conspicuously in most of his films. The director's passion for the medium, however, is most manifest in *8 femmes*, where inter-filmic allusions go on almost ad infinitum. The opening credits, for example, suggest that Ozon still had *The Women* in mind when he edited *8 femmes*. In Cukor's comedy every actress's name is announced by a title and the picture of an animal, whether wild or domesticated, each intended to reflect the personality of the characters. The opening of *8 femmes* is almost identical, except that a flower garden replaces Cukor's menagerie. The credits show us in succession the eight actresses' names in pink font along with close-up shots of various flowers, which in retrospect can be understood as symbolic representations of each protagonist's temperament: an orchid for the wealthy and beautiful lady of the house; a carnivorous flower for her bitter maiden sister; a white daisy for the seemingly innocent younger daughter; a sunflower for the loyal, cheery governess; a red rose for the father's scandalous, seductive sister; and so on.

There are two additional types of citations in *8 femmes*, one American, the other French. The most evident North American influences are the 1950s Hollywood melodramas directed by Douglas Sirk, such as *There's Always Tomorrow* (1956) and *Imitation of Life* (1959). *8 femmes* particularly quotes the same director's *All That Heaven Allows* (1955), a doomed love story between a wealthy widow (Jane Wyman) and a younger, lower-class nurseryman (Rock Hudson): in addition to opting for a winter/Christmas setting and shooting numerous scenes through or in front of windows (a recurrent visual motif in Sirk's work), *8 femmes* opens with the lyrical image of a female deer while Sirk's psychological drama ends with that of a male, antlered version of the same animal. (Todd Haynes's *Far from Heaven*, released the same year as *8 femmes*, clearly positions itself in relation to *All That Heaven Allows* as well, attesting to the patent fascination of contemporary gay directors for the 1950s period and in particular for Sirk's melodramas.) The atypically bright chromatic palette of Ozon's film and its eight distinct musical numbers also evoke the primary-colored musicals of (non-émigré) Vincente Minnelli, two typical representatives of which are *The Band Wagon* (1953) and the period piece *Brigadoon* (1954). More generally, *8 femmes*'s actresses and their opulent, perfectly tailored wardrobe (designed by Pascaline Chavanne) pay homage to stars of classic Hollywood: Lana Turner (Darrieux), Lana Turner and Marilyn Monroe (Deneuve), Agnes Moorehead (Huppert), Kim Novak and Grace Kelly (Béart), Rita Hayworth and Cyd Charisse (Ardant), Audrey Hepburn (Ledoyen), Leslie Caron and Sandra Dee (Sagnier), Hattie McDaniel and Juanita Moore (Richard) (Ozon, *8 femmes* 36–63).

If *8 femmes* mimics the aesthetics, costumes, and genres of postwar Hollywood cinema, it is also deeply rooted in the French tradition. The second type of intertextuality makes explicit or indirect references to French films of all periods, creating, in the same fashion as the American references, a meta-filmic continuity between Ozon's work and that of his cinematic fathers. As Lalanne notes, *8 femmes* "is as much *a film about* as *a film with* Catherine Deneuve, Fanny Ardant, Isabelle Huppert . . . François Ozon has managed to direct the most deliberately *meta* film in all of French cinema ("Les actrices" 82, Lalanne's emphasis). Examples are virtually endless. Béart/Louise's leather boots are directly inspired from those Jeanne Moreau wears in Luis Buñuel's *Le journal d'une femme de chambre* (*Diary of a Chambermaid,* 1964). The picture of Austrian-born actress Romy Schneider that Louise shows Gaby is a reminder that Béart replaced Schneider, after her real-life suicide, as director Claude Sautet's *actrice fétiche.* By confessing to Gaby, when talking about the photograph of her former employer (Schneider), that she "loved her," Louise ventriloquizes Ozon's own feelings for Schneider and his profound childhood admiration for the *Sissi* film series (Rouyer and Vassé, "Danger" 21). It also arguably alludes to Schneider's starring role in Francis Girod's *La banquière* (*The Woman Banker,* 1980), in which she plays a bisexual woman—lesbianism being, as we shall see, one of *8 femmes*'s unveiled secrets.

The very presence in *8 femmes* of Danielle Darrieux—French cinema's unrivaled doyen, who made her acting début in 1931, and whose career spans over seventy years—points back to numerous film projects in which she participated. The *huis clos,* gender-imbalanced format of

8 femmes harkens back to Darrieux's performance in *Marie-Octobre* (Julien Duvivier, 1959), a dramatic, single-set production in which she plays a lone woman in an all-male cast of former Resistance members, one of whom is guilty of treason. By having the same actress assume the role of the family's matriarch, who used poison to kill her husband (an army colonel), *8 femmes* indirectly makes reference to three previous films in which Darrieux and Deneuve were mother and daughter—including Demy's *Les demoiselles de Rochefort* and Téchiné's *Le lieu du crime* (*Scene of the Crime*, 1986)—and another Demy musical where Darrieux incarnates a colonel's widow, *Une chambre en ville* (*A Room in Town*, 1982). Going further back in time, Mamy's spouse-killing past evokes 1950s productions in which Darrieux plays a poisoner: her former husband Henri Decoin's *La vérité sur Bébé Donge* and *L'affaire des poisons* (*The Poison Affair*, 1955). Deneuve's vampy singing number "Toi jamais" recalls three Demy films in which she starred and sang: *Les demoiselles de Rochefort*, *Les parapluies de Cherbourg* (*The Umbrellas of Cherbourg*, 1964) and *Peau d'âne*. Similarly, Ledoyen's performance of the sugary song "Mon amour, mon ami" is suggestive of a more recent French musical where she assumes the lead (singing) role: Olivier Ducastel's and Jacques Martineau's *Jeanne et le garçon formidable* (*Jeanne and the Perfect Guy*, 1998). Moreover, Ledoyen hides her pregnancy in *8 femmes,* as she did in Claude Chabrol's *La cérémonie* (*A Judgment in Stone*, 1995); anecdotally, the actress was really carrying a child (a daughter) during the shooting of Ozon's film, which prompted Darrieux to jokingly rename the film "9 femmes" during interviews. When Pierrette accuses Huppert/Augustine of being like the heroine of Alexandre Dumas's romance novel *La dame aux camélias* (*The Lady of the Camellias*), she cleverly refers to Huppert's performance as Alphonsine in the Italian film adaptation of this French novel, Mauro Bolognini's *La storia vera della signora dalle camelie* (1981). One last example, more personal to Ozon's cinema: Sagnier's crazed dance choreography as she sings Sheila's "Papa t'es plus dans le coup" in the company of her mother and sister recalls Sébastien's performance of another Sheila song in *Une robe d'été* as well as Sagnier's own participation in the famous dance in *Gouttes d'eau sur pierres brûlantes* (fig. 8).

The screenplay further distances itself from *8 femmes*'s theatrical source and insists that beyond cinematic references the film is very

Figure 8. Gaby, Catherine, and Suzon
in *8 femmes*.

much in line with Ozon's previous achievements. At the same time, it also mentions another (this time literary) "parent text" written by one of France's most celebrated queer authors: "On a deeper level, François Ozon revised Robert Thomas's play by drawing themes from his own cinematic universe: the absence of the father, sexual ambiguity (already present in his previous films), and a criticism of the family circle and the perverse relationships between masters and servants, just as Jean Genet did in *Les bonnes* [*The Maids*]" (Ozon, *8 femmes: Scénario* 5).

Let us now turn to the question of sexual ambiguity, rightfully mentioned here as a recurring theme of Ozon's. With so many female characters confined together in this enclosed space, it is hard to imagine that he resisted the temptation to introduce some sexual tension and provide some of them with the opportunity to fulfill their heretofore hidden same-sex desires. The film contains an "official" lesbian couple and advances the possibility of one or two more alliances. The first uncovered lesbian relationship has blossomed long before the beginning of the story. As the investigation progresses, it transpires that the cook, Madame Chanel, has been having an affair with the father's sister, Pierrette. Pierrette, in turn, is a former prostitute whom the seemingly righteous wife and mother of the family, Gaby, hates and has forbidden from seeing her own brother because of her loose morals. As the characters attempt to establish everybody's whereabouts the night of the murder,

Louise divulges that Pierrette was in the house the night of Marcel's stabbing; she had apparently come to visit both Marcel and Madame Chanel. This revelation causes Pierrette to acknowledge regular secret meetings with her sibling and also forces the two female "culprits" to acknowledge their love for each other; it is better to come out of the closet than be accused of murder, even in the conservative 1950s.

Lesbianism is altogether absent from Thomas's play, where Madame Chanel's only shocking secret is that she plays cards behind her employers' back. Ozon once joked that his decision to turn her and Pierrette into lesbians would have made the playwright furious and confessed: "[Thomas's] heir and beneficiary admitted to me that he absolutely hated lesbians and that, out of the eight women, he identified with Pierrette the most! But that is the beauty of adapting the work of deceased authors, such as Fassbinder or Robert Thomas . . . They can't come and tell you off!" (Mellini 53). If the presence of same-sexuality is hardly surprising coming from our director, lesbianism is portrayed in the film in a rather ambivalent fashion. After Pierrette and Madame Chanel's liaison comes out in the open, Gaby and her mother are appalled at the idea of having an *"invertie"* in the house, and the maid withdraws to the kitchen; Mamy's heavy gasping upon hearing the news and her subsequent use of the old-fashioned, pejorative term *inverti(e)* (inverted) to describe lesbian identity is a cause of amusement for the contemporary viewer and a reminder that the story does not take place in 2002. Madame Chanel's musical number follows, as she, alone in her own domestic space (the kitchen), sings a song titled "Pour ne pas vivre seul" (originally sung by Dalida in 1972). The doleful ballad is about lonely people who would do anything not to be on their own: some adopt a dog, some worship a cross, others grow roses, and so forth. The second verse asserts that same-sex relationships occur for the exact same reason: "So as not to live alone, girls love girls, and sometimes we may see boys marry boys." As the screenplay contends, most of the musical numbers are aimed at disclosing the characters' true inner thoughts. However, it remains unclear whether the film suggests that Madame Chanel herself became a lesbian out of sheer loneliness, or whether the line, within this particular context and given the scene that precedes it, pokes fun at assumptions about homosexual desire.

The apparently random lesbian kiss between Pierrette and Gaby, which occurs later in the story, is equally difficult to interpret. Although the two women loathe each other, they unexpectedly reconcile after a violent fight that has brought them to the floor; the battle commences after they realize that they have the same lover, an extramarital affair in Gaby's case, and one of two disclosed skeletons in her closet. A lengthy, passionate kiss ensues, and although the narrative has somewhat "prepared" the spectator for other possible lesbian liaisons besides Pierrette and Madame Chanel's (Louise flirts with Gaby in an earlier scene), the kiss comes as somewhat of a surprise, even for those familiar with Ozon's output (fig. 9). What is certain is that it provides both shock value (it is, after all, two immensely popular French actresses kissing) and comic relief: the rest of the women walk in on them and witness the embrace, flabbergasted. I have already mentioned Lalanne's dismissal of the Deneuve/Ardant kiss as a lesbian display of affection and his contention that it should rather be read as an ephemeral coming together of two effigies of François Truffaut's cinema ("Les actrices" 83). David Ehrenstein, an openly gay American critic, has a similar opinion, albeit for different reasons; he argues in the *Advocate*, "[T]hat embrace isn't meant to examine same-sex passion so much as it is to recall plush A-picture romance in all its Hollywood glow" (60). What may prompt both Lalanne and Ehrenstein to read the kiss as something that is not fundamentally homosexual is that, to the film's merit and in spite of the

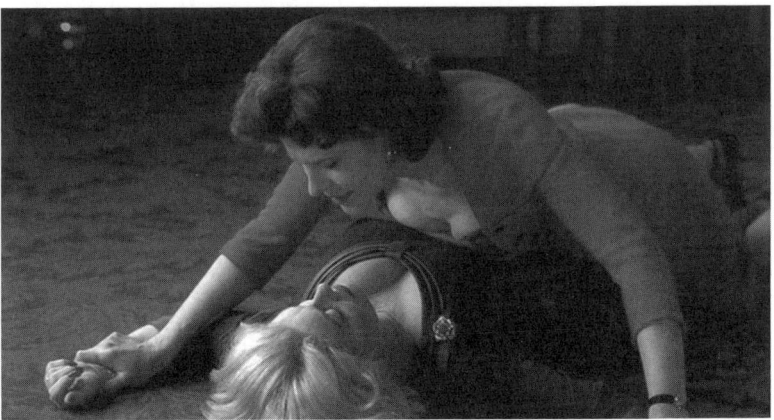

Figure 9. Pierrette and Gaby in *8 femmes*. I

plot's introduction of homosexuality as something "scandalous" according to some family members, lesbianism is generally treated without recourse to weighty stereotyping, thus rendering it as "natural" as heterosexuality. Even though these remarks—Lalanne's particularly—are potentially problematic in their suggestion that the Deneuve/Ardant romp is a "sexually neutral" activity, it is true that the women's interaction carries strong intertextual undertones that may well take precedence, in the auteur's mind, over the film's narrative coherence. The two actresses' physical altercation most evidently pays homage to Truffaut's *La femme d'à côté* (*The Woman Next Door* [1981], Ardant's first film with partner Truffaut, the illustrious fight of which is recreated in *8 femmes* with Deneuve in the role of Gérard Depardieu), while the ensuing kiss is probably intended to recall Tony Scott's *The Hunger* (1983) and Téchiné's *Les voleurs* (*Thieves*, 1996), in which Deneuve famously plays the part of a lesbian.

There are additional winks at Truffaut in *8 femmes,* some that cite his cinema and others that reference the real-life love relationships he had with the two present actresses—Deneuve in the late 1960s and early 1970s, Ardant in the 1980s. During a mother-daughter talk between Deneuve/Gaby and Ledoyen/Suzon, in which Suzon learns that Marcel is not her biological father, the mother repeats a line ("te voir . . . c'est à la fois une joie, et une souffrance" [seeing you brings me joy, but also makes me suffer]) said to Deneuve by two men (Jean-Paul Belmondo and Depardieu) in two Truffaut films, *La sirène du Mississippi* and *Le dernier métro* (*The Last Metro,* 1980). As soon as she utters those words, Deneuve seems more affected by the memory of Truffaut and the films she made with him than her diegetic conversation with her daughter. Similarly, the abnormally long (twenty-two-second) close-up shot of Ardant (who overhears the line) that concludes the scene suggests it is the memory of her late companion that brings her to tears rather than the fictional context of the film.

Undeniably, a large part of *8 femmes*'s interest and enjoyment lies in the spectator's ability to engage in a cinephilic Clue game of sorts that consists in identifying the various filmic citations, including some from Ozon's own filmography, that the director playfully inserted throughout the story. But it would be a mistake, and simply inaccurate given the film's success in non-French markets, to reduce the film to a whodunit for cinephiles and dismiss it as a whodunit tout court. Certainly most commentators spend a large part of their reviews listing those inspirations, sometimes to the detriment of other elements (see, for example, Boujut; Mellini; Masson), and I realize that the present discussion may be guilty of the same crime. At the same time, almost half of the red-velvet-covered, two-hundred-page color book that was released concomitantly with the film (published by La Martinière, 2002) also highlights in great detail Ozon's filmic homages and his commitment to celebrate, through this project, his favorite movies, directors, and actresses. Ozon conceded that the murder investigation and its surprising final twist were "a pretext" to put together a rare, and probably never to be reproduced, bouquet of French actresses of various generations and adeptly toy with their cinematic baggage. Yet he also insists that he took the story seriously and that the plot and its intricacies are ultimately what seduced the public and made the film a tremendous popular success both locally and internationally. *8 femmes* was viewed by 3.7 million spectators in French theaters. It went on to receive Lumière and Etoile d'or awards and was nominated for no less than twelve César awards; it subsequently won two prizes at the reputable Berlinale, one prize in Boston, and one in Russia (Huppert's wired, Louis de Funès–like performance was particularly rewarded). Ozon explains his intentions:

> I did not want to be condescending towards [the whodunit] and its motifs. I really wanted to treat them seriously, and the script supervisor and I made sure that everything was plausible: one must be able to watch the film again knowing its dénouement. Although the interest of the film may lie elsewhere, all sorts of audiences responded to it: children, for example, had a very different way to look at it and paid close attention to the plot and its plausibility . . . The element of surprise [at the end of the film] is not essential, but this type of storytelling is always a source of pleasure. My desire to make films is before anything else a desire to tell stories, and to see an audience shiver and laugh [while watching *8 femmes*] is truly exciting to me. (Delmotte, "Entretien" 88)

Ozon greatly simplified Thomas's original story line by omitting numerous details that he judged secondary, but kept the dénouement, which the filmmaker claims was not Thomas's idea but rather that of celebrated Gallic dramatist Jean Anouilh (Rouyer and Vassé, "Danger"

19). Despite plot simplifications, Ozon rendered the narrative more complex by introducing, in addition to lesbian intrigues, two of his favorite ingredients: unreliable flashbacks, already present in *Sitcom* and *Les amants criminels,* and abruptly erupting musical numbers, which may be traced back to his short work and in this case significantly modify the film's generic fabric and narrative flow. There are six brief flashbacks, presented to us at multiple points in the narrative, as characters provide their subjective credible recollections of the night of the murder: Louise serves herbal tea to her master around midnight, Pierrette threatens Marcel to make him give her money, Suzon visits her father in the middle of the night to announce her pregnancy, Gaby (wrongly) speculates on Pierrette killing Marcel and on later trying to shoot Chanel so she would not reveal that Pierrette is the murderess, and so on. These flashback motifs have been read as self-consciously "useless," especially because "two of them contradict one another," and mere pretexts to break the rhythm and give the viewer access to certain rooms that the theatrical, single-location nature of the main mise-en-scène would not otherwise permit (Masson 18). More pragmatically, the flashbacks further delay, in true whodunit fashion, the final narrative pirouette revealed to us by Catherine in the form of a seventh, longer flashback sequence.

The eight musical performances, in which each character sings a solo with or without back-up accompaniment, are more unbalanced in their textual function and may have a destabilizing effect on the spectator. Having taught *8 femmes* several times in a university course on French cinema, I can affirm that their precipitous, unannounced incursion may be off-putting to the traditional viewer, even one familiar with classic American musicals. Several factors may explain such reaction. Ozon's design was to be "democratic" and give each actress "her [own] moment of musical bravura" as well as to use songs to "reveal the secret failing [*faille*] of every character, their motivation" (Mellini 52). But in the name of artifice, theatricality, Brechtian "distanciation," and sheer pleasure, four concepts that Ozon frequently mentions in interviews when discussing *8 femmes* and some of his previous films (especially *Sitcom* and *Gouttes d'eau sur pierres brûlantes*), the eight songs intentionally rupture the film text and arguably interrupt, temporarily but repeatedly, suspension of disbelief. Ozon, however, would disagree with their potentially unsettling character: "While shooting, I made sure these interludes were introduced progressively. But as I edited the film, I realized that the pill would be easier to swallow if women started singing without warning. Absolutely no intellectualization, it's all about pleasure" (Rouyer and Vassé, "Danger" 19). The absence of "warning," however, and the impetuous changes in tone and style these episodes create engender a jolting reaction in the spectator. The latter must, for example, embrace the fact that Pierrette bursts into laughter seconds after finding out that her beloved brother has been assassinated and, more generally, relish these performances as suspended moments of "pure entertainment."

The musical intrusions are highly stylized, strictly choreographed (courtesy of Sébastien Charles), and intended to recall the heyday of the Hollywood-crafted musical: women perform in playback for the camera, lights occasionally go dim, non-diegetic music supplements the solo acts, and in the case of Pierrette's black-glove striptease, which quotes that of Rita Hayworth in *Gilda* (Charles Vidor, 1946), further tributes are paid. According to Alain Masson, these fragments give actresses temporary license to "break loose from their characters" and unknowingly proclaim, through the lyrics they sing, "lucid maxims" that are relevant to their current situation (17). What I find particularly interesting about these recitals is that if most of the women are shown as sexual objects to be looked at, all of this occurs without the presence of the proverbial mediating male gaze in narrative cinema (recall, for example, the mixed but predominantly male crowd attending Gilda's singing act "Put the Blame on Mame"; for feminist discussions of the "male gaze," see De Lauretis; Mulvey, "Visual Pleasure"; Mayne). This departure from traditional female performance on film, where non-singing (women) characters are presented in countershots as enthralled, admiring spectators, intensifies the film's queer tension, sometimes forecasting lesbian romances that the text will later divulge (Chanel/Pierrette; Gaby/Pierrette), other times advancing possibilities that remain unfulfilled (Augustine/Louise; Gaby/Louise).

In order to situate *8 femmes* within the context of the present section on "paternal monsters" as well as the director's overall filmography, it is useful to revisit momentarily Lalanne's convincing contention that Ozon's films position father figures in strict binary terms: they are either present and abusive in one way or another or altogether absent, leaving behind them a world filled with chaos and insanity ("Les actrices" 83).

While Jean in *Sitcom,* the ogre in *Les amants criminels,* and, as we shall see, Léopold in *Gouttes d'eau sur pierres brûlantes* and Gilles in *5x2* roughly fit the first category, Marcel, the virtually unseen father in *8 femmes,* although abusive in various ways, better fits the second; so do Jean in *Sous le sable* and, to an extent, John in *Swimming Pool* (notice the recurrence of the name "Jean" or its English equivalent in both categories). Going back to *8 femmes,* it should be clear by now that although many conversations in the film revolve around the male kind—echoing *The Women's* tagline that despite their on-screen absence, the film is "all about men!"—Ozon's creation works hard to prove that men are unnecessary, if not a nuisance to women. Gaby's lover has betrayed her by sleeping with Pierrette, who gave the same man a large sum of money with which he ran off to Mexico. Pierrette admits to often preferring the delicate touch of women because "men have disappointed [her] so often," and Mamy avows the murder of her husband, whom she says she "could not abide." Even before the discovery of Marcel's daggered body and long before secrets are revealed about his own monstrosity (he had an ongoing, in-house affair with Louise and possibly impregnated his daughter Suzon), Catherine's first musical number expressly establishes the father as an outdated concept: "Papa, t'es plus dans le coup" roughly translates as "Daddy, You're Not With It Anymore." But just as the rat reappears on the father's grave at the end of *Sitcom,* questioning the possibility of a bona fide matriarchal society, Marcel's death turns out to be all but a fallacy. The film's conclusion reveals a fake murder ploy: the father, alive and well, has been hiding in his room all along, listening to what has transpired in and around the house. Catherine confesses to the seven women that she and Marcel masterminded the murder scheme in order to prove to her father that she is the only one worthy of his affection. The film, however, regales us with one last *coup de théâtre:* disgusted at the behavior of his wife, sister, sister-in-law, older daughter, mother-in-law, and maids, Marcel finally commits suicide in front of Catherine, making his death "the result of the murder investigation rather than its cause" (Masson 16).

The last musical number, Darrieux's rendition of Georges Brassens's "Il n'y a pas d'amour heureux" (There Is No Happy Love), follows this tragic event and prompts the other characters to engage in a mournful ballet. After the song, all eight women stand next to one another in a perfect line, inhabiting the same shot for the first and last time. This is the last image of 8 *femmes,* one that is particularly rich in significance and a final reminder of the work's trans-generic, inter-filmic qualities (fig. 10). The unorthodox, symmetrical composition conjures up another that is especially familiar to American crime film enthusiasts: a police lineup, which, in addition to being an ultimate homage to the police thriller genre, intimates that the women are all in some way guilty of the father's quietus. The shot also invokes the world of the theater, and one expects the eight actresses to take a bow in front of the camera, especially after they slowly start holding hands. However, they refrain from bowing, and the spectator is left to contemplate this unique sample of four generations of French actresses. Darrieux, who was eighty-five years old in 2002, has enlightened the silver screen since the early talkies, while Deneuve, Huppert, and Béart are undoubtedly three of the most recognizable actresses working in France today. But the image also serves as a suggestion that the next generation, personified by Ledoyen and Sagnier, is well on its way. Notably, the oldest and youngest performers (Darrieux and Sagnier) stand in the very center of the line. When the two of them join hands, the veteran of French cinema offers a symbolic relay baton to the rising star, a hopeful gesture signifying that the future of the medium Ozon cherishes so much is now secure. This final shot is dramatic in both senses of the term and operates outside the film's

Figure 10. The last shot of 8 *femmes.*

narrative reality. Evidently, its artifice and near-perfect symmetry point back to the harmonious visual composition of the musical interludes. But perhaps more interestingly, the fixed image denotes the characters' apparent disconnection from the reality of the father's suicide, a lack of interest or denial reinforced by the fact that no one rushes to Marcel's side to verify Catherine's affirmation that he has indeed perished. In contrast to the trauma initially caused by the father's emotional absence in *Sitcom,* the patriarch's inadequacy is already established in the first minutes of *8 femmes,* making this last shot consistent with the characters' longing for a fatherless fate.

As I have already suggested, the complexity of Ozon's cinema prevents the articulation of a formula (beyond the simple one proposed by Lalanne) that would accurately describe the ways in which male characters are portrayed in his films and, more particularly, the relationship between patriarchy and queer identity. While the presence of the father is shown to be incompatible with the queering and overall evolution of the family in both *Sitcom* and *8 femmes,* the paternal figure in *Les amants criminels* is, in contrast and despite his explicit monstrosity, the one facilitating both the queering and maturation of the film's male teenager. Symptomatically, some critics have proposed markedly divergent readings of the ogre, one commentator seeing Manojlovic's character as "the bad father, a hypocritical voice of morality . . . [and even] something outside the parameters of humanity" (Hain 285) while another opined that the woodsman is a "rare exception" in Ozon's cinema in that he is the only character in the film that is "vaguely moral or sensitive" (Gilbey, "Criminal Lovers" 39). Ozon's portrayal of women is no less complex, as the next section will demonstrate. In the following three films discussed, Ozon scuttles the unapologetic, "excessive" world of artifice and camp and draws a realistic, intimate, and compassionate portrayal of two women and a gay man in pain.

Mourning Sickness: *Sous le sable, Swimming Pool,* and *Le temps qui reste*

Ever since his early filmmaking projects, and long before the vanishing fathers described above, François Ozon's films have dealt with loss. Most of them revolve, in different ways, around the disappearance of someone or something and around the consequences, whether welcomed or grievous, of such bereavement. In the case of *Photo de famille* and *Victor,* the elimination of the mother and father ignites a process of liberation, transforming the protagonist in the first short film into a macabre, yet self-satisfied, photographer and enabling the character in the latter to become a parricidal but nonetheless freed sexual being. The absence and subsequent loss of Paul's father in *La petite mort* and the earlier death of Tatiana's infant in *Regarde la mer* convert the protagonists into individuals who engage with others in a manner that may be considered socially inappropriate, if not ill-willed. Oftentimes, these films are concerned not so much with loss itself but with how the mourner-protagonists cope with that deficit and how their grieving affects others, be they relatives or strangers.

Such is precisely the case in *Sous le sable* (2000), *Swimming Pool* (2003), and *Le temps qui reste* (2005), Ozon's fourth, sixth, and eighth feature films. In addition to sharing a sense of loss, these films stand out in their sobriety and, to a certain extent, their minimalism, in contrast to the colorful, plot-twisted, studio-shot, ensemble-cast narratives that characterize Ozon's first two feature films and *8 femmes.* Introspective in nature and slow in pace, these three works have much in common. Filmed mostly on location, they focus on lonesome characters who, because of various types of mourning sickness, have taken refuge in narcissistic isolation. Their *mourning* sickness also beacons an absence of *morning* sickness. The two heroines of *Sous le sable* and *Swimming Pool* are childless, and there are reasons to believe that part of their suffering stems from that lack. The hero of *Le temps qui reste* does father a child, but for him the joys of parenthood are off-limits. In order to allow the tormented, self-absorbed protagonists to gaze at their own reflections and contemplate their fates, mirrors, rivers, pools, and oceans abound in the three stories, which all begin and end beside a body of water.

The opening sequence of *Sous le sable* features, in an uninterrupted take, three components that are crucial to the ensuing narrative: the liquid element, the beach, and the city of Paris. The film opens to a long-shot view of Notre Dame Cathedral. The camera, placed on the Pont d'Austerlitz, then tilts down to a high-angle shot of the river Seine; the title of the film appears in red font upon the surface of the rippling water, which occupies the entire frame. A horizontal panorama shot reveals sunbathers lying on the river's right bank and, even farther right, cars whizzing by on a four-lane road. It is late summertime. Marie Drillon (Charlotte Rampling) and her husband, Jean (Bruno Cremer), leave the capital and drive south to their vacation home in Lit-et-Mixe, in the Landes region of southwestern France. Marie sits behind the wheel, Jean is half asleep next to her, at the *place du mort*, and both are silent for much of the journey. Their muteness, which implies either great marital familiarity or, conversely, deep communication problems, continues as they reach their destination, settle into their cottage, and drive to the deserted, lifeguard-free nudist beach the following morning. Marie, slim and toned in her brown, one-piece bathing suit, reads Balzac's *Le lys dans la vallée* (one of Ozon's favorite novels) on the sand; Jean, a physically imposing man, goes for a swim in the Atlantic Ocean and never returns. After an unsuccessful attempt by a lifeguard crew to find his body, dead or alive, Marie spends one more evening in the empty country house, revisits the desolate beach at night, and returns to Paris by herself the next day.

These are the first twenty minutes of the film. By the time the location shooting ended in the summer of 1999, these few scenes constituted the extent of Ozon's skeletal scenario. The disappearance of a man, the uncertainty about his future and that of his wife carry a strong autobiographical element; this sequence is in fact based on a particular event in the director's life, a traumatic childhood recollection:

> I witnessed that very event as a child. I must have been 9 or 10; I was on vacation in the Landes with my parents. Every day, we would see on the beach a Dutch couple, each about 60 years old. One day, the husband went into the water and never came back. A helicopter landed on the sea, the wife spoke with the lifeguards. This event profoundly shocked me and my siblings, and disrupted the rest of our vacation. No one wanted to swim anymore. The image of that woman leaving the beach, alone with her husband's belongings, has often haunted me. I've always wondered: what happened next? (Ozon, "Entretiens *Sous le sable*")

More than twenty years after the episode, Ozon was still eager to imagine the future of the Dutch woman, now transformed by his fictional rendition of the story into an English-born teacher in Paris. Unfortunately, shortly after the completion of the summer shoot, one of the project's main production companies declared bankruptcy and money ran out. The fate of the film and that of its central character were both uncertain. Producers were disinclined to fund the project and much less desirous than Ozon was to find out "what happened next." Fidélité Productions, the director's ever-so-faithful production company, was still on board. But the Centre National de la Cinématographie rejected a request for an *avance sur recettes* (advanced funding later recovered with box office profits), and no television channels were willing to step in as coproducers (Charcossey 44). The reasons invoked were manifold, but some of the main concerns were that Charlotte Rampling and Bruno Cremer, who had already starred together in Patrice Chéreau's *La chair de l'orchidée* (*Flesh of the Orchid*, 1975) twenty-five years earlier (the same number of years *Sous le sable*'s Jean and Marie have been married), were no longer "marketable" actors. Neither was a seemingly depressing story of death and mourning (S. Johnston 13).

Luckily, foreign producers did not share these concerns, and thanks to presale money from Japan, the Benelux, Italy, and Canada, where Ozon had acquired some notoriety, French pay channel Canal Plus purchased the television rights to the film. In addition, Haut et Court, a French production company specializing in independent cinema, agreed to both coproduce and distribute *Sous le sable.* The project was saved, but money was still less than abundant. These financial difficulties forced Ozon, who briefly considered filming with a less onerous digital video (DV) camera but was unsatisfied with the results, to shoot the remainder of the film in Super 16 (a 35mm camera was used to film the first twenty minutes). In retrospect, Ozon enjoyed the varying visual results rendered by the two shooting formats and even appreciated the fact that the second part had to be filmed six months later, in the middle of winter: "[These changes] are not a problem, because they coincide with a different season and match the film's narrative rupture. The first part, in the summer, is a prologue of sorts, the exposition of a real event. The film then spreads its wings in the winter. Everything becomes very introspective, events are more uncertain: we are in Marie's head, and her life journey is more ambiguous, less resolute, more blurry, more fragile, a bit like quicksand" (Ozon, "Entretiens *Sous le sable*"). The quicksand (or *sables mouvants*) metaphor echoes and in some way elucidates the film's title, but may also apply to the writer's block Ozon experienced in crafting the second part of his project.

Marie's post-estival existence was nebulous, even in Ozon's mind. All he knew at first was that the concluding sequence would take place on the beach in Lit-et-Mixe, with Marie crying and burying her hand in/under the sand as if to inter the memory of her husband, but he "did not know what Marie would have to go through to end up there" (Ozon, "Entretiens *Sous le sable*"). He originally intended to turn the film into a police thriller of sorts, with a proverbial series of leads and red herrings (tales of nervous breakdown, money trouble, adultery, illegitimate child, suicide) that would eventually bring a resolution to the story and explicate Jean's vanishing. Rampling was willing to go along for the ride, no matter what that ride would be like, but Ozon was having difficulties and needed assistance. Novelist Emmanuèle Bernheim, who at the time had worked as a scenarist on minor film and television projects, came to his rescue. Bernheim was shown the film's prologue and provided, in Ozon's words, a "feminine point of view." She confirmed the instincts of the filmmaker, who at that point had refocused all his attention on Marie and transformed the story into one of mourning, of coping with death without a body. Bernheim endorsed Ozon's theories about the plausibility (and possibility) of Marie's future sexual life. She refined the character of Vincent (Jacques Nolot), Marie's temporary lover, more generally helped Ozon "clean up and tighten the scenario," and encouraged him to opt for a simple rather than convoluted plot (Ozon, "Entretiens *Sous le sable*").

The ensuing plot is indeed uncomplicated, but as one French critic rightfully points out, *Sous le sable* is "a falsely simple work" (Blouin 78). It is a work where fantasy merges with actuality; a work deeply anchored in social reality that nonetheless manages, in a virtually seamless fashion, to flirt with the fantastic. The second part opens to another high-angle shot of the Seine, this time at night, in the winter. A slow pan up reveals a building on Paris's exclusive Ile Saint-Louis. We are in the home of Amanda (Alexandra Stewart), Marie's best friend and fellow English literature professor at a local university. An impeccably dressed, chignoned Marie is all smiles at the dinner table, with five other guests. Amanda has invited her husband's friend Vincent in the hopes that Marie might enjoy his company and move on from her life as a widow. The dinner host's second wish, revealed in the privacy of the kitchen, is that her grieving friend will consult a psychiatrist, but Marie vehemently refuses.

The evening is nevertheless quite pleasant until Marie begins to talk about Jean as though he is still alive and currently living with her at their Paris apartment. This does not deter Vincent from driving Marie home and kissing her on the lips. She pushes him away, and as she steps into her apartment, Jean is there, waiting for her.

Is it a flashback sequence, so frequent in Ozon's cinema? Or has Jean suddenly returned without telling anyone? No, it is simply Jean as Marie imagines him to be, a broad shoulder for her to rest on, her longtime companion (fig. 11). For Marie is in denial about Jean's disappearance and likely death. And why wouldn't she be, since no body has yet been found? Thus Marie continues to live as a married woman and conjures Jean, whom the spectator sees just as she does, whenever she pleases. In the next scenes, Marie appears to lead a normal life: she exercises at the gym, goes for regular swims at an indoor pool, teaches her literature classes (her students are studying the writings of Virginia Woolf), meets Amanda for lunch, and goes shopping for expensive clothes, for herself and for Jean. In each of these scenes, however, something seems off. And the harder Marie strives to bury her head in the sand, the more circumstances work against her: her bank card is denied (the likely result of a reduced household income); a sixty-something man with a physique reminiscent of Jean swims alongside her in the pool; Amanda

Figure 11. Marie and a spectral Jean
in *Sous le sable*.

continues to insist that she see a mental specialist; and, worst of all, one of the lifeguards who looked for Jean the summer before attends her literature course and at the end of a lecture reminds her of the traumatic incident. Still, Marie manages to stay in her head for a little while longer. In a famous sequence where the (clothed) Englishwoman is seen upside down in separate high-angle close-up shots of her feet, crotch, breasts, and face, she lies down on her bed and fantasizes a ballet of hands (Jean's, Vincent's, and her own) caressing her body at the same time (fig. 12). Later still, even when she finally succumbs to Vincent's advances and sleeps with him one rainy afternoon, she tells him that she has never been unfaithful to her husband before. The relationship is short-lived: Marie ultimately chooses the memory of her absent husband over the physical presence of Vincent and coldly tells her enamored, patient lover that he does not "measure up" to Jean ("tu [ne] fais pas le poids" is her exact, untranslatable phrase), physically (Vincent is tall and slender) as well as emotionally.

Although the skeptical viewer may judge that Marie's entrenched denial, one that would enable her to behold, touch, and talk to a phantom, is rather inconceivable, Ozon took only measured risks in envisioning the behavior of his main protagonist: "I talked to a psychoanalyst to

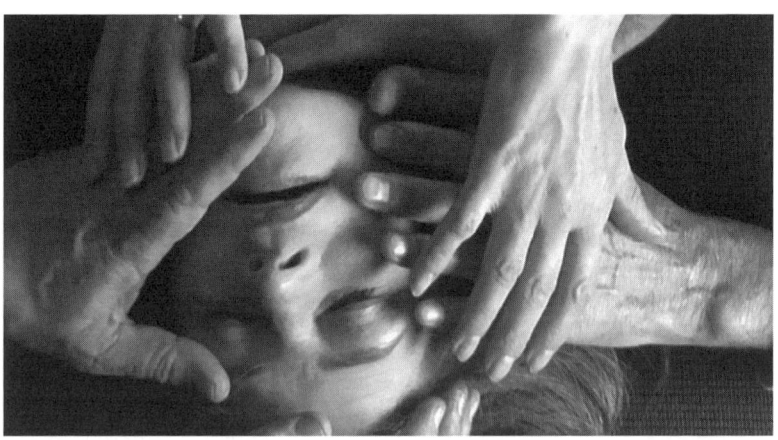

Figure 12. Marie and a ballet of hands
in *Sous le sable.*

check if I wasn't mistaken about the character's process of denial. He said it was entirely probable that a woman in this situation would see her husband as a ghost, and that it wasn't a sign of madness, it was a way of saving herself. She creates an inner world to alleviate her loss" (S. Johnston 13). Marie's refusal to accept the loss of her spouse is in fact a refusal to mourn, a liminal, in-between state that renders proper mourning impossible.

In "Mourning and Melancholia" Sigmund Freud distinguishes between the two mental states of his essay's title, between these two possible reactions to a lost object. Opposing the melancholic condition to "normal" mourning, the Austrian psychologist contends that in mourning the past is declared resolved, finished, and dead, while in melancholia the past remains steadfastly alive in the present (Eng and Kazanjian 3–4). Freud, however, challenges the idea that the mourner's ability to declare the object dead and move on should be considered "normal" and that the inability of a melancholic person to do so (such as Marie in *Sous le sable*) should be seen as pathological. David L. Eng and David Kazanjian conclude, after analyzing Freud's theories: "Ultimately, we learn, the work of mourning is not possible without melancholia" (4). Marie's melancholia should thus be understood, as Britt-Marie Schiller argues, not as an *alternate* to mourning but rather as a "prelude to mourning" (218). The same critic also provides crucial extra-filmic insight on Rampling's role as Marie and on the actress's own mourning process. As it turns out, she, too, used a traumatic memory to shape her character, a memory that far exceeds the trauma Ozon experienced on the beach as a child: "Rampling was asked about her convincing portrayal of Marie's denial of the truth. She revealed that she acted the same way when her sister committed suicide at the age of 20. It was such a shock; Rampling experienced such violent pain, that she erased it totally from her mind. She simply did not think about it until thirty years later. But, she added, 'the repressed returns, and at some point you have to deal with it'" (218). The return, or uncovering, of the repressed is what Marie is ultimately faced with in *Sous le sable*. A number of events, in addition to the aforementioned "reality checks," lead to the end of Marie's denial phase.

The forced return to reality that triggers Marie's winter trip back to the Landes is progressive and combines both external circumstances (out of Marie's control) and decisions she makes of her own volition. A turning point in the story occurs during a moving, lyrical musical sequence in a neighborhood supermarket, where Marie does her shopping shortly after consummating her relationship with Vincent. As a smiling Marie navigates her cart through the aisles and picks up various items from the shelves, we hear the first two verses of the melancholy song "Septembre (Quel joli temps)" (September, Such a Lovely Time of Year) by French chanteuse Barbara. Here is an English translation of the lyrics heard in the film (and subtitled on the U.S. DVD):

> Never has the summer's end seemed so magnificent
> This season's vines will make only the finest grapes
> In the trees we can see swallows gathering
> But we must part ways, even though we like each other
> September, what a lovely time for saying good-bye
> What a lovely night for feeling like we are twenty again
> Rising with the smoke of cigarettes
> Love trails away, my heart ceases to beat.

This moment, where Marie seems truly happy, possibly from her recent tryst with Vincent, brings us back to the summer segment, to the time when Jean and Marie abruptly parted ways. Though Ozon affirms on the commentary track of the DVD that the ballad is extra-diegetic and thus heard only by the spectator, it nevertheless signals a shift in Marie's state of mind, a shift from a melancholic stage to one that will enable mourning to betide. In this sense Barbara's therapeutic intrusion mirrors, in its capacity to express emotions outside the film's narrative space and without resorting to spoken dialogues, other musical sequences that pervade Ozon's cinema. The sung melody, which can be viewed as Marie's interior monologue, propels the woman back to the world of the living, marks the beginning of the end of her torpor, and precipitates events that will guide her to the truth.

The first, perhaps most pivotal of such events occurs in the sequence immediately following that of the grocery store. A telephone message from a police officer in Lit-et-Mixe who has information about a dead body found at sea awaits Marie when she returns home. After listening to the message, the distressed woman searches for Jean throughout the apartment, but he is nowhere to be found; the only image that is available to Marie is her own reflection in the mirror. It is shortly after this point that the film begins to resemble the police investigation narrative that Ozon had envisaged in his original screenplay. But it does so gently, without giving us the impression that *Sous le sable* is switching generic gears in the way that, say, *Les amants criminels* does once the lovers enter the ogre's forest. For Marie, not a police officer, becomes the case's main investigator. Rummaging through Jean's office papers, she discovers sleeping pills as well as prescriptions for an unfamiliar drug she did not know her spouse was taking. She pursues her inquiry at the pharmacy, where she learns that the medication in question is an antidepressant. All the pieces of the puzzle begin to come together, and suicide proves to be the most likely cause of Jean's death. After terminating her affair with Vincent, Marie must go back to the Landes and find out if the body retrieved by the authorities is indeed her husband's.

Before discussing the film's conclusion, let us pause momentarily and consider the tremendous success of *Sous le sable,* for both filmgoers and critics, and the impact it has had on the future of Ozon's career. Like the convalescent character it depicts, the film, which cost next to nothing by industry standards (nine million francs), made a spectacular recovery if one considers the financial obstacles that earnestly threatened its very production. In the three days following its release on February 7, 2000, *Sous le sable* was seen by 115,000 spectators in France. The eighty copies of the film failed to respond to increasing demands, and by the second week an additional sixty-six copies had to be made. By week four, 450,000 spectators had seen the film, and by the following August, almost 700,000. *Sous le sable* was then distributed worldwide, and close to 300,000 people saw it in the United States alone. In France film critics, who, according to Laure Charcossey, "were never particularly fond of Ozon," unanimously supported his latest creation, including the "four aces" that can make or break the success of a film: *Cahiers du cinéma, Les Inrockuptibles, Le Monde,* and *Libération* (Charcossey 44). Ozon had finally conquered the press and directed a film worthy of its attention. Better yet, he had done so without compromising his artistic vision and unique ability to push cinematic conventions. As one *Cahiers du cinéma* critic contends at the end of his glowing review, Ozon's is "a 'French film' as a genre in and of itself that the filmmaker turns on its head" and adds: "Ozon did not sacrifice his radicalism [*radicalité*]. He simply managed to find its proper place" (Blouin 78).

The latter comment is obviously condescending toward the film-maker's previous work, since the phrase "managed to find its proper place" implies that his earlier films failed to do so. Nonetheless, I believe that the term *radicalité* is used positively here, highlighting Ozon's unparalleled capacity to recount familiar stories in an unfamiliar way. As an example, the same commentator mentions, among other scenes, the supermarket sequence as one particularly audacious moment where the film and its character tread "less charted territories" (78). Here, Marie is seen in a different light and the story suddenly becomes airier, more contemplative, less expected. Of course, one may also argue that despite its relative radicalism, *Sous le sable* is a more "familiar" work simply because of the more "universal" qualities of its subject matter.

It is useful to repeat that *Sous le sable* is the first entry in Ozon's filmography from which queer characters are altogether absent. Even his later, seemingly "straight" *5x2*, which documents in reverse chronology five moments in the life of an opposite-sex couple, contains two gay protagonists in supporting roles. The brief but noted presence of the two men provides a crucial counterpoint to the (unsuccessful) heteronormative existence led by the film's main couple. Yet despite this apparent absence, there *is* something queer about *Sous le sable.* I am not suggesting that the film itself is queer, but rather that Ozon's queer sensibilities surface in indirect ways. In addition to Jean's conjured image, the spectral presence of bisexual English novelist Virginia Woolf infuses the narrative: Marie reads a long excerpt from *The Waves* to her students, recites from memory Woolf's suicide note during a dinner date with Vincent, and, at the film's conclusion, approaches the waters of the Atlantic Ocean as though she, like Woolf (and perhaps Jean) before her, may decide to end her life by drowning herself.

I have already mentioned, particularly in the context of *8 femmes,* Ozon's cinephilic propensity to devise multilayered films that acquire different meanings depending on the spectator's sensibility, interests, and prior knowledge. Usually the films function both on a literal level and, sometimes more crucially, in how they reference other (often cinematic) works or even the actors' own biographies (in *8 femmes* the scene in which Deneuve indirectly evokes the memory of the late François Truffaut in the presence of Ardant, his real-life widow, comes to mind).

In the context of *Sous le sable,* the casting of Jacques Nolot in the role of Vincent is an interesting choice. On the level of the narrative, the weight, both literal and figurative, that Nolot's character bears on the life of the protagonist is worth analyzing. For Vincent's (unknowing) influence on Marie modifies her behavior and, in my view, alters the way she sees herself in relation to others. When Marie and Vincent make love for the first time, something unexpected or "unfamiliar" happens. Up until that moment, the newly formed couple's gender roles and sexual behavior seem almost excessively traditional, given Ozon's previous output: Vincent and Marie lie in bed naked, their two bodies are neatly tucked under the covers, and Vincent is positioned on top of his female partner. But as he begins to penetrate her vaginally, Marie inexplicably bursts into uncontrollable laughter (fig. 13). Clearly perturbed by such behavior, one that is certainly unfitting given the context of their lovemaking, Vincent demands an explanation. Marie manages to utter between two tee-hees: "There is something bizarre" ("about you," the phrase implies). Vincent remains perplexed and insists that she explain herself. "I'm sorry, but you are just so incredibly . . . light(weight); I'll just have to get used to it," she giggles.

This moment of light comedy, which most evidently foreshadows Marie's later observation that Vincent cannot "measure up" to Jean, is a rare opportunity for the spectator to express amusement at the heroine's generally more doleful existence. But unlike Marie and the viewer,

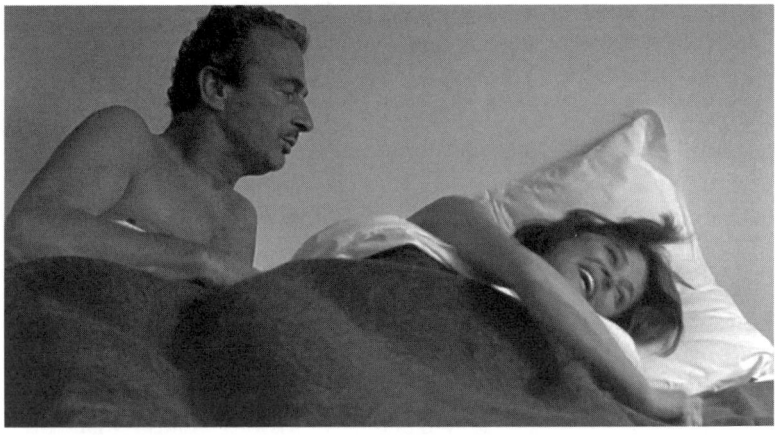

Figure 13. Vincent and Marie in *Sous le sable*.

who are both aware of Jean's corpulence, Vincent fails to understand Marie's remark; the film's published screenplay indicates that even after her explanation, Vincent continues to look at her "in a skeptical way" (Ozon, *Sous le sable* 62). The phrase implies that for Marie there is "not enough man" in Vincent to fill in the space left behind by Jean. But for Vincent, Marie's hurtful statement conveys a different meaning and insinuates that he is "not man enough," that she is unable to take him seriously as a potential sexual lover. In both interpretations of Marie's reaction (Vincent's and the viewer's), such unruly mirth intimates that Marie adheres to a fairly rigid definition of masculinity, one that is shaped principally by her twenty-five-year history with Jean, whom she "never cheated on" before.

Marie's mockery of Vincent's masculinity is complicated on an extra-filmic level by the fact that actor and director Jacques Nolot is a self-identified gay man. Nolot is known for staging his own life as a (morose) queer individual in the films he both stars in and directs. While some viewers may not be aware of that fact (Cremer and Rampling are more well-known than Nolot), Ozon certainly is. When asked about the casting of Vincent, Ozon confesses to having been touched by Nolot's demure performance as Jacqui in *L'arrière-pays* (*Hinterland,* 1998), released two years before *Sous le sable.* Ozon also contends that Nolot's previous work as a director helped the actor understand his character, particularly Vincent's "effaced" quality (Ozon, "Entretiens *Sous le sable*"). Also significant is the fact that *L'arrière-pays* is the first installment in a trilogy of films that, like *Sous le sable,* are all concerned with loss: that of a mother, of close friends, and in Nolot's latest film, *Avant que j'oublie* (*Before I Forget,* 2007), the loss of the protagonist's own youth.

It is remarkable, to go back to Vincent and Marie's sexual congress, that this unwanted, laughter-filled interlude actuates a physical and verbal reversal of gender and sexual roles. The two resume their lovemaking, but Marie assumes at her initiation the controlling position as she flips Vincent over, sits on top of him and directs his caressing moves: "Close your eyes," she orders, before instructing, "Now caress my hips, my breasts . . ." Thus, through her sudden, post-laughter change in behavior, reminiscent of Hélène Cixous's plea for woman's liberation in her influential essay "The Laugh of the Medusa," Marie is initiated into a novel embodiment of sexuality that allows her to emancipate herself and evolve from a self-effaced wife to an effective single woman.

Marie's emancipation continues as she makes her way southward. Before reaching Lit-et-Mixe, the Englishwoman visits a nursing home in order to notify her mother-in-law of Jean's possible death by suicide. The pit (and dare I say pitiful) stop is another sequence in the film that Patrick Blouin regards as "audacious," as less neatly delineated for what he calls a "French film" (78). Belgian-born actress Andrée Tainsy accepted the role of ninety-year-old Suzanne after Danielle Darrieux, who was eager to work with Ozon but unwilling to incarnate an old woman living in a retirement home, turned down the director's offer (Ozon and Bernheim). Although relatively brief, Tainsy's intense performance leaves a lasting mark on the spectator and concomitantly exhibits Marie's newfound inner strength. Saying that the two women's exchange is heated would be an understatement. When Marie verbalizes, for the first time in the narrative, the possibility that Jean killed himself, Suzanne refuses to accept such a hypothesis. The elderly woman affirms that, unlike Marie, she was aware of Jean's depressive tendencies and declares: "No one in the Drillon family has ever committed suicide . . . The truth is crueler. He disappeared because he was bored, or rather, because you bored him . . . Plus, you were never able to give him a child." Marie, although disconcerted, manages to give Suzanne the cold, hard facts about the probable discovery of Jean's body in a fishing net and spews, as if to end the conversation, "We should have sent you to a psychiatric hospital rather than a nursing home." Suzanne replies acridly and without missing a beat, "I think you'll end up there before I do." Given Ozon's cinephilia and his knowledge of actors' biographies, Suzanne's phrase possibly references Rampling's role in *La chair de l'orchidée,* in which her character, Claire, lives in a mental institution; it may also relate to the actress's own mother, who had to be institutionalized following the death of her daughter, Rampling's sister (Ciment and Tobin 11).

The scenario indicates that this arduous conversation leaves Marie "discomposed" but also, paradoxically, "reinvigorated" (Ozon, *Sous le sable* 94–95). These two apparently opposed sentiments in fact reflect rather accurately those that Marie experiences at the morgue in Lit-et-Mixe and, later, on the sand at the film's conclusion. Against the advice of both the police investigator and the medical examiner, Marie asserts her need to behold Jean's decomposed, unrecognizable body. The two men wish to spare her such a traumatizing sight, especially because genetic analyses have unequivocally confirmed that the corpse is indeed that of Jean Drillon. Marie insists, "I want to see the body . . . It's important for me." This would suggest that only the physical presence of the body can lead to the acceptance of Jean's death, the final stage of her mourning process. The look on Marie's face as she observes the cadaver and Ozon's paced mise-en-scène recall for the cinephilic viewer another story of "death without a body" and a similar sequence at a mortuary in Henri-Georges Clouzot's crime thriller classic *Les diaboliques* (*Diabolique,* 1955). In Clouzot's morgue scene, Christina, whose husband disappeared without a trace after she and a female accomplice drowned him and later dumped the body in a murky swimming pool, is shown a dead man who turns out *not* to be her spouse. In Ozon's morgue segment, Marie is shown an unidentifiable body that the doctor affirms *is* that of her spouse. But Marie struggles to accept it and, after another incongruous burst of laughter, maintains that the body and watch found on the dead man's wrist are not Jean's. In the two morgue scenes Christina and Marie utter exactly the same French phrase: "C'est pas lui"/That's not him.

It is only after Marie revisits the barren, windswept beach at low tide, the very site of Jean's disappearance, that she is able to shed the tears that evince her mourning process has finally begun in earnest. The static, medium close-up of Marie records her first tears since Jean's vanishing, her lowest ebb. Though the uninterrupted shot of the weeping widow lasts "only" one minute and ten seconds in *Sous le sable,* it was partially inspired by the conclusion of Ming-liang Tsai's Taiwanese film *Vive L'Amour* (1994), in which we see the heroine cry for a total of six minutes and twenty-five seconds (Ozon and Bernheim). However, in contrast to Tsai's work, which finishes on that note after a simple fadeout, this is not the end of Ozon's story. When Marie catches sight of a lone man standing on the beach in the distance, her tears give way to a faint, hopeful smile, and the reinvigorated woman begins to run toward him. The credits roll before Marie reaches the (imagined or real) masculine silhouette. This last image, an extreme long shot of Marie running away from the camera, invites two possible interpretations. One may read her heady run as a regression, a flight from reality or, conversely, a thrilling thrust toward a future without Jean, whether on her own or with another companion. (Marie does seem to be heading toward the enigmatic figure, but her trajectory is slightly misaligned, as though she did not really intend to reach him.) In the latter reading, which seems more probable, this final beach episode represents a milestone for Marie, one that pushes her forward, no matter where that destination might be. It is perhaps this openness, the unresolved character of *Sous le sable*'s dénouement (and, more pragmatically, the immense success of the film) that motivated Ozon to partner with Rampling again three years later, in *Swimming Pool.*

The latter film was released immediately after *8 femmes,* which itself came out between the two Rampling-starring opuses. Golden Palm nominee *Swimming Pool* echoes *Sous le sable* in its intimacy as well as its dealings with loss, with absence. Despite its intimate feel and the limited number of actors in the cast, *Swimming Pool* feels like a family reunion of sorts. Emmanuèle Bernheim, with whom Ozon did not collaborate to adapt *8 femmes* (he preferred to solicit Marina de Van for his indoor whodunit), was on board again as cowriter for this exterior thriller. Rampling shares the lead role with a physically metamorphosed Ludivine Sagnier, whose participation in Ozon's first (predominantly) English-language film marks her third collaboration with the filmmaker. But one may travel further back in time, back to Ozon's featurette *Regarde la mer,* to discover a link between the story starring Sasha Hails and the two Rampling-led works. I have already pointed out Frédéric Bonnaud's contention that *Regarde la mer* may be seen as a "rough draft" of *Sous le sable* (53). Earlier in this study I offered the term "trilogy on female desire" to describe these three films, which share a thematic bond in the isolation of these three Englishwomen in a remote vacation spot, the obsessive staging of their sexual urges, and the sudden death of one of the characters.

An explicit stylistic connection bonds the latter two films, as the opening of *Swimming Pool,* a high-angle shot of the river Thames in London, unambiguously quotes the first few seconds of *Sous le sable.* In the Paris-based narrative the camera pans down to the water after showing, as I already mentioned, a view of the French capital's most famous gargoyle-adorned cathedral. In *Swimming Pool* the camera tilts up from the flowing river to reveal a panorama of Big Ben and the Parliament. In both instances, the title of the film appears against the surface of the water, in capital letters, in the same font.

Because of the profession of the heroine and its principal narrative developments, *Swimming Pool* is, of the three films, the closest in genre to a crime thriller. London-based crime novelist Sarah Morton (Rampling) lives a gloomy life in the house she shares with her feeble, elderly father. The brusque, conservatively dressed wordsmith was once successful at producing the renowned Inspector Dorwell franchise books that middle-aged Englishwomen devour on the underground train. But she now appears weary, slightly alcoholic, and, to make matters worse, experiences a writer's block that delays the release of her next Dorwell book. She accepts the offer of her publisher and occasional lover, John Bosload (Charles Dance), to stay at his secluded vacation retreat in the Luberon, in southeastern France, where the glorious weather and large swimming pool will surely inspire the struggling author. She settles in, but the tempestuous arrival of John's daughter Julie (Sagnier) hampers her productivity. Julie's nightly sexcapades with older, unattractive men annoy Sarah, but also fascinate her. Sarah is inspired by the secret diary of the blonde bombshell, abandons her *Dorwell on Holiday* project, and begins to work frantically on a new piece temporarily titled *Julie*. At dinner Sarah learns of Julie's French mother, who once wrote a romance novel that was never published. Upon discovering that the writer has stolen her journal, Julie seeks revenge by bringing home and seducing local waiter Franck (Jean-Marie Lamour), whom she knows Sarah finds handsome. Sarah spies on the couple as Julie unsuccessfully attempts to convince Franck to sleep with her. The next morning, Franck has disappeared and Sarah begins to investigate. Franck has not gone to work and his house is empty. She also learns that Julie's mother died in a terrible accident, the circumstances of which remain unclear. Sarah finds blood by the swimming pool, and Julie eventually confesses to killing Franck "for [Sarah], for the book." The women bury the body in the backyard. The next day, Sarah offers herself to the gardener, Marcel (Marc Fayolle), to prevent him from discovering Franck's burying place. Julie leaves for Saint-Tropez and gives Sarah a copy of her mother's book for inspiration. Back in London, John rejects Sarah's novel, *Swimming Pool,* but the shrewd woman has already sold the rights to another publisher. As she leaves her former lover's office, she catches a glimpse of John's daughter Julia, whom she has never met. The film ends by the villa's swimming pool, as Sarah waves successively at Julie and Julia.

In the numerous publicity posters that were designed for the promotion of *Swimming Pool,* both in France and abroad, one may notice two distinct taglines. The most recurring—"On the surface, all is calm"—teases the spectator into believing that someone or something may be hidden below the surface of the country home's initially tarpaulin-covered pool. The line also points figuratively to the quiescent rhythm of the narrative, to Ozon's measured, unhurried method of easing the viewer into Sarah's world in the same way someone would dip his or her toes into the water for fear that it might be too cold. If the first phrase underscores the importance of the film's aquatic environment, the second (French-language) tagline—"Tout les oppose, un secret va les réunir" (They are polar opposites, but a secret will unite them)—places more emphasis on the two heroines and their primarily rivalrous relationship. Up until Franck's disappearance, Sarah appears as restrained as Julie is hedonistic, as tight-lipped as Julie is clamorous, as buttoned-up as Julie is undraped (fig. 14).

Ludivine Sagnier astutely analyzed this spectacular clash of characters, both within the narrative and in relation to Ozon's oeuvre: "By choosing Charlotte and me, François has united two trends in his own

Figure 14. Sarah and Julie in *Swimming Pool.*

filmmaking. I come from the artificial, conceptual and theatrical trend epitomized by *Gouttes d'eau sur pierres brûlantes* and *8 femmes,* while Charlotte emerges from *Sous le sable,* a much more naturalistic work. In *Swimming Pool,* these two trends collide and power the relationship between Julie and Sarah. Julie is shallow, almost vulgar, whereas Sarah is more mental and introspective. The characters collide and eventually evolve: Julie becomes more inward, while Sarah blossoms" (Goudet, "*Swimming Pool*" 16). Sagnier's discourse corresponds to Ozon's own declarations about the film, which is quite possibly his most personal work. The director willingly admits in interviews that he *is* Sarah Morton and that *Swimming Pool* is about his own creative method:

> It's a self-portrait. I reveal a lot of things about the way I work . . . I show the writing process in its most concrete form, talk about the little habits we may have before starting to write, the need to reorganize the world around us in order to be able to produce . . . I wanted an English novelist in this role because I love them! I enjoy the personality of these strictly dressed women, these generally unpleasant, sex-deprived spinsters who write stuff that looks nothing like them. I enjoyed this contrast. People often tell me that I am not like the characters in my films. Apparently, they think that I'm much more perverse than I actually am. I like the discrepancy between what you create and what you are willing to show of yourself in real life. (Marvier 15)

The latter idea is rendered explicit in the first scene, when the famous Sarah Morton coldly tells a woman who recognizes her on the London underground, "I am not the person you think I am." In order to mask his autobiographical intentions and devise a film that works on multiple levels, both as a self-portrait and a proper tale of murder, Ozon abandoned his original title, *Ecrire* (To Write or Writing), and favored *Swimming Pool.* When asked why he chose this particular English-language title, which emphasizes an essential inanimate object in the narrative, Ozon replied jestingly, citing the title of a famous French film: "Well, I couldn't possibly call it *La piscine!*" (Marvier 19).

If the English-title-phobic Québécois *did* end up choosing the French translation of Ozon's work for its Canadian release, the filmmaker's comment refers to a filmic antecedent that cannot be overlooked when discussing *Swimming Pool.* Jacques Deray's 1969 crime drama, *La piscine,* stars Rampling's compatriot Jane Birkin alongside Maurice Ronet and screen legends Alain Delon and Romy Schneider, one of Ozon's preferred postwar actresses. Filmed in Saint-Tropez (Julie's final destination in *Swimming Pool*), this sizzling, tension-filled thriller stages most of its action around the swimming pool of an out-of-the-way dwelling. Like its 2003 counterpart, it features a heavily accented, bikini-wearing young woman (Penelope/Birkin and Julie) whose sex appeal will have deadly consequences for one of the lustful male characters. The love triangle and its ensuing jealousies narrated in Deray's work are suggested in Ozon's film in a dance segment I will analyze later. But one may search further back in cinematic time to find in *Swimming Pool* allusions to another classic, one I already mentioned as a potential inspiration for *Sous le sable*. As Ryan Gilbey notes, "The women's criminal collusion, and an exquisitely tense scene in which Sarah anticipates the discovery of a corpse in the pool, nods to *Les diaboliques*" ("*Swimming Pool*" 66). All tributes aside, most of Ozon's inspirations for the film, on both thematic and stylistic levels, are to be found in his own cinema: "*Swimming Pool* reflects my personal obsessions about creating and, since it's a film about inspiration, contains many references to my other work. [The] caressing shot [in which the camera pans up slowly from a character's feet to face] is also in [*Gouttes d'eau sur pierres brûlantes*]. The relationship between Ludivine and Charlotte refers back to [*8 femmes*]. *Swimming Pool* also resembles [*Sous le sable*], since both those women live in their heads" (Abeel).

What distinguishes *Swimming Pool* from its forebears, whether internal or external to Ozon's oeuvre, is that although it is a thriller in its own right, it also functions as a metaphor for the filmmaking process. However, unlike Godard's Brigitte Bardot–starring *Le mépris* (*Contempt*, 1963), Truffaut's *La nuit américaine* (*Day for Night*, 1973), or, more recently, Catherine Breillat's *Sex Is Comedy* (original French title, 2002), all three of which are (semi-) autobiographical works that take place on a film set, Ozon here hides behind a (female) protagonist and concentrates on the practice of scriptwriting rather than film shooting. Sarah's painstaking care is highlighted as she first prepares to write. The published screenplay reads: "[Sarah] must now set up her desk. She pushes a night stand against the window, places a small lamp on it and takes her laptop, her printer, a power strip, an adaptor, sheets of paper and a small pencil case out of a big bag. She meticulously places each object where it belongs, the printer on the floor, the laptop at the center of the table. Once everything is in place, she takes three steps back and observes, satisfied, her new installation" (Ozon, *Swimming Pool* 21–22). This written description corresponds rather accurately to its visual equivalent in the film's final cut and is but one example of the care Ozon took in detailing Sarah's obsessive routines, especially those associated with her writing, (healthy) eating, and even strolling habits. Writing, nonetheless, consumes most of her time, and the spectator is offered on multiple occasions the sight of Sarah sitting behind her computer or editing her manuscript on printed pages, whether in her bedroom or on the patio. Also clearly recorded is the brain wave caused by Julie's arrival and the sudden burst of inspiration that Sarah enjoys as a result of this unanticipated distraction.

One sequence in particular spells out visually and quite cleverly the initial flow of Sarah's creative juices. It is the morning after Julie's arrival, and Sarah sits down to write on the balcony. Julie has left traces of her passage throughout the property—the kitchen table is filthy, a blood-red inflatable mattress lies on the edge of the pool—but has not yet awakened. Time passes, Julie finally arises, and Sarah observes the blonde from above as she walks indolently down the steps that lead to the pool. Later still, Sarah glances down at the swimming area. The tarpaulin has been partially uncovered, revealing a patch of water sullied by autumn leaves. We see, from Sarah's point of view, a naked Julie emerge from under the black pool cover, eventually reaching the surface and taking her first breath after an underwater swim (fig. 15). Julie's pose, her open arms and upward gaze, recalls that of Ophelia in Sir John Everett Millais's 1852 painting; the unwelcome vegetation on the surface of the pool mimics the lush foliage surrounding the river where the long-haired, singing woman floats in Millais's artwork. Ophelia's chanting is also evoked via Philippe Rombi's original music, which accompanies Julie's swim. Ophelia and Julie float, surrounded by leaves, and are both on a threshold: Ophelia is on the verge of death, while Julie metaphorically begins her life as Sarah's muse.

Evidently, Sarah's muse is also Ozon's, and her winsome image here and elsewhere celebrates the role Sagnier has played within his oeuvre since their first collaboration in *Gouttes d'eau sur pierres brûlantes*. On the level of screenwriting, however, one could also easily argue that Julie

Figure 15. Julie emerges from the water
in *Swimming Pool.*

is to Sarah what Emmanuèle Bernheim is to François Ozon: a script doctor who cures the director's occasional writer's block, a fine-tuner who deflates his insecurities about the writing process, a fellow artist who motivates him in his creation. Bernheim and Ozon's second partnership particularly seduced reviewer Stéphane Goudet. The Frenchman compares *Swimming Pool* to a millefeuille (literally, "thousand-leaves" or "thousand-sheets"), a Gallic delicacy made up of multiple layers of custard and puff pastry. In this context the name refers both to the critic's voracious pleasure in consuming the unfolding story and the myriad word-processed pages Sarah prints out as she becomes inspired. The cunning metaphor also aptly describes, all autobiographical references aside, the narrative's multiple strata of meaning. Goudet designates the countless "superimpositions" created by the film's recurring motifs (the pool and river water), objects (a postcard, a reappearing crucifix, a recovered novel), images (a "fake" corpse that becomes a "real" one), and people (Julie once mistakes Sarah for her mother) ("*Swimming Pool*" 17). These layers anticipate the narrative twists created by Sarah's own investigation after Franck's vanishing, as a noticeable acceleration of the narrative's rhythm occurs in the last thirty minutes. Though the viewer is never given access to the content of Sarah's novel *Swimming Pool,* the layers of meaning also possibly imitate the intricacy of the novel that the Englishwoman completes before leaving the Luberon.

Assuredly, the pool itself assumes the starring role in this superimposing game. I already pointed out the possible use of the film's title "character" as a canvas for Ozon's personal rendition of Millais's *Ophelia*. A more essential clue lies in the bluish hues of Sarah's computer screen, a mirror image of the water's surface that has been read as one evocative of an author's "blank page in the typewriter" (Gilbey, "*Swimming Pool*" 66). When, after Franck's disappearance, Sarah slowly unspools the tarpaulin cover for fear that his lifeless body may lie underneath, she metaphorically flips open the cover of her new book. But since the film also concerns Ozon's own professional activity, the ever-changing surface of the pool (at times dirty, clean, blanketed, or bare) typifies the moving images projected on a cinema screen. More generally, this liquid, polymorphous space also represents the adaptability, sexual or otherwise, of Ozon's characters as well as the numerous waterside films he directed before *Swimming Pool*.

Unlike the chain-written, money-making Dorwell series, Sarah's new project sparks her creativity and gives her a second wind as a novelist, an exhilarating process that fills her with pride and satisfaction. For Sarah, composing a story inspired by Julie's life has salutary repercussions, and the woman undergoes an exhaustive transformation that the film records avidly: she trades her Diet Cokes and fat-free yogurts for French wine and chocolate-drenched profiteroles; she takes a swim in the pool despite originally voicing her aversion for human-made bodies of water; she takes pleasure in conversing with Franck, overcoming her earlier misanthropy; her blouse becomes increasingly more undone, eventually coming down altogether when she seduces Marcel to keep Julie's murderous act a secret; and, finally, she frees herself from John's loveless, greedy claws as she switches publishers at the film's conclusion. Although originally perceived as an invasion, Julie's arrival engenders a profound sense of fulfillment that retrospectively exposes the extent of Sarah's deficiencies. Rampling describes Sarah thusly: "My character suffers from an identity crisis. She feels a void within her and has no idea how to fill it" (Ciment and Tobin 10). The void in question is multiform, a consequence of Sarah's inability to maintain stable relationships with others, the waning of her career as a successful novelist, the looming reality of her father's imminent death, the vacuity of a life without a child of her own.

Ozon's intention in *Swimming Pool* was to design for the English actress a character in total opposition to Marie: "In *Sous le sable*, the character was Charlotte Rampling herself. The project consisted in filming her as she is, in daily situations. Whereas in *Swimming Pool*, she had to incarnate someone completely different from who she is. It is only later that I realized the connections between the two films, a similar effort to represent fantasy" (Marvier 15). As it turns out, the similarities between Sarah Morton and Charlotte Rampling, both in terms of her private life and screen personas, are more pronounced than Ozon may have imagined. Ginette Vincendeau references the actress's longtime, well-documented struggle with clinical depression, the end of her marriage to French musician Jean-Michel Jarre in the mid-1990s, and her evident "loss of status as a film star" (28) until her fecund encounter with Ozon, the only director with whom she has worked more than once. The critic also points out a traceable continuity between her film personas, which tend stereotypically to "play on [her] Britishness," from the 1970s to the present: "From *The Night Porter* [Liliana Cavani, 1974] and *Paris by Night* [David Hare, 1988] to *Swimming Pool*, her films have explored the gap between her characters' impeccably groomed appearance . . . and 'improper' sexual behaviour—sado-masochism, murder, bestiality" (28).

Rampling's quest for fulfillment through art, a survival mechanism that followed the family tragedies of her young adult years, is something the actress has freely discussed, particularly with regard to Ozon's films. She has also disclosed the origin of her character's first name:

> In *Swimming Pool*, we have a woman who had an upbringing similar to mine, very harsh, severe, with no tenderness. As a consequence, she quickly sought refuge in writing, to protect herself. When you meet Sarah, you feel a desperate solitude within her . . . I know I have that in me too. My father had it, he gave it to me, and up until now I managed to avoid dealing with it. I'm glad I did it [thanks to Ozon]. Sarah is the name of my sister, who committed suicide. In *Sous le sable,* I mourned her death; here, I borrowed her first name. Every creative act helps you. Acting can really help you. (Ciment and Tobin 15)

The generational distance Ozon stages by confronting Sarah with the youthful Julie (the name of Ozon's younger sister, who appears in *Photo de famille*) intimates a desire to celebrate what Vincendeau calls

Rampling's "ageing beauty": "[S]hots of Sarah gazing at Julie semi-naked at the poolside suggest Rampling contemplating her distant youth" (28). This reinforces Ozon's choice *not* to use filters to smooth Rampling's wrinkles in either *Sous le sable* or *Swimming Pool*. The most explicit representation of that gap, of the confrontation between young and aging, occurs in the dance sequence during which Sarah and Julie compete for Franck's attention.

Julie unexpectedly brings Franck home one night after learning of Sarah's attraction to him. Julie convinces Sarah, who has politely excused herself in order to leave the couple alone, not to go to bed right away. At that point, the viewer, unlike Sarah, knows that Julie has discovered the theft of her journal and suspects that the intentions of the young seductress are malicious. During the conversation, Franck seems more interested in Sarah than in Julie, driving the latter to initiate a musical diversion. Steve Everitt's sex-oozing dance tune "Mirrorball (Let's Do It)" does the trick: Julie drags Franck away from Sarah, and the two engage in a luscious dance (fig. 16). But in Julie's mind, her sultry moves will appear even more seductive against those of a repressed middle-aged Englishwoman. Julie consequently invites Sarah to join in the swaying festivities. Sarah's stiff, awkward movements negate her earlier remark that she participated in the "swinging London" of the

Figure 16. Sarah, Julie, and Franck
in *Swimming Pool*.

1970s, or at the very least suggest a drastic transformation since then. To Julie's dismay, Franck ends up preferring Sarah's clumsy dancing company over her own. Her "revenge" unfolds in the ensuing sequence, in which Julie kills the object of Sarah's desire—the murder remains off-screen until a flashback later displays Julie's vicious pounding of Franck's head with a massive poolside rock. But the dance segment may also be read as an effort for Julie to seduce both Franck and Sarah. In fact, the original scenario envisaged a lesbian sex scene in which Franck would also participate (Marvier 19). Ozon's decision to drop the possibility of a ménage-à-trois privileges a more maternal relationship between the two women, a more logical choice, given Julie's later mistaking of Sarah for her own mother and their (sisterly or mother/daughter) contrivance in getting rid of Franck's body.

The Hitchcockian attributes of *Swimming Pool*, with its gradual tension-building, single-location setting, various cases of mistaken identity, and twist ending, particularly seduced the public. In the United States alone, box office profits exceeded ten million dollars and the film showed in theaters for three and a half months, an infrequent success for a French-produced work. If certain critics lauded the film and its conclusion, which "[l]ike *The Usual Suspects* [Bryan Singer, 1995] . . . ends with a revelation that substantially alters what has gone before" (Gilbey, "*Swimming Pool*" 64), others were less bedazzled by Ozon's product. Frenchman Charles Tesson titles his review of the film "Eau plate" (Flat Water) and accuses Ozon of "surfing on the unexpected and well-deserved success of *Sous le sable*" with an unconvincing work whose "lone good idea" is to merge reality and fantasy (48). The title of American Stephen Rebello's *Advocate* review, "The Shallow End," echoes Tesson's in its aquatic pun and its contention that the film is simply too bland for his tastes. Rebello's reasoning, however, differs from that of his French colleague. *Swimming Pool*, although homoerotic at times and featuring a character who is "an embodiment of dykey photos of such real-life thriller writers as Patricia Highsmith and Ruth Rendell," is ultimately a disappointment for Rebello because it "packs less muscle than we're hoping for" (57). Herein lies the irony of Ozon's critical reception over the years: while chastised at the dawn of his career for being too extreme, he is now incriminated (on both sides of the Atlantic) for being too dull and, in Rebello's case, for not being "gay enough."

While Tesson particularly dislikes the film's dénouement (48), Rebello sees it as a meager but nonetheless noteworthy redeeming quality (57). I would argue that the extraordinary success of the film, particularly in North America, comes precisely from the "buzz" created by its startling epilogue. When Sarah sees John's daughter Julia for the first time, the attentive spectator immediately notes the similarities between Julie and Julia's ages, first names, as well as the length, texture, and color of their hair. As a fantasy sequence (devised by Emmanuèle Bernheim) stages, presumably from Sarah's perspective, the blonde women's joint, chimerical return to the pool area in the Luberon, the viewer realizes suddenly that Julie (a prettier, sexier version of Julia) may simply be a figment of Sarah's imagination. This would signify that most events, including the murder, were simply a visual representation of Sarah's new book. If François Ozon refuses to decide whether the film's developments have "really" occurred or whether they were fantasized (Marvier 20), many spectators *needed* to know. These viewers' categorical refusal to accept the ambiguity of the last segment generated a veritable flooding of entertaining message boards on the Internet Movie Database website. Some of these commentators report their confusion ("I just don't get the ending") or frustration ("This is why I don't watch foreign films") at Ozon's creation, while others claim to hold "the truth" about its conclusion: "The ending explained," "Everyone is over-thinking this," and "I think I figured it out" are just three of many similar message board titles one may find on the website. I can attest to the fact that analogous conversations were occurring on the street as the film was showing in movie houses in North America. This undoubtedly helped its promotion and partially explains its long run in the theater circuit.

Like Ozon, English critic Ryan Gilbey is untroubled by the indefiniteness of *Swimming Pool*'s closing sequence and sees it as a strength rather than an infirmity: "[T]he ambiguities intensify the picture's hothouse atmosphere, making it all the more impressive that Ozon maintains such a consistently cool touch" ("*Swimming Pool*" 66). Ozon's "cool touch," his unbending composure, is preserved in *Le temps qui reste,* the next and last mourning film of this section. Released two years apart with only one film (5x2) in between them, *Swimming Pool* and *Le temps qui reste* share more than a melancholy protagonist. If Sarah's profession as a novelist parallels that of Ozon the scriptwriter, Romain's job as a fashion photographer may be interpreted as an illustration of Ozon's engagement with the visual aspects of filmmaking.

In their frontal dealings with literal death, their Parisian locale, and partiality for the ocean rather than the artificiality of the swimming pool, *Sous le sable* and *Le temps qui reste* also share a sisterly bond. They are in fact the first two installments of Ozon's proposed trilogy about death and mourning. Jeanne Lapoirie, who was Ozon's cinematographer in *Sous le sable*, returned to photograph *Le temps qui reste*, the filmmaker's first work in Cinemascope. However, in contrast to Marie's story, Romain's is about self-mourning, about preparing for one's own quietus. The film follows Romain (Melvil Poupaud), a haughty, thriving fashion photographer who is diagnosed with terminal cancer. The thirty-one-year-old gay man, who has suspected AIDS rather than cancer, declines chemotherapy treatment after learning that his chance of survival is less than 5 percent. This choice grants him only three remaining months of existence. He is unable to announce the news to his parents (Daniel Duval and Marie Rivière, whose characters remain nameless) during a dinner gathering and instead favors a verbal confrontation with his sister, Sophie (Louise-Anne Hippeau), a proud mother of two. Following an affectionate exchange with his father, Romain ends his relationship with his German boyfriend, Sasha (Christian Segenwald), and visits the backroom of a gay club but does not participate in the action. Romain's grandmother, Laura (Jeanne Moreau), whom he visits shortly thereafter, becomes the only confidante of the young man, because, in his words, "like [him], [she is] going to die soon." Driving home from Laura's country home, he converses with Jany (Valeria Bruni-Tedeschi), a rest-stop waitress who served him the day before. With the consent of her sterile spouse (Walter Pagano), Jany asks Romain to impregnate her. The dying man refuses, claiming an aversion for children. Romain makes peace with Sophie on the phone after receiving a warmhearted letter from her. Without revealing his impending death, Romain asks Sasha to have sex with him "one last time" but is rebuffed. He finds Jany and sleeps with her in a gentle threesome with her husband. Romain shears his black locks, making his face appear thinner. Two months later, a pregnant Jany and her husband act as witnesses as Romain bequeaths all of his possessions to the unborn child. Romain, now pale and emaciated, heads to the coast of Brittany. After a swim in the ocean, he lies on the beach and remains there until the sun goes down.

Two crucial motifs accompany Romain throughout his solitary journey toward death: his digital camera on the one hand and conjured images of his childhood self on the other. Ever since learning of his upcoming demise, Romain avidly snaps pictures of various individuals: strangers in a public park and on the Breton beach, his sleeping boyfriend, Laura, his sister, and her child. With the exception of his grandmother, he does so without the knowledge or consent of his subjects. In Ozon's first feature film to center exclusively on a masculine figure, it is difficult not to see a correspondence between Romain's compulsive desire to record the present through photographs and the filmmaker's much discussed (and often chided) impetus for shooting at least one film a year since his début. In his tepid *Le Monde* review of the film, Jean-Luc Douin asserts that Romain photographs his surroundings "a bit too much" ("Chronique"). This criticism echoes that of reviewer François Bégaudeau; this *Cahiers du cinéma* critic frowns upon Ozon's filming velocity and claims that *Le temps qui reste* was shot and released quickly because, like all of his films, this latest creation tells the same old rambling story (66–67).

Less faultfinding, Olivier de Bruyn regards *Le temps qui reste* as a "personal film on more than one account" (105), while Pierre Murat advances that Romain is probably "the more or less admitted double of his creator" ("Portrait"), a claim reinforced by Poupaud's physical resemblance to Ozon as well as repeated shots of Romain gazing at himself in the mirror (fig. 17). Murat's keen reasoning is that Ozon went from being adulated by critics as the king of short films to being vilified as the master of cynicism. Ozon's decline in the eyes of the critical establishment is cleverly metaphorized in *Le temps qui reste*. Romain's triumph as a photographer is underscored to the point of caricature in the sunlit, Eiffel-Tower-featuring rooftop locale where his fashion photo shoot takes place; like Ozon himself, Romain is a hands-on artist who inquires about the models' hair and makeup and insists on personally selecting their clothes ("I can't photograph such a hideous thing," he tells the costume assistant on the set about a dress she shows him). This picture-perfect, if arrogant, image of success rapidly goes downhill: Romain faints at

Figure 17. Romain gazes as himself
in *Le temps qui reste.*

the end of this outdoor sequence, and his boss later suggests that he let someone else go to Japan for an important shoot. Finally, after an initial, brief period of denial following the news of his death sentence, he decides to take an unlimited leave of absence. This does not keep Romain from remaining a ravenous photographer, the only difference being that his subjects become increasingly more personal.

This tendency to examine ever more intimate subjects may well apply to Ozon's own filmography. However, the fanatic photographer is far from being a new figure in his cinematic realm. Max Cavitch identifies a "photographer-as-wayward-son figure," which, though fully developed in *Le temps qui reste,* already appeared in embryonic form in his very first short, the late-1980s *Photo de famille* and his mid-1990s, twenty-five-minute *La petite mort* (318). Commenting on Romain's endmost desire to leave an offspring behind after his death, Cavitch contends that the film "returns us to the melodramatization of the narcissistic will to self-perpetuation for which the family may be the universal alibi" (319). The three films Cavitch analyzes all explore, in one way or another, the relationship between photography, kinship, and death. The latter trio inevitably points to Roland Barthes's seminal, swan-song essay, *Camera Lucida: Reflections on Photography* (1980), in which the French philosopher reflects upon the effects of photographs on those who look at them (especially himself) and at the same time pays tribute to his beloved late mother. One excerpt from Barthes's book cited by Cavitch in relation to *Photo de famille* particularly applies to Romain's cruel but heartfelt admission that he has no interest in photographing his parents or his sister's children. Barthes wonders: "What did I care . . . about the photograph as family rite[?] . . . nothing but the trace of a social protocol of integration, intended to reassert the Family" (318). Romain's wish to separate himself from his family and its social constraints is partially explained when, after his mother deplores the fact that Romain may never have children, the son curtly replies: "You're out of luck, your son's a fag, no descendants on my end."

In this early sequence, Romain's animosity toward his mother and, as the evening progresses, toward his sister, Sophie (who shares a first name with the daughter in *Sitcom*), begs two possible interpretations. In this context, the announcement of his homosexuality (the first time the spectator hears it) and his disapproval of Sophie's maternal habits ("your children are your things") may denote a genuine desire to live outside heteronormative norms. In contrast, it may also betray deep regrets for not having access to the same privileges those norms confer. The latter theory seems to prevail as the story unfolds. In the scene immediately following his altercation with Sophie, Romain asks his taciturn father to take him home. In a moment altogether unique in Ozon's output, Romain questions his father about the longevity of his relationship with his wife, Romain's mother, despite multiple adulterous affairs (initiated by the father only), a situation already alluded to in Ozon's 1990 Super-8 short, *Mes parents un jour d'été.* The simple yet honest response Romain receives (that the father never left his wife, because he still loves her) drives him to tenderly caress his father's cheek, a gesture that reveals Romain's respect for conjugal life and the (possibly envious) acknowledgment of its difficulties. This desire to conform, to be part of a traditional family structure, takes precedence as he photographs his relatives (Sophie, his nephew, Laura) and, later, as he consents to fathering Jany's child, a half-selfish, half-altruistic decision that belies his earlier proclamation that he dislikes children and wants "no descendants."

The role of photography as a socially anchored exercise has further implications besides what Cavitch calls "a mass social practice for integrating and protecting the family" (318), and those implications are particularly relevant to our discussion of *Le temps qui reste.* According to Barthes, photographers are also "agents of death" in our increasingly more secular societies: "Death must be somewhere in our society; if it is no longer (or less intensely) in religion, it must be elsewhere; perhaps in this image which produces Death while trying to preserve life. Contemporary with the withdrawal of rites, Photography may correspond to the intrusion, in our modern society, of an asymbolic Death, outside of religion, outside of ritual, a kind of abrupt dive into literal Death. *Life/ Death:* the paradigm is reduced to a simple click, the one separating the initial pose from the final print" (*Camera Lucida* 92, Barthes's emphasis). The removal of a church sequence from the final cut (available in the deleted scenes section of the DVD), in which Romain tells a priest that God has left him long ago, coupled with the photographer's zealous recording of life before his own extinction, take on a new significance in light of Barthes's argument. Romain's need to document "the time that remains" (the literal translation of the film's title), his compulsion to catalog his life and that of his kin, would then be a way (for Romain and perhaps his creator) to reconcile with and prepare for death in the absence of religion, and not simply an attempt to preserve life.

The other vital agent in Romain's mourning process is the periodically conjured image of his childhood self. Ozon exhibits notable creativity in the various ways in which he makes young Romain (Ugo Soussan Trabelsi) appear to the spectator, whether on his own, with little Sophie, or in the company of his young (male) crush. Equally notable is the fact that those brief scenes featuring Romain as a child are the only ones in the film from which Poupaud is absent; short of a few countershots, the actor otherwise occupies all remaining frames. The importance of Romain's preteen alter ego is stressed as early as the film's first shot, a medium close-up of a boy with long, curly hair (filmed from behind) sitting alone on the beach. The name of Melvil Poupaud appears first, to his left. This device signals a connection between the swimsuit-wearing boy and the actor and, in retrospect, frames the film with two seaside images of a solitary Romain. The child stands and walks toward the ocean without reaching it (referencing the conclusion of *Sous le sable*), and the film cuts to an adult image of Romain sleeping next to his companion, whose gender remains unidentifiable to the spectator.

The oneiric character of the child's apparition is thus immediately established. But as it turns out, most other materializations of the youngster will occur not in Romain's slumber but in his daydreams: a dissolve shot makes the child appear in the mirror, where, after snorting a line of cocaine, Romain glares at himself in his parents' bathroom (a continuation of fig. 17); the brown-haired boy appears playing in the forest with his sister as Romain walks alone in the woods behind Laura's house (the adult Romain is shot in *nuit américaine* [day for night], a contrast from the brightness of the daydream sequence); minutes later, the boy strolls the woods with his father and laments the death of a wild rabbit (the repetition of a forest scene with the animal-loving Alice in *Les amants criminels*); later still, Romain enters a church to light a candle and "sees" himself urinating in the holy water stoup in the company of a friend. The most innovative, and perhaps most moving, manifestation of the photographer's juvenile spirit emerges at the film's close, when Romain catches a runaway blue ball that turns out to be . . . his own. A boy comes to retrieve it, and Romain gazes up at him(self). The two smile at each other, but the poignant exchange remains silent. These episodes, which have been condemned for being slightly naïve (de Bruyn 105), substantiate Romain's design to "distance himself from his job and relatives to make peace with himself" (Rouyer, "*Le temps qui reste*" 22).

In addition to the fanciful (wordless) dialogue between Romain and his child persona, the two connections he establishes prior to his death are with people who, like him, are experiencing a lack: Laura and Jany. The two women are also, not coincidentally, the only ones who are made aware of Romain's calamitous fate. Jeanne Moreau's appearance as Romain's caring grandmother is short-lived, but her impact on the viewer is long-lasting. As Emma Wilson observes, "Moreau was missing in Ozon's panoply of French actresses in *8 Women;* he gains the chance to make a loving tribute to her fading beauty in this later film . . . [Moreau's presence here and in lesbian filmmaker Josée Dayan's *Cet amour-là* (2001)] increases the sense that Ozon taps into the vein of affection for aging women in queer culture" (21). After finding out that Romain is going to die, Laura tells her grandson that she wishes she could "leave with [him]." In light of Ozon's tendency to blur the divisions between actor and character, the statement reads as an extra-filmic affirmation (or regret) that Moreau's fifty-six-year-old career is coming to an end. On a narrative level, Laura comprehends both Romain's impeding death and his estrangement from his family. After the death of her husband, Laura was unable to cope and abandoned her son when he was still a child, something for which, Laura maintains, Romain's father "never forgave [her]." While she had numerous lovers, Laura was never able (or willing) to build a steady relationship with another man.

In a sense, Jany is Laura's converse. The young server shares a solid, amorous bond with her partner, Bruno, but is unfulfilled because of their inability to procreate. The spectator may find Jany's timid yet strikingly spontaneous request that Romain "sleep with [her]" hard to believe. That Romain eventually agrees to it, and copulates not only with Jany but with her husband as well, may be deemed both shocking and inconceivable, especially for viewers who are unfamiliar with Ozon's style. Wilson contends, "It is in [the couple's] tryst with [Romain] that, for some, the film will lose justice and credibility," but the scholar advances the possibility that, given Ozon's record, the sequence may only be happening in Romain's mind (21). Regardless of whether it is real or imagined (I am inclined to believe the former) the threesome indeed proves that Ozon is true to his last name, a homophone for *"osons,"* the imperative form of the French verb *"oser"* or "let's dare/let's be daring." One *New York Times* commentator finds this plot development "both breathtakingly poignant and very close to ridiculous" (Scott, *"Time to Leave"*). These contradictory feelings are understandable and possibly stem from the fact that the threesome resembles not mechanical breeding (with the sole purpose of Jany's impregnation in mind) but voluptuous lovemaking. After an awkward start, Jany asks her husband to undress. Bruno complies and joins her and Romain on the bed. The three then take turns kissing one another tenderly before Romain gently penetrates Jany.

The mixed feelings of this *New York Times* journalist vis-à-vis Ozon's narrative and aesthetic choices are far from isolated. Particularly striking are the varying responses the film as a whole has generated in critics. I would even argue that the drastically opposed ways in which *Le temps qui reste* has been read (or, more accurately, "experienced") make it stand out in Ozon's filmography. Most commentators agree that Romain's unpleasant, gruff behavior is unexpected when compared to the heroes in other "terminal illness movies." One critic calls Romain "antipathetic, presumptuous" (Defoy 58) while another unceremoniously judges him to be "for lack of a better word, a bastard" (Wisniewski). They also notably comment on the fact that Romain's mournful journey avoids excessive sentimentality, unlike, to cite but a few films mentioned, *Steel Magnolias* (Herbert Ross, 1989), *Philadelphia* (Jonathan Demme, 1993), *My Life*

Without Me (Isabel Coixet, 2003) and *Son frère* (Chéreau, 2003) (de Bruyn, *"Le temps qui reste"* 105; Wilson, *"Time to Leave"* 20; Defoy 58; Scott *"Time to Leave"*; Douin, "Chronique"). But what they disagree on, interestingly, is whether evading *pathos* equates to removing all *feelings*. "One essential thing is missing from [the film]: emotion," states Douin, while Stéphane Defoy esteems Romain's story neither "touching" nor "poignant" (58). In contrast, the subtitle of Pierre Murat's review of *Le temps qui reste* reads, "François Ozon's latest film is heart-breaking" (*"Le temps qui reste"*), and Philippe Rouyer propounds that Ozon's narrative ideas are "strong and impressive, in line with a film that travels without a net into emotional territory" (*"Le temps qui reste"* 22).

These reactions undeniably vary according to whether or not the critics in question (most of whom are familiar with Ozon) "like" the filmmaker and his previous creations. This is not, however, the only reason. As Wilson confesses, her first theater screening of *Le temps qui reste* left her "disappointed." But the opportunity to watch it again on DVD led to a different viewing experience, one that allowed her to find the film "acquiring different contours" and appreciate its "brilliance" (*"Time to Leave"* 24). Having watched *Le temps qui reste* multiple times over the course of a few years, I can relate to these statements. I have concluded that my spectatorial response to the film depends not solely upon what it shows (and does not show), but upon the mood I am in when watching it. One may of course make a similar argument for *any* film, but Ozon's stands out in its starkness, in how its creator shows only what he deems essential, with neither "fillers" nor "filters."

The proof is in the pudding of deleted scenes that are included in the DVD extras. At eighty-one minutes, *Le temps qui reste* is the shortest of all Ozon's full-length pictures. The DVD offers a full eighteen minutes of segments that were cut during the editing process, evidence that making a shorter film was not Ozon's original intention. Some omissions are merely aesthetic choices. For example, Ozon favored in the final cut a simple voice-over of Sophie reading her letter to Romain over a visual image of the actress projected onto the window of her brother's apartment. In other instances, conversations are cut short, such as one in which Romain inquires about his father's use of Viagra. Other scenes are missing altogether: sequences of Romain's childhood in a swimming pool with friends, on a bed with Laura, in the backyard playing games with Sophie. Also missing is the aforementioned conversation about God between Romain and a priest and one in which the protagonist tells his doctor that he "like[s] nobody." Ozon does not provide a commentary for these scenes, or an explanation for their deletion, but one can surmise that they were simply too distracting, too much of a space filler for a tale Ozon wished to keep simple. As a last example, one deleted segment in the rest-area bathroom shows Bruno looking at Romain with insistence, a gaze that the photographer wrongly mistakes for gay cruising.

Another element that distinguishes *Le temps qui reste* from Ozon's previous pictures and depletes its potential to be an "intimate" or "emotional" film is the use of the widescreen aspect ratio. This new format for the director is decisive in accenting "the solitude of the protagonist in close-up shots," as his face "appears isolated in the middle of large portions of empty space" (Rouyer, "*Le temps qui reste*" 23). Exceptions to this precept, such as the radiant two-shot close-up of Romain and Sasha that our character conjures after his breakup, only serve to underscore the hero's estrangement following the news of his incurable illness (fig. 18). The impossibility of framing Romain's face in classic close-ups potentially hinders the spectator from properly connecting with him on an intimate level.

Mirroring the rest of the film, the closing sequence of *Le temps qui reste* is at once penetrating and strangely distant. The director's will to shoot on the northwestern coast of Brittany rather than in the more Ozonian Landes region alludes to the site of Eric Rohmer's *Conte*

Figure 18. Sasha and Romain
in *Le temps qui reste*.

d'été (*A Summer's Tale*, 1996), in which a twenty-something Poupaud plays an inexperienced beach vacationer who cannot decide between three potential female love interests. Like Poupaud's character, Gaspard, in Rohmer's coming-of-age opus, Ozon has Poupaud/Romain eat a chocolate ice-cream cone as he gazes at the ocean, a patent tribute foreshadowed in the casting of the Rohmerian actress Marie Rivière as Romain's mother. Gaspard's guitar, a recurring object in Rohmer's tale, is replaced by Romain's digital camera in *Le temps qui reste* (fig. 19). The reference to Gaspard, a character whose adult life is nascent and full of possibilities, further dramatizes that of Romain, whose existence is coming to a close. While Gaspard is spoiled for choice, Romain is desperately alone. The paleness of Romain's skin further differentiates him from the other tanned bodies, and his immobility contrasts with the vivacity of his fellow beachgoers.

If Ozon defies expectation in other portions of the narrative, the film's last images are almost predictable. I am not suggesting that the sight of Romain lying alone on the beach as the sun slowly goes down above his face is "predictable" in the sense of mundane or commonplace. Like cinema itself, this last image plays with our persistence of vision, and it is predictable simply because we have already "seen" it, because the narrative has carefully prepared us for it. The film's first shot of Romain's child persona on the same beach; the constant play with light and shadow through images overexposed by Romain's camera flash; the luminous recollections of his past, which contrast with the film's

Figure 19. Romain at the conclusion
of *Le temps qui reste*.

numerous night scenes (in the forest, at the gay club, on the street), all point to a trajectory resembling life itself, a trajectory from lightness to darkness captured beautifully in the final image of a sunset.

Of course, for those acquainted with Ozon's prior exercises, the ultimate shot of *Le temps qui reste* is familiar territory for additional reasons. In its ability to call forth previous visions of lone characters on the beach (Luc in *Une robe d'été*, Sasha in *Regarde la mer*, Marie in *Sous le sable*), Romain's final portrait reminds us that in Ozon's coastal world, water, sand, and sky coalesce to generate joy and excitement, but also peril, mourning, and death.

Foreign Affairs: *Gouttes d'eau sur pierres brûlantes*, *5x2*, and *Ricky*

The last three feature films considered in this study, *Gouttes d'eau sur pierres brûlantes* (henceforth, *Gouttes d'eau*), *5x2*, and *Ricky*, span nine years of Ozon's career. Released in 2000, 2004, and 2009, respectively, Ozon's third, seventh, and tenth full-length projects all focus on a couple (or a combination of couples) and on the difficulties that connubial life entails. Veering away from the self-absorbed, solitary universe epitomized in the characters of Marie, Sarah, and Romain, these tightrope exercises in couplehood are either adaptations of literary works (a Fassbinder play for *Gouttes d'eau*, a Rose Tremain novella for *Ricky*) or, in the case of *5x2*, a picture strongly inspired by two other films (from directors Ingmar Bergman and Jane Campion) and reminiscent of *Betrayal*, a play by Harold Pinter. These reinterpretations of already existing works are more than intertextual references; the acknowledged inspirations infuse the three narratives not anecdotally but on a deeper level. I have already pointed out Ozon's taste for non-French-native actresses, from Sasha Hails and Lucia Sanchez to Valeria Bruni-Tedeschi and Charlotte Rampling, and, more seldom, for nonnative actors (Miki Manojlovic). It is significant that all of Ozon's inspirations in the films under discussion draw from non-French sources and also employ at least one foreign-born performer. In addition, the first two films, *Gouttes d'eau* and *5x2*, take place partially or completely outside of France (Germany and Sardinia, respectively), while *Ricky* unfolds in a lower-class suburb outside of the French capital. This last, previously unseen, un-Ozonian location (if one excludes the eight-minute *X2000,* commissioned for television) signals a marked departure from the familiar, a departure all the more conspicuous with *Ricky* being Ozon's first film to plunge so deeply into the realm of the fantastic.

The Teddy Award recipient *Gouttes d'eau* is, like *Sitcom,* an interior, single location *huis clos.* The film was shot between the summer and winter episodes of *Sous le sable* and released the same year as Marie's tale. For *Gouttes d'eau,* Ozon disinterred and adapted an unstaged play that Rainer Werner Fassbinder wrote in 1965 when he was nineteen years old. At the time, the Bavarian-born (soon-to-be) playwright had left his divorced mother to rekindle his relationship with his father. Fassbinder's papa, a fallen doctor who had lost his license after performing illegal abortions, strongly disapproved of his son's homosexual conquests. While Fassbinder was desperately looking for paternal love, he received only disdain (Landrot). Fassbinder's play was written in this emotionally taut context and certainly incorporates autobiographical tidings. Given Ozon's record for portraying ineffective father figures, it is unsurprising that Léopold's character in Fassbinder's play appealed to him. The same-sex, intergenerational, master-and-slave relationship spotlighted in his previous film *Les amants criminels* returns in full force in *Gouttes d'eau.* Ozon's adaptation retains the theatricality of the play's original four-act structure as four distinct segments are announced in the film via a (Godardian-style) intertitle. On a formal level, Ozon's work borrows from both Fassbinder (the film director) and émigré, German-born Hollywood filmmaker Douglas Sirk while still remaining distinctly Ozonian. The geographical setting is, as in the 1965 play, an unidentified German city, the time period slightly later than Fassbinder's, in the 1970s.

Gouttes d'eau recounts (in French, not German) the piquant, dysfunctional relationship between a fifty-year-old salesman named Léopold Bluhm (Bernard Giraudeau) and Franz Meister, a twenty-year-old student (Malik Zidi). In act 1 Léopold (who was only thirty-five in Fassbinder's story) invites Franz to his one-bedroom apartment (the film's lone setting) and seduces him after a ludic round of Ludo, a board game involving miniature horses and dice, and a conversation about Franz's (limited) sexual experience with boys at boarding school. The first act ends as Léo reenacts in his bedroom Franz's narrated dream, in which he sleeps with a father figure dressed in an overcoat. Act 2 begins six months after Franz has moved into Léo's apartment. The lederhosen-wearing Franz revels in playing the submissive role of the stay-at-home housewife. Despite Franz being at Léo's beck and call, the middle-aged bachelor grows tired of his younger protégé. Léo reiterates a remark from the first act ("It is so hard for me to take pleasure in things"), and although the two bicker constantly, the incredible sex they have every weekend keeps them together (Léo travels for work and is away on weekdays). This segment ends as Léo and Franz reenact the same dream, only this time Franz wears the overcoat. Act 3 stages the first love scene between the male couple (all previous sexual acts have been suggested, not seen), but tension mounts even further outside the bedroom. Franz drops his apron and packs his suitcase, but the two somehow reconcile and the young student stays. Franz's former fiancée, Anna Wolf (Ludivine Sagnier), telephones Franz and visits him while Léo is away. They make love and make up. In act 4 Anna tries to convince Franz to leave with her, but the young redhead hesitates, confessing his enduring love for the older man. Léo returns and does not mind Anna's presence. Later still, Léo's former transsexual lover, Véra (Anna Thomson), also shows up at the door, turning the relationship into a complicated ménage-à-quatre. Franz is frustrated with the situation while Anna and Véra enjoy being at Léo's service. There follows a campy, perfectly choreographed musical sequence during which the four protagonists interrupt all daily activities in order to swing to the strains and German lyrics of Tony Holiday's "Tanze Samba mit mir" (Dance the Samba with Me).

This high-powered dance is a prelude to a group sex act in which Franz refuses to engage. Instead, Franz fantasizes a sequence during which he kills Léo while the latter is having sex with both Anna and Véra. Like the father in *Sitcom,* however, Franz does not act on his murderous impulse. Feeling unloved, he instead swallows poison, determined to end his life. During the (real, not fantasized) threesome, Véra feels overlooked, as Léo is more aroused by the younger Anna, and the middle-aged blonde joins Franz in the living room. She confesses to having had a sex change for the sole purpose of pleasing Léo, whom, like Franz, she still adores. She suggests that she and Franz "try something together," but learns he has poisoned himself. Franz calls his mother to announce the news, and her unemotional reaction is to wish him "bon voyage." Franz dies. Véra summons Léo into the room and explains what happened. Undeterred, Léo sends a hysterical Anna back to the bedroom, phones Franz's mother to confirm her son's death, and resumes lovemaking with Anna. The film closes as Véra, visibly shaken by the incident, unsuccessfully attempts to open the window to catch some air.

Although the subject matter of both the film and the play is melodramatic, the tone is, with the notable exception of its conclusion, generally comedic and occasionally farcical. The translation into French of Fassbinder's play, which Ozon used liberally for his adaptation (most dialogues draw from the written text, translated by Jean-François Poirier), subtitles the play "A Comedy with a Pseudo-Tragic Ending" (Fassbinder 4). Because of the film's subject matter, its literary and cinematic influences, and Ozon's previously acquired reputation, *Gouttes d'eau* is often seen as an updated, queered version of the melodrama, a genre that Laura Mulvey opposes to most other male-centered traditions and describes as representing "pent-up emotion, bitterness and disillusion well known to women" (qtd. in Handyside 216). Given the generic instability of postmodern films, and notably Ozon's, and in light of the fact that Ozon consistently revisits genre in unpredictable ways, some critics, especially those of Gallic descent, have concluded that *Gouttes d'eau* is nothing other than a shallow pastiche devised by "a young homo spoon-fed on queerness" (Bingham 2), or simply "a postmodern *exercice de style*" (Handyside 207). Despite the undeniable fact that the majority of Ozon's films rely heavily upon intertextual allusions for signification, I oppose this view and adhere to Fiona Handyside's belief that *Gouttes d'eau* is far more than a parodic, queer appropriation of various traditions and conventions. Instead, it can be regarded as "a complex re-negotiation of cinematic history that stresses the continuities and inspirations between different filmic cultures and the role of genre film-making in the contemporary French cinematic landscape" (207).

It is noteworthy that Ozon chose to retain the German setting and approximate time period of the play, announced in the dated postcards of German urban landscapes during the opening credits sequence, to stage this renegotiation. Such a process of defamiliarization is consistent with Ozon's overall, and already discussed, reticence to fit within the boundaries of mainstream French cinema, making most of his works virtually (and, for commentators, frustratingly) unclassifiable. A further attempt at defamiliarization—one may also call it, as Ozon does, distanciation, in the Brechtian sense of the term (Ozon, "Entretiens *Gouttes d'eau*")—is captured in the very title of the film. For French audiences, Ozon's enigmatic *Gouttes d'eau sur pierres brûlantes* (translated literally from German) fails to evoke what the original idiomatic expression *Tropfen auf heisse Steine* does for a German-speaking reader or spectator. The singular "Ein Tropfen auf den heißen Stein" refers to something utterly inconsequential or a failed attempt at something. In the context of Fassbinder's play, the phrase points to the illusory and evanescent nature of love, to the hopelessness and meaninglessness of human relationships: it is hot at first, but their condensation and flow eventually evaporate. The rough equivalent of the French expression "une goutte d'eau dans l'océan" (a drop in the ocean), which the French translation of Fassbinder's play (*Gouttes dans l'océan*) retains, is admittedly a far less sizzling title but one that clearly strives to be culturally intelligible; it is also one that Ozon chose not to keep. In looking at posters from four different countries (France, Germany, the United States, and Japan), we note that the metaphor manifestly speaks to a German audience (Fassbinder's original title remains unchanged). It also holds a distinctive meaning for the Japanese public, as the expression "yakeishi ni mizu" (literally, "water on hot stone") signifies "something bound to fail." As for the English translation (*Water Drops on Burning Rocks*), it is catchy but far from the equivalent phrase "a drop in the bucket."

While we are on the subject of promotion, there is something to be said about the varying marketing strategies employed by these four countries. The French, German, and American posters all show, with different backgrounds, Franz, Anna, and Léopold sitting on the mature man's sofa, with Anna sitting in the middle. On the French and German posters, Véra is seen behind the couch, staring at Léo. In the American image, however, she disappears, a surprising detail given Anna Thomson's New York City origins and her earlier participation in successful American films such as Tony Scott's *True Romance* (1993) as well as her lead roles in independent U.S.-produced films by Israeli-born Amos Kollek (notably, *Sue Lost in Manhattan* in 1997). On the French and American posters, both Franz's and Léopold's right hands caress one of Anna's bare knees, the one spatially closest to them. The men are clothed (courtesy of Pascaline Chavanne), Franz in lederhosen, Léo in a dark business suit, whereas Anna wears nothing besides her turquoise-colored underwear. On the German poster the picture was digitally (and quite cleverly) modified to show Franz's and Léopold's hands unite on top of Anna's lap, pointing to the two men's sexual connection. On the German and American images the background is a different but equally kitsch and psychedelic version of 1970s wallpaper fabric. On the French poster the background instead exposes the bare buttocks of the four protagonists. These aesthetic choices may well point to what is culturally acceptable in each country to show on a film poster: the four bare derrières on the French version, oddly but perhaps not coincidentally reminiscent of French singer Michel Polnareff's exposed backside on his infamous concert poster from 1973, have disappeared upon crossing the Rhine and the Atlantic. If Germany chose not to show naked bottoms, it significantly did not shy away from promoting the film as one involving a same-sex intrigue.

Japan took an altogether different route, and the Nippon poster is a still from the dance sequence, with digitally added brown 1970s wallpaper in the background. The same country heavily promoted the film as a "musical," as the poster would suggest, and even published additional advertisements intended to teach the Japanese audience the exact steps of Ozon's (or rather, Sébastien Charles's) "Tanze Samba mit mir" choreography. In addition to highlighting cultural differences, these varying advertising materials reveal the generic instability of Ozon's film and the difficulty of describing its exact content and, consequently, of promoting it adequately. Is *Gouttes d'eau* a risqué *comédie de moeurs* (comedy of manners)? Is it a comedy tout court? A psychosexual thriller? A retro-kitsch musical? It is indeed difficult to tell. It is also important to underscore that with the exception of Germany, most of those images deceivingly heterosexualize the story, a problematic choice if one considers that Franz and Léo's sexual affair in reality dominates the diegesis; Anna does not appear until the third act, forty-four minutes into the film, while Véra, who rings the doorbell twice while Léo is unavailable, does not make a proper appearance until the fourth and last act.

The malleability of sexual behaviors and gender identities, mostly absent from the posters, already present in the play, but further exacerbated in the film is, as we know, a crucial part of Ozon's landscape. I have already mentioned the continuum suggested by queer theorist

Eve Sedgwick in her "universalizing view" of the homo/heterosexual definition, a particular way of seeing same-sex object choice "as an issue of continuing determinative importance in the lives of people across the spectrum of sexualities . . . [and also] as a matter of liminality or transitivity between genders" (1). I want to propose that the "transitivity" theorized by Sedgwick manifests itself throughout Ozon's film text not simply on a narrative level, but stylistically as well by way of an innovative, ever evolving, multiple-angle framing of its characters. Several critics, including Richard Falcon, have read Ozon's cinematic choices as devices borrowed from Fassbinder and Sirk that emphasize the confinement of the four protagonists:

> Having already established his credentials as a *pasticheur* in *Sitcom* (1998), Ozon here adopts some of the most obvious stylistic traits of mid-period Fassbinder. There is the claustrophobic single-interior location . . . and the use of overt theatricality for specifically cinematic aims . . . The one exterior shot, repeated throughout the movie, isolates the characters—first Franz and Léopold, then Franz and . . . Anna, then Franz and . . . Véra—from each other within the apartment's window frames; and when the prowling camera rests, it entraps the characters within a constricting *mise en scène* similar to that in Fassbinder's Douglas Sirk–inspired melodramas." (*"Water Drops"* 64)

Ozon employs two additional framing techniques that are markedly distinct from the obsessive use of windows (and, by extension, mirrors) evocative of Fassbinder, Sirk, and, I would argue, framing master Jean Renoir. These two methods turn, in my view, Ozon the "pasticheur" into an astute innovator. Throughout the narrative, all four characters frequently, almost constantly, stand on thresholds and walk inside long hallways, repetitively crossing the metaphorical lines evoked by Sedgwick. Within the context of the film, these dramatized back-and-forth movements complicate visions of sexuality and suggest that "crossing over" is as easy as passing through a doorframe. In one particular sequence we see Léopold standing in a glass doorway in the background while the entire scene, which includes Franz in the middle ground as he talks on the phone, is framed by another (wooden) doorway in the foreground (fig. 20). The moment is decisive: Anna phones Franz for the first time since their separation, hoping to arrange a rendezvous

Figure 20. Léo and Franz in *Gouttes d'eau*. |

with her former fiancé. Though Léo later pretends to be unaffected by Anna's request, he listens in as an enthused Franz tells her to come visit him in the near future. As we have seen, this invitation will change the dynamic of Franz and Léo's relationship. Anna's trespassing into Léo's airtight universe turns the previously straight-identified but recently gay-acting Franz momentarily straight again while it gives Léo, who generally prefers the company of men, the opportunity to enjoy that of the opposite sex. It also causes Franz to forsake his status as Léo's "servant," a role that both Anna and Véra eagerly take over. The framing and shot composition of this particular phone sequence, along with many others in the film, are *not* ensnarement maneuvers but rather pictorial apparatuses that emphasize the fragility of the gay/straight border as well as the mutability of the socially constructed masculine/feminine (and in the case of Véra, the biological male/female) delineations. Like the narrative itself, they also present homosexuality as unproblematic. They propose, in Ozon's words and like Fassbinder's *Faustrecht der Freiheit* (*Fox and His Friends,* 1975), "a universal vision of couplehood" (Ozon, "Entretiens *Gouttes d'eau*").

Beyond this inventive imagery, significant effort has been deployed to dispel the sentiment that we are watching "filmed theater," an easy trap into which other directors may have fallen, given the film's theatrical origin and studio-shot locus. The camera thus insists on making its presence known in a variety of ways. Reducing traditional short reverse shots to a minimum, the camera zooms in and out, frames characters in high angles, circles invasively around Franz and Léo during conversations, unexpectedly switches angles and distances, pans right, pans left, and, at the end of the first and second acts, takes pleasure in slowly caressing overcoat-wearing Léo and Franz from their feet to their head.

From a thematic standpoint, Ozon uses the majority of Fassbinder's translated dialogues and maintains the play's principal developments. However, he takes two crucial liberties in the fourth and final act. First, he transforms Véra's character from a biological woman to a post-op male-to-female transsexual who decided to obtain a sex change not because of gender dysphoria, but in a dire attempt to please Léopold, who had grown tired of him; she tells Franz that Léo had suggested he would marry Véra if she were a woman. This was a failed endeavor, and Léo ended the relationship shortly after the operation. It is undeniable that Véra's forced transsexualization represents, within the context of the story, a horrific act of self-mutilation and castration that equates Léopold, who forcefully dominates all three characters, with a ruthless monster. Although grave, Véra's transsexuality is presented in a way that encourages comic relief. Léo plainly announces that "he [Véra] had his dick cut off in Casablanca," news that causes both Anna's and Franz's jaws to drop as they spring off the sofa in unison to greet her. Perhaps paradoxically, this is one of the film's lightest moments and further evidences Ozon's distanciation designs. But as we shall see, Franz's tragic demise and Véra's ensuing solitude are presented in a much darker fashion at the film's conclusion. This denotes that Ozon's recourse to comedy, which culminates in the musical sequence, should not be regarded as a wish to undermine the tragic character of Fassbinder's tale and its severe condemnation of human behavior.

The second substantial modification to Fassbinder's story is the added dance sequence, which forcibly alters the film's complexion. It is undeniable that this musical segment, though dazzling, feels incongruous. However, even spectators who have missed the film's trailer, which features the swinging foursome, have been somewhat prepared for it, for *Gouttes d'eau* is a film that exhibits chronic melomania, particularly of the Teutonic kind. Léo's stereo system sits prominently in the living room. In the first scene, the old bachelor plays a record aimed at setting the mood for what he hopes will lead to same-sex frolicking. Later on, he and Franz argue about who damaged the needle of the record player after Léo demands that Franz turn down the music. If Verdi's *Requiem* makes an appearance, most melodies heard in the film aim to emphasize its German milieu. Those tunes also arguably compensate for the fact that actors speak in Molière's, not Goethe's, tongue. On the classical side, the sound track includes excerpts from Handel's coronation anthem *Zadok the Priest* and Beethoven's Symphony No. 4. On the retro kitsch side, we hear, in addition to the samba of Hamburg-born (closeted) pop singer Tony Holiday (1977), the sorrowful German-language song "Träume" (Dreams, 1969) by French yé-yé chanteuse Françoise Hardy. The self-proclaimed Germanophile François Ozon elected not to subtitle the songs or the poem "Lorelei" by Heinrich Heine (recited twice in the original German by Franz), because he wanted to force French spectators, who "associate [the German language] with a difficult historical period," to "perceive this language differently, in its musicality, its mystery" (Ozon, "Entretiens *Gouttes d'eau*") (conversely, the U.S. DVD of *Gouttes d'eau* offers as special features two "sing-along" versions of "Tanza Samba mit mir," one with English, the other with German subtitles, as well as a subtitled English translation of Heinrich's poem recited by Franz).

The crazed musical foursome, which occurs sixty-one minutes (or two-thirds) into the narrative, begins after Véra's spontaneous, simple request: "Léo, may I play a record?" The film then cuts to a close-up of Léo's boogying derrière, followed by Véra's, Anna's, and Franz's, four consecutive shots that the French poster references in nude form. An ensuing medium four-shot reveals the dancers in their aligned hip-shaking and arm-waving splendor (fig. 21). Sagnier, who speaks some German, lip-synchs to the song, while the others remain close-mouthed but equally enthralled. Cinematic variety is added as the camera frames the dancers in medium close-ups, panning from left to right then from right to left. Sagnier's and Thomson's wide smiles betray the fact that the actresses, not the characters, are dancing here. Zidi is a particularly inept dancer, an attribute that fits his character, as we shall see. Giraudeau, however, takes the performance seriously. He remains impressively concentrated throughout the exercise, which lasts slightly over one minute.

Figure 21. Anna, Léo, Véra, and Franz
in *Gouttes d'eau*.

The choreography, loosely inspired from Holiday's feeble moves in the song's YouTube–available recorded (lip-synched, not live) performance, ends as Léo abruptly turns off the stereo and convenes everyone into the bedroom. The two women shriek with anticipation, but Franz shows no reaction.

By now we know that intrusive musical interludes are one of Ozon's trademarks. In its eccentric nature and highly stylized theatricality, the dance in *Gouttes d'eau* recalls other films by the same auteur, notably, the opening sequence of *Une robe d'été* and the eight distinct singing numbers in *8 femmes*. In all three films, the fourth wall is violated, the choreography is symmetrical and previously rehearsed, and actors perform for the viewer, not an unseen diegetic character. In addition to the obvious comic relief the scene provides and the added campiness it injects into Fassbinder's somber fable, the question of its exact function must be posed. In "Entertainment and Utopia," film theorist Richard Dyer suggests that the Hollywood musical is an escapist and utopian form of entertainment that offers us as spectators "the image of 'something new' that our day-to-day lives don't provide," and that musicals in fact compensate for "specific inadequacies in society" (qtd. in Bolton). Dyer lists abundance, energy, intensity, transparency, and community as recurring concepts that are part and parcel of the genre (qtd. in Bolton). It would seem, then, that the fast-paced choreography in *Gouttes d'eau* waltzes the spectator, if only for a few seconds, into a world of "pure entertainment" where all sexual beings are "in sync" and love tales end happily.

This is a plausible argument, but *Gouttes d'eau* does something else, something that traditional musicals strive to avoid at all cost. It lays bare the very artifice of this entertainment piece, first, by letting the sequence "sneak up on us" (we know we are *not* watching a musical) and, second, by exposing Franz (who dies shortly thereafter) as unable to keep up with the beat. The poor lad stumbles, scrutinizes the others' dance moves, and eventually gives up dancing altogether. In this light, the scene does not convincingly function as escapist entertainment, partially preventing the viewer from suspending disbelief and undermining the utopian values it is supposed to promote.

The imperfect but nonetheless genuine delight provided by the musical segment contrasts, as I already pointed out, with the solemnity of the film's conclusion. It is interesting to note that *Gouttes d'eau* closes on Véra's character, perhaps the most tragic of the four, rather than on the main (remaining) protagonist, Léo. Before exploring this finale further, the question of Ozon's casting should be examined. The youngest two performers were relative newcomers in the year 2000: Sagnier had played small parts as a child and adolescent actor but was mostly unknown when the film came out; Zidi's first screen appearance dates to 1998. Giraudeau and Thomson, on the other hand, are not neophyte actors. For the part of Léo, Ozon was determined to hire a famous performer. This turned out to be a difficult task, as many refused to play a homosexual man. Giraudeau, notorious in the 1980s as a (female-seducing) Casanova character, accepted willingly. Ozon discussed his casting choice of the actor, who had fallen from grace in the 1990s, and described Giraudeau's participation in a way similar to how he described Rampling's in *Sous le sable:* "Giraudeau's presence did not help us get funding from television channels . . . I [on the other hand] liked the idea to have a fifty-year-old actor who is still handsome. There are few of them in French cinema. Giraudeau was a star in the 1980s, and I found it interesting to use him now that he is older and no longer able to hide his wrinkles" (Higuinen, *"Gouttes d'eau"* 40).

Ozon's project was felicitous for the actor as well. Giraudeau admitted to suffering from depression before the shoot and professed a drastic, long-lasting shift in his mood caused by the atmosphere on the set, a sound stage in Saint-Denis, outside of Paris. He also confessed that he was not afraid of incarnating a homosexual character, because he had already played one three times before (Gorin, "Vive le déguisement").

It is probable that Ozon opted to make Fassbinder's thirty-five-year-old Léopold into a fifty-year-old man as a result of Giraudeau's inclusion in the cast. To my knowledge, Ozon has not commented on the casting of Anna Thomson (sometimes credited as Anna Levine) for the role of Véra, but her presence is equally fascinating. If Véra is, as I mentioned, a biological woman in Fassbinder's work, and if the thought to make her a transsexual was indeed Ozon's, the French filmmaker actually borrowed the idea from Fassbinder's film *In einem Jahr mit 13 Monden* (*In a Year with 13 Moons*, 1978), which features a male-to-female transsexual character named Erwin/Elvira. Ozon resolved to bring more depth to Véra's character in order to "pose the question of the character's identity in parallel to that of Franz" (Ozon, "Entretiens *Gouttes d'eau*"). What remains unexplained, however, is why an American female-born actress was chosen to play the part. While the film explores the complexity of Véra's identity, particularly in her emotional conversation with Franz shortly before his death, the narrative fails to pose the question of Véra's cultural and linguistic otherness. No mention is made of her national origin or her foreign accent; the actress speaks good French, but is clearly identifiable as an Anglophone by a French-speaking audience. This absence of explanation is uncharacteristic of Ozon's cinema, which usually finds ways to "acknowledge" the national origins of its performers, whether stereotypically (consider the characters of Maria in *Sitcom* and Sarah in *Swimming Pool*) or, in the case of Marie in *Sous le sable*, in more nuanced ways. Perhaps one may explain this deficit by arguing that *Gouttes d'eau* already had to work overtime to justify the German setting and origins of its French-speaking, but occasionally German-reciting and lip-synching, characters. Admittedly, adding a layer of Americanness to this mix may have overcomplicated the story.

At the same time, the film *does* acknowledge Véra's double otherness as a transsexual and nonnative French (or German) speaker in circuitous, subtler ways. It is accidental that Véra's name is homophonic to the future tense of the French verb *voir* (to see; *elle "verra"* [she "will see"]). It is, however, a happy coincidence, for Véra is indeed a "seer," someone who observes, notices, and comprehends. Thanks to those abilities, she differs from the other characters as someone closely in touch with reality and its harshness. Véra is alone with Franz when he dies; she is the only (crying) witness of his demise. In their final conversation, she is the one who helps Franz fathom the extent of Léo's ruthlessness, who consoles the young man when even his mother shows little compassion.

Because of Véra's singular capacity to see, and see through, people, Ozon revised the ending of Fassbinder's play in order to heighten the importance of her character. In the play, Léopold is indifferent to Franz's death. Véra urges him to call the police, but Léo answers: "We'll do that later. Get undressed and lie down on the bed next to Anna, a gorgeous woman if I may say so. I'm quickly going to brush my teeth, then I will join you." Véra replies, "Oh yes," the play's last two words (Fassbinder 61). In the film a similar dialogue occurs, but Véra's "Oh yes" turns into "You don't need me," to which Léo retorts, "But *you* need me." The film's remaining seconds, not present in the play, will prove Léo wrong. Echoing the cross-gender clothing exchange in *Une robe d'été*, Véra goes to retrieve her fur-lapel coat, which Franz had put on earlier because he was cold. She changes her mind and instead shrouds the young man with it. She then walks to the window to open it, but is unable to do so. The camera frames Véra through the window, slowly tracking away from the mentally drained woman as the extra-diegetic melody of Hardy's "Träume" fills the air. Véra *is* trapped here, as she stands by a threshold that cannot be crossed (fig. 22). But unlike the seemingly insouciant, though genuinely unhappy Anna and Léo, Véra is acutely cognizant of her confinement.

The entrapments of passion are further explored in *5x2*, released four years after Ozon's adaptation of Fassbinder's play. The screenplay of *5x2*, published at the same time as the release of the film, renders explicit the connections between the two works: "After *Gouttes d'eau sur pierres brûlantes* . . . François Ozon returns to the couple, but concentrates this time on a heterosexual union: a man and a woman of today, who work and have a child. Of course, *5x2* provides a similar, cruel description of the illusions that temporarily cement any love story; but it seems as though this story treats, more specifically, questions of divergence and

Figure 22. Véra at the conclusion
of *Gouttes d'eau.*

solitude within the couple" (Ozon, 5x2 3). The "look" of 5x2, shot mostly on location with many exterior scenes, could not be further from that of *Gouttes d'eau;* yet its division into five distinct episodes recalls the four-act structure of Léo and Franz's love affair. The doomed relationship in *Gouttes d'eau,* formally indicated via intricate framing methods, is stressed in 5x2 by way of an obsessive inclusion of transitory spaces. These spaces include elevators, cars, and stairs as well as long, tunnel-like corridors where the two main characters walk alone or together, depending on the state of their relationship.

5x2 is a powerful story about the disintegration of a marital union, about the long-term impossibility of living together harmoniously. Ozon recognized in interviews his debt to *Scener ur ett äktenskap (Scenes from a Marriage,* 1973), a highly successful five-hour television miniseries by Swedish director Ingmar Bergman (Abeel). This six-episode series was later released in theaters in an edited, three-hour version, and went on to win multiple awards, including a Golden Globe. Bergman's story closely follows the relationship between Marianne and Johan (names strangely reminiscent of Marie and Jean in *Sous le sable*) over the course of a few years, detailing the ups and downs of their union, which ends in divorce. The series has little action and few secondary characters, preferring instead to convey the trials and tribulations of the couple, which include tales of abortion and extramarital affairs, via lengthy conversations that take place indoors. During the screen tests for *5x2,* Ozon's scenario was unfinished, and the director used conversations extracted from *Scenes from a Marriage.* One such screen test was filmed and made available as an extra feature on both the French and American DVDs of *5x2.* We see actors Stéphane Freiss and Valeria Bruni-Tedeschi (*5x2*'s future couple) as they recite a (post-divorce) scene translated into French from the original Swedish. The DVD viewer does not find out until the end credits of this short segment that the scene is Bergman's, not Ozon's. At ninety minutes, *5x2* is obviously less verbose than *Scenes from a Marriage,* but Bergman's excerpt featured here fits well with the rest of Ozon's narrative. Without information about its origin, Freiss and Bruni-Tedeschi's exchange could be mistaken for a deleted scene from Ozon's film or a scene that was written, screen-tested, but never shot.

Like *Gouttes d'eau* and *Scenes from a Marriage, 5x2* is divided into acts or episodes, which present five pivotal stages in the life of middle-class, Parisian couple Gilles (Freiss) and Marion (Bruni-Tedeschi). The title *5x2* refers to the five segments in the life of those two individuals, and the film recounts their relationship in reverse chronology, from their last interaction as a married couple, signing divorce papers in front of a judge, to their initial meeting, as both are visiting the Italian island of Sardinia. Unlike Bergman's work, Ozon's five episodes do not have titles, but for now I propose to describe them succinctly in the following way: (1) the divorce; (2) family life after the birth of their son; (3) the baby's birth; (4) the wedding; and (5) first encounter. The film's screenplay does not provide titles either, but names the episodes numerically, in a countdown from 5 to 1. Although the choice of an inverted narrative will undoubtedly evoke Christopher Nolan's *Memento* (2000) and in the French context Gaspar Noé's *Irreversible* (2002), both of which predate *5x2,* Ozon acknowledged a lesser-known source of inspiration: a made-for-television movie titled *Two Friends* (1986). This film by New Zealand–born director Jane Campion chronicles in reverse chronology the story of a crumbling friendship between two female adolescents of different social backgrounds; the viewer anticipates a specific event that would explicate the end of the friendship, but their social difference is the lone subtle "revelation" of the film's close (Ozon, "Entretiens *5x2*").

Given the fact that *5x2* refuses to overtly provide a *reason* for the failure of the marriage, Campion's film indeed appears much closer in spirit to Ozon's than those of Nolan and Noé. Although unacknowledged as an inspiration, *5x2* is also close in both spirit and structure to *Betrayal*, a 1978 play by English author Harold Pinter. The play is composed of nine scenes that move back in time from 1977 to 1968 and relate the affair of Emma and Robert from their breakup to the declaration of their feelings for each other.

In *5x2* the five episodes are self-sufficient, in the sense that they contain a clear beginning and an end, with a specific story line that could potentially be told on its own. These moments, however, take full significance only in relation to the other four. On the level of form, each segment is separated from the next by a fade to black, which marks the passage of time, and outmoded Italian love songs (sung mostly by men), which anticipate the last sequence in Italian-speaking Sardinia and arguably point to the national origin of actress Valeria Bruni-Tedeschi. (In contrast to Véra's character in *Gouttes d'eau,* the film justifies the ability of French-born Marion to speak Italian well by inserting a sequence in episode five in which she states that her ex-boyfriend was Sicilian.) Each episode in *5x2* bears a different aesthetic, following a clear trajectory from a darker color palette to a lighter one, from the indoor to the outdoor. With some exceptions, the tone of the film also evolves from somber to lighthearted. Ozon's comments about the film's construction reveal his desire to toy with the medium: "Within each part, I tried to evoke a different style of cinema. We start with an intense psychological drama and in the second part of the film, which is more socially anchored, we move on to something more conventional for French cinema. For the wedding, American cinema was my main reference and for the first encounter, I wanted to recreate Eric Rohmer's summer films . . . On the set, I would often say jokingly: 'we start with Bergman and end with [Claude] Lelouch'" (Ozon, "Entretiens 5x2"). The mention of Rohmer, a crucial inspiration for the ending of *Le temps qui reste,* along with other filmmakers and cinematic traditions, confirms Ozon's vision of cinema as hybrid, referential, and experimental.

Within each episode "something" happens, making the reasons for the divorce potentially more and more understandable to the spectator. But as I already noted, the film does not point to a single event, and it is probable that each viewer will draw different conclusions from the information presented on screen. As Philippe Rouyer argues, "The project's interest is contingent upon the fact that there are no secrets behind the door, no lovers in the closet, no obvious explanation for the couple's emotional bankruptcy, but rather a multitude of signs that the spectator may notice, assemble and interpret differently, depending on his or her sensibility" ("*5x2*" 28). Rouyer is slightly wrong about the absence of a lover, as we shall see. He is right, nonetheless, in pointing out the fact that nothing excessively dramatic happens, although, again, the film leaves it up to the viewer to decide. Some, myself included, may in fact find the events I am about to describe quite tragic.

Beyond the tragedy that is obviously intrinsic to any divorce, *5x2* exhibits signs of a much darker experience. Indeed, one could find alternate titles to those I provided above in an attempt to describe each episode's "main event." Episode one (the divorce) may thus be renamed "the rape": after finalizing their divorce papers, Marion and Gilles go to a hotel room together in the middle of the day. The exact reason is not made explicit. One can surmise that they want to have sex "one last time" before separating in earnest, something that is confirmed when Gilles immediately undresses and encourages Marion to do the same. She complies, even asking Gilles to kiss her. Perhaps realizing the damage that a last sexual intercourse can potentially cause, Marion quickly changes her mind and tells Gilles to stop caressing her. Instead of complying, he pins Marion down and sodomizes her as she screams for him to stop. The segment ends as Marion walks out on her ex-husband when the latter suggests that they "try again" (to live together). Episode two, which I tentatively named "family life," may be rechristened "the orgy": during a dinner with Gilles's brother, Christophe (Antoine Chappey), and his younger boyfriend, Mathieu (Marc Ruchmann), the conversation revolves around fidelity. Christophe and Mathieu admit to having an open relationship. Encouraged to give his point of view, Gilles proceeds to relate in graphic detail events of a party during which he engaged in group sex with both men and women. Marion confirms the story, and we also learn that she refused to participate in the orgy.

It may be more accurate to retitle the third episode (the birth) "single mother": when he learns that Marion is about to give birth prematurely, Gilles panics and does not come to the clinic until several hours after the delivery, leaving the role of caretaker to Marion's mother, Monique (Françoise Fabian). In the fourth episode (the wedding), which could alternatively be titled "sex with a stranger," there is an expectedly joyous ceremony but no wedding night—at least not between the bride and groom: Gilles is too inebriated to perform his conjugal duty, which leaves Marion wandering alone in the forest behind the hotel. There, she meets a handsome American tourist, who kisses her and, the film connotes, makes love to her. Finally, the fifth and last episode relates Gilles and Marion's first proper encounter in Sardinia; they had met briefly in Paris, but knew nothing about each other. However, what could be a lovely story of nascent love is tarnished by the fact that Gilles is on vacation with his girlfriend of four years, Valérie (Géraldine Pailhas). Before the film's "happy ending," which shows Marion and Gilles bathing in the Mediterranean at sunset, we see a close-up of Valérie's troubled face: she has understood Gilles's attraction to Marion and knows that her relationship with him is coming to an end. "Adultery" is my choice of substitute title for this section.

I realize that the above description of 5x2's "dark sides" may be seen as a partisan reading that, perhaps more so than other films, depends entirely on my subjective experience. But it is precisely the unusual elasticity of 5x2, its capacity to provoke various, if not opposed, spectatorial responses, that makes it particularly special in my view. Discussing his work on the screenplay and in the editing room, Ozon affirmed his refusal to take sides, his attempt to "erase moments when the couple's relationship was made too explicit," and his determination not to "psychologize" Gilles and Marion's union (Ozon, "Entretiens 5x2"). I, on the other hand, *will* take sides and argue that the film spends significantly more time stressing Gilles's shortcomings than Marion's. In addition to the observed rape sequence, the recounted group sex experience, and Gilles's inexplicable (and ultimately unexplained) absence from the clinic, an accumulation of details all point to his failings as a spouse and father.

At the conclusion of episode one, Marion leaves the hotel room to avoid an argument. As she opens the door, Gilles unceremoniously suggests that she leave and "go get fucked by someone else." Gilles complains to being "fed up" in episode one after a day home preparing dinner and taking care of their son, Nicolas. In episode three, when Monique takes him to see Nicolas in the incubator, Gilles refuses to accept that this tiny infant could be his and instead waves in the direction of a bigger, healthier baby (the father in Ozon's short *La petite mort* also refuses to accept his son when he first sees him). In episode five, when Valérie confesses to being "touched" by Marion, whom she finds both pleasant and attractive, Gilles retorts: "Are you trying to sell her [Marion] to me? Would it turn you on if I banged her?" These moments, which question Gilles's ability to be faithful on the one hand and to act as an adequate father on the other, cannot be offset by Marion's single faulty action in the film: her brief encounter with the American on her wedding night. As if to belittle the long-term impact of Marion's impulsive action, to underrate it as something that can potentially be excused, the film presents Marion's adulterous affair as something she may have only imagined—first, by situating the scene outside the reality of the wedding venue (in a quiet, starlit forest), and, second, by cutting to the next scene immediately after the kiss, leaving the rest to the viewer's imagination. The screenplay includes a morning-after scene between Marion and the stranger that was edited out of the final cut, and the text indicates that the Adonis "has disappeared" when Marion turns around to look at him one final time, inferring that the mysterious man may not be real (Ozon, *5x2* 71).

Despite these developments, which encourage reflection on the part of the spectator, *5x2* stages numerous opportunities for viewers to *interrupt* reflection and instead lose themselves in the whirlwind of the couple's life. Knowing Ozon, it should come as no surprise by now that these intervals are conveyed musically. Referencing a slightly tacky but nonetheless engaging song by French pop singer and dancer Claude François, Rouyer subtitles his review of *5x2* "Comme une chanson populaire" (Like a Popular Song) (28). The critic does not mention any specific musical sequence, but I am guessing that he is referring to the 1950s and 1960s transalpine love songs by Bobby Solo and others that are featured at the hinge of each episode. There are two additional melodic moments in the film that I see as temporary respites from the austere reality of the couple's relationship. The first one occurs in episode two, during the couple's evening with Gilles's brother, Christophe, and his partner, Mathieu. Tension between Gilles and Marion is palpable after Gilles confesses to having cheated on his wife with multiple partners. In a sequence similar to that between Sarah, Julie, and Franck in *Swimming Pool*, a dance follows. Paolo Conte's Italian-language "Sparring Partner" dominates the sound track, and we see Marion and Christophe swaying together in the background while Gilles and Mathieu converse in the foreground. Complicity between each temporary couple is obvious (see Phil Powrie's "Haptic Moment" for a close reading of this sequence). But what the spectator retains from this segment is not necessarily how it underscores the duo's failing marriage but, rather, its ability to deflate the tension in the air; to make us forget, however momentarily, that this love story will end (or, rather, did end) tragically.

The second moment of temporary respite occurs at the marriage reception, in episode four. The wedding party is dancing, reveling in the union of the new, clearly elated couple. Gilles and Marion dance with each other in the center of a circle of guests, itself surrounded by clapping friends and relatives. Suddenly something happens to the sound track as well as the image track. The party's blithe accordion rhythm and background cheering fade to give way to Philippe Rombi's more somber music as the camera records, in a closer shot and in slow motion, Gilles and Marion kissing tenderly. The wedding reception ends thusly, for both the newlyweds and the spectator. Rombi's notes continue as we see a high-angle shot of Gilles and Marion climbing up a spiral staircase, into the nuptial bedroom (fig. 23). I see this sequence as a beautiful yet

Figure 23. Marion and Gilles in *5x2*.

haunting moment of "suspension" that breaks into the narrative, one that intrudes quietly, announced only by the director's choice of slow motion coupled with the solemn non-diegetic music. On the surface, this segment is one that facilitates a kind of pure spectatorial pleasure, of rejoicing at the sight of bliss. On a deeper level, however, this intrusion brings the viewers "back to the future" of Marion and Gilles's life together. After all we have seen, it becomes virtually impossible to enjoy the moment as romantic or utopian in the same way we might have done if the film unfolded in chronological order. In this light, the staircase to happiness becomes one that leads to agony.

Yet it is still possible to "forget," if one chooses to do so, the events of the past (that is, of Gilles and Marion's future). In episode five the narrative incites us to join in the festivities of the Sardinian, all-inclusive beach club—to enjoy the bright sun, to participate in a lesson of water aerobics, to dance along with Marion to Whigfield's "Saturday Night," to feel, as the song suggests, "the air getting hot." Comparison with *Sous le sable* is interesting here. Ozon interrupted the shooting of *5x2*, which was filmed in the same order as the spectator sees it, for five full months. Episodes one, two, and three were shot in the winter, four and five in the summer. In between the two shoots, Ozon wrote the "ending," the wedding reception and Sardinian vacation. In contrast to the financial trouble he encountered with *Sous le sable*, which halted the production of the film, Ozon's choice here was deliberate. This allowed the two actors to "prepare themselves physically so they could look younger"—Ozon asked both of them to lose weight for the summer segment—and gave the director additional time to think: "I wrote the first three parts very quickly, then found I was blocked, especially about the initial encounter. As I shot the first part, I had a vague notion that when they met, Marion would be mourning a boyfriend who had died. But inserting something so major at the end would totally alter the way people interpret the film. The long break kept me from falling prey to such easy screenwriting solutions" (Ozon, "Interviews *5x2*"). Bruni-Tedeschi confessed in an interview that she suffered from that long interruption and feared she would "fall out of character, [that her] life would move on, [and that her] mind would be elsewhere" (Ozon, "Interviews *5x2*"). The actress's remark about her fear of "forgetting" fits well with the intentions of the narrative, as it matches the emotional distance created by the happy atmosphere of the final episode.

It should be clear by now that the appeal of the film rests principally in its rearward progression toward the onset of the pair's relationship. On the French DVD of *5x2*, Ozon proposes, as he did for *Les amants criminels,* an alternate version of the story. The second version, titled *2x5,* moves chronologically from the initial encounter to the divorce. Viewing it is inspiring, not as a separate work, but in comparison to the original. As Jean Douchet observes, this chronological reedit "is a *reductio ad absurdum* which proves that the film's interest lies not in what it tells but in how it is constructed." Douchet then adds that this exercise demonstrates that the original inversion of the narrative "gives [Ozon] the chance to tell a love story in its singularity (the characters have distinct personalities) as well as its generality (the characters, at the same time, are archetypes)" (67). *2x5* is described on the French DVD as "a playful experimentation rather than a film that its creator intended to direct" since "*5x2* was conceived, written, filmed, and edited as a story told in reverse chronology." *2x5* opens in Paris with a scene shot but edited out of *5x2*'s final cut in which Marion meets Gilles briefly at a business meeting. We then travel to Sardinia before going back to France for the wedding, the birth, the dinner with Christophe and Mathieu, the divorce settlement in the judge's office, and the events in the hotel room.

Significantly, Ozon used the same music for the last image of *2x5*, a shot of Marion entering an elevator to leave the hotel, as he did for *5x2*'s ultimate, and perhaps most well-known, frame. The latter shot, however, is crucially missing from *2x5*, for obvious reasons. At the conclusion of *5x2*, Gilles meets Marion on a deserted beach while his girlfriend, Valérie, is hiking in the Sardinian hills. Marion is surprised to see him alone and asks why he did not accompany Valérie. Gilles claims that he wanted to sleep in. But as Gilles inquires about Marion's personal life and her past relationships, one can surmise that he has joined Marion with the intent to seduce her. Marion suggests that they go for a swim, and we see a gorgeously photographed, long-lasting image of the couple swimming in the sea at sundown (fig. 24).

In light of what we have seen, the sequence, although seemingly simple and straightforward, takes on a new significance. Echoing in its

Figure 24. The conclusion of *5x2*. |

function the slow-motion segment of the wedding reception, the beach at sunset in *5x2* is a cinematic trope that is at once predictable, as a trite image in Hollywood film repertoire, and disturbing, for the critique it offers of a "happily ever after." Because *5x2*'s intentions are clearly to turn the conventional romance film on its ear, this ultimate shot self-consciously represents what Douchet names "the cliché of all clichés" and an image "evoking nothing but melancholy" (602). For that reason, and despite Ozon's aforementioned claim to have been inspired by American cinema, *5x2* is an anti–*When Harry Met Sally* (Rob Reiner, 1989). For those familiar with Ozon's own visual vocabulary, Gilles and Marion's aquatic union is, however paradoxically, more evocative of Marie's sadness at the close of *Sous le sable* than Luc's jovial beach encounter with Lucia in *Une robe d'été*. As the screenplay of *5x2* notes, "When Gilles and Marion swim together in a calm sea under the sunset, we understand that Nature itself traps these two bodies" (Ozon, *5x2* 3).

Before turning to *Ricky,* the last film to be discussed in this study, it is useful to mention Ozon's ninth film, *Angel* (2007). Like *Ricky,* it is the adaptation of a literary work by an English woman writer. Based on Elizabeth Taylor's novel from 1957, *Angel* was shot and released between *Le temps qui reste* and *Ricky.* Notably, it is Ozon's only feature film not to have received a theatrical or DVD release in the United States (the DVD only came out in French-speaking Canada). Such a lack of interest on this side of the Atlantic may come as a surprise, given *Angel*'s all-English cast. The film, which had been gestating in Ozon's mind since he read the novel in 2000, had a difficult genesis. Producers, including those in Taylor's home country, were uninterested in funding the adaptation by a Frenchman of a costume drama based in England during the Edwardian era. Though Ozon did eventually gather enough funds to direct the film, thanks to French, British, and Belgian producers, it fared quite poorly at the European box office. This partially explains its limited release on the international market and its failure to find distributors in the Western Hemisphere, despite Ozon's notoriety (the United States–based IFC Films announced the release of *Angel* on DVD sometime in 2010, but the film is not yet available as I write). Things may have turned out differently had Ozon not changed his mind about who should incarnate the part of the title character. Ozon initially proposed the role to Nicole Kidman, who accepted it, but later retracted his offer when he realized that he needed a younger actress (Rouyer, "L'ironie" 23). Newcomers Romola Garai and Michael Fassbender were eventually chosen for the parts of Angel and Esmé, Angel's husband, and Charlotte Rampling was cast in a supporting role.

Angel represents a departure for Ozon. This is the director's first period piece (*Gouttes d'eau* not really qualifying as one), his first film shot exclusively in English, and one that includes the largest cast of any of his films to date. From a thematic standpoint, however, *Angel* is a calculated departure and is in line with some of Ozon's previous creations. The press kit introduces the story in this way: "England, 1905. Angel Deverell, a young prodigal writer, experiences a spectacular climb and realizes the dream of all young girls: success, glory and love. But isn't it too much for one person?" (Wild Bunch 3). For those familiar with the trajectory of Ozon's career, the character of Angel feels a bit like the filmmaker's alter ego. As Ozon confesses: "When I read [Taylor's novel], I devoured it. I recognized myself in the story . . . You can say that *Swimming Pool* was born from my desire to adapt *Angel*. One could already find [in Sarah Morton's story] the relationship between writer and editor, between fantasy and reality and, for a portion of it, the English dialogues" (Rouyer, "L'ironie" 21). Beyond its connections with

Swimming Pool, Angel revisits nostalgically, as Ozon did in *8 femmes,* the Hollywood melodrama of the Technicolor era (see Asibong for a detailed discussion of *Angel*).

If Angel does not have wings, the title character of *Ricky,* Ozon's next feature, does. In a sense, *Ricky* also signals a shift for the director, from the centrality of Paris to its peripheral suburbs and, insofar as the characters are concerned, from the bourgeoisie to the struggling working class. In addition, *Ricky* diverges more markedly from actuality, submerging itself more headily in the domain of the fantastic. The back cover of *Ricky*'s French DVD characterizes the film as a "poetic, disturbing, modern fairy tale" and summarizes the story in the following way: "When Katie, an ordinary woman, meets Paco, an ordinary man, something magical and miraculous happens: they fall in love. Out of their love comes an extraordinary baby: Ricky." The end credits indicate that *Ricky* was "freely adapted" from English author Rose Tremain's short story "Moth" and mentions Emmanuèle Bernheim as Ozon's collaborator in the screenwriting process. "Moth" was published in 2005 as part of a Tremain's collection of novellas titled *The Darkness of Wallis Simpson and Other Stories.* These stories have been described by an English journalist as "modernist fairy tales of motherless children and childless mothers." The same reviewer adds that in the "mystical stories 'Nativity Story' and 'Moth' . . . [it] is the combination of the weird and the everyday that makes them so unusual" (Guest). The juxtaposition of the words "weird" and "everyday" in this citation echo the ordinary/ extraordinary divide in *Ricky,* as the synopsis mentions.

Detailed summaries of both "Moth" and *Ricky* are helpful in that they reveal the similitude between the two works as well as the copious liberties Ozon took in adapting this short text. Tremain, who is a native of London, situates the twelve-page-long story of "Moth" far from the quotidian reality of England, in a trailer park named Sunny Lawns outside of Knoxville, Tennessee. Further distance is established as the tale of this extraordinary baby is told in the past tense by a third party, a friend of Ricky's mother named Annie. The forty-year-old single, childless woman lives in the trailer home next to Pete's, the mother of five-year-old Lisa and baby Ricky (the fact that Pete is usually a man's name is mentioned but ultimately unexplained). Annie, who dreams of becoming a writer, speaks in the first person and narrates the events one year after they occurred. Annie describes Pete, a single mother, as a good friend whose main occupation (and lone passion) is to sew appliqué patterns onto laundry bags, cushion covers, and aprons and sell them in a craft village somewhere in the Smoky Mountains. The narrator mentions two men in Pete's life, "a flaked-out hippie in that village who had a thing for her" and Pete's ex-lover and father of her two children, a 911 dispatcher who is introduced in the following way: "His name was Chester and he had an appetite so big, he used to snatch food off Pete's plate and stick it in his mouth. He weighed down the trailer. And his shit wouldn't flush away, it was that huge" (Tremain 168). The crude language Annie employs throughout the novella matches that of the characters in the transcribed dialogues. It also establishes the narrator as a plain-speaking, down-to-earth woman who can be trusted. After a relatively long introduction of Pete's character, Annie is ready to tell us "this true story of Pete and Lisa and Baby Ricky." She announces, approximately one-third of the way into the text: "So I'm going to put this all down. Everything happened real fast, but in a way it was long and complicated, like a book can be" (170).

Ricky was nine or ten months old when Pete first voiced concerns to Annie about the baby screaming for no apparent reason. The two women examine Ricky together and discover two lumps on his shoulder blades. They decide not to consult a doctor and wait, but a few days later Pete awakens Annie in the middle of the night to declare, panicked, "Ricky's on the ceiling" (171). As the story progresses, we learn that Ricky is a flying baby who, like a moth, enjoys zigzagging around light fixtures. This fascinates his sister, Lisa, who also wishes she could go up on the ceiling. The two friends evoke the possibility of calling "a surgeon, for example," but are mistrustful of the medical profession and instead hope that Ricky's wings will fall off (173). Annie suggests advertising Ricky's special gift and charging patrons to come and see the baby flying around the park, something that will undoubtedly make Pete a billionaire. Instead of preventing Ricky from flying, the mother lets him zoom around the trailer, which makes the baby happy. Pete thinks of Annie's proposal, but hesitates to turn her son into a circus freak. While shopping at a Kroger supermarket, Ricky flies away from the shopping cart. At Annie's request, the manager turns off all the lights, and Ricky finally circles down and lands "in a box of apples" (175). The news of the flying baby travels fast, and the local, national, and international press "crammed into the trailer park" (175). Pete makes a deal with ABC News, and money-hungry Chester returns to the mother of his two children to declare his unconditional love for her. Along with Ricky, Chester attracts most of the attention as the proud father while Pete remains in the background. One night, as the sun sets on the park, journalists gather by the lake and a cluster of oaks behind the trailers. Chester lets go of Ricky, who flies away and never returns. Chester reunites with the twenty-two-year-old woman he dated before his recent reappearance. The story ends as Annie announces Pete's death by suicide. Lisa goes to live with Annie, who becomes her surrogate mother.

Ozon's filmic rendition of Tremain's short story incorporates numerous developments from "Moth," but significantly modifies the structure of the narrative as well as the characters' contours and, one is tempted to say, souls. Instead of the storyteller Annie, who disappears in Ozon's tale, it is the mother, Katie (Pete in "Moth"), who frames the narrative. With some exceptions, we see the story unfold from her point of view, which causes the narrative to lose the emotional distance that Annie provided in "Moth." The geographical distance established in Tremain's story between center (the city) and periphery (the trailer park) is cunningly transposed in Ozon's film, which takes place in a penurious housing project outside of Paris. We are shown early in the narrative a succession of tall, monochromatic buildings. One of them houses Ricky's family in a one-bedroom apartment. The edifices stand next to a few trees and a lake where migratory birds gather. With the exception of a sequence near the end, gray, overcast skies loom above the low-income suburb, matching the spirits of its inhabitants, all of whom seem to struggle to make ends meet.

Ricky opens in the office of a social worker. The camera frames Katie (Alexandra Lamy), who is at wit's end: her Spanish boyfriend, Paco, has left her. She has difficulty raising her son and wonders whether she should temporarily send the baby to an orphanage. The scene cuts to a lake view, and a caption takes us "Several months earlier." We are introduced to seven-year-old Lisa (Mélusine Mayance), Katie's daughter. Lisa, who sleeps in the apartment's sole bedroom, is motherly to Katie, who sleeps on the couch: the girl awakens her mother, who confesses not wanting to go to work, but Lisa insists that Katie rise. Katie drives

Lisa to school on a motor scooter and goes to work in a factory. There, she meets Paco (Sergi López), and the two have sexual intercourse in the restroom at lunchtime. That night, Katie masturbates herself to sleep. The following night, Katie dines with Paco. Back at her place, they make love while Lisa listens in. Katie introduces Paco to Lisa. The girl, who does not know her father, rejoices at the thought of having "a new family."

After an ellipsis, we see Paco and Lisa at the hospital. As they wait for Katie to deliver her baby, the girl suggests that they name her brother Ricky but is unable to explain why. Once the new family is home, Paco toasts to his son, "the world's most beautiful baby." Ricky (Arthur Peyret) cries often, straining the couple's relationship. Paco feels rejected, and Lisa sees him conversing with another woman outside the building. Paco stays home alone with Ricky, and Katie later finds bruises on Ricky's back. Suspecting abuse, she confronts Paco, who denies it. The man moves out, and the bruises begin to swell. Lisa and Katie find Ricky sitting on top of an armoire and discover his wings. Hoping they will fall off, they keep Ricky from flying out of bed by securing a blanket onto his crib with clothespins. In a series of dissolves, we see the wings develop further, and Katie begins to accept the situation. She buys Ricky a helmet and, in Lisa's presence, lets him take his first proper flight (fig. 25). A scene in the grocery store follows, and events unfold there the same way as in

Figure 25. Katie, Ricky, and Lisa in *Ricky*.

Tremain's novella. The media seize the story. A doctor (André Wilms) wishes to keep Ricky in the hospital and run a series of tests on him. Katie refuses and instead takes Ricky home. Television crews harass the family everywhere they go. Paco returns and Katie apologizes to him. The man resumes his role as spouse and father. After Ricky hurts himself flying, the same doctor makes a house call and proposes to remove the wings surgically. Katie and Paco refuse. Paco negotiates with the media, and the couple meets a horde of journalists outside their building. Ricky flies away, disappearing into the sky. Thinking her son has perished, Katie jumps into the lake with the intent to drown herself. Ricky returns, saving her life. After professing her love to him, Katie lets Ricky go. Katie returns home and embraces both Paco and Lisa. Next, Katie is shown lying on her couch, pregnant. Paco takes Lisa to school on Katie's scooter. A close-up of Lisa, who smiles as she holds on to Paco, concludes the film.

Despite the fact that François Ozon was immediately seduced by Tremain's story, the mood and trailer park location of which reminded him of Jean-Pierre and Luc Dardenne's *Rosetta* (1999), the usually intrepid filmmaker initially emitted reservations about the possibility of adapting "Moth" to the screen: "Although I liked the way an extraordinary, amazing event disrupts the characters' otherwise bleak existence, the fantasy elements frightened me. It seemed impossible to render. But then I realized that what touched me about the story wasn't so much the fantasy elements as the way it talks about family, our place in it, and how a new member—a new partner or a new child—can shake up the balance" (Le Pacte 5). In order to make the arrival of a winged baby function inside a social-realist context reminiscent of films by Ken Loach and the Dardenne brothers, Ozon's strategy was to mimic Tremain's and "introduce elements of humor and distance [that] come in to release tension and make the scene work" (Le Pacte 5). The maneuver proved effective, and the film weaves genuinely amusing moments that evoke Annie's colorful language and unconventional storytelling methods in "Moth." These instants often emerge from the surprisingly straightforward ways in which Katie and Lisa deal with Ricky's new feathered limbs. Instead of being frightened, they are intrigued, but not in a morbid kind of way.

Katie regularly measures Ricky's wings, as one would monitor the growth of a child. Visual and verbal comparisons between the anatomy of a chicken and Ricky's peculiar appendages abound in the film. Lisa's candid reactions to her brother's singularity are often humorous ("they suit him well," she remarks about Ricky's wings, as if talking about an outfit), and so are Katie's. In the meat section of the supermarket, the young mother measures the wings of a rooster. She then unblinkingly asks the perplexed butcher to give her precise information about the proportions of the animal and how its weight should compare to the size of its wings. In the bookstore, Katie inquires about their selection of "books on wings." Although the outside reactions to the discovery of Ricky's special gift are often unhealthy and voyeuristic, especially on the part of the media, individual strangers verbalize the nonsensicality of the situation in comic ways. As Ricky flutters up and down the aisles of the supermarket, a customer expresses his desire to purchase a "remote-controlled baby," asking where he can find one in the store. Later, a middle-aged woman sarcastically asks Paco, whom she saw on television, if he would be willing to make love to her so that she might enjoy her own flying baby (this remark also suggests that in people's minds, Paco is responsible for his son's anomaly, not Katie). On a literal level, these moments work to counteract the bleak reality of the characters' lives: the financial woes, the arguments between the couple, the accusations of child abuse. But given the audacity of the subject matter, humor in *Ricky* is also crucial in the way it deflates possible reservations on the part of the skeptical viewers, encouraging them to laugh at the unfolding events rather than at the film itself. After Ricky vanishes, Paco and Lisa walk the streets of the neighborhood and distribute posters that read: "Have you seen Ricky Sanchez? Blond, blue eyes, missing since December 23. Distinguishing mark: two wings on his back." By self-consciously recognizing the asininity of its topic, *Ricky* potentially saves itself from being deemed asinine.

Ozon's strategy paid off, and several French reviewers have praised the film for its daring qualities while simultaneously pointing out the director's sense of humor (see, for example, Lorrain; Le Floch; Douin, "*Ricky*"; for a negative review, see Icher). One of them jestingly judges *Ricky* to be a destabilizing, haunting "UFF (Unidentified Flying Film)" (Delcroix 31). However, *Ricky* proved too venturesome an enterprise for Ozon's longtime partners from Fidélité Productions (now called Fidélité Films), Marc Missonnier and Olivier Delbosc. Despite having financed every project by Ozon, whether short or full-length, since he graduated from the Fémis school in 1994, Fidélité refused to support *Ricky.* They were unconvinced by the story, skeptical about its suburban setting, and apparently hostile to Ozon's choice for the lead actress, Alexandra Lamy (Sotinel; Douin). This hostility stemmed from the fact that Lamy is a "TV actress" who is especially well-known for her comedic part as Chouchou in the French series *Un gars, une fille* (A Boy, a Girl). According to a film critic in *Le Monde*, who angrily calls Fidélité's rejection "shameful," the producers doubted Lamy's ability to play someone other than the character that made her famous. Ozon nonetheless managed to convince Claudie Ossard, the producer of Jean-Pierre Jeunet's record-breaking hit *Le fabuleux destin d'Amélie Poulain* (*Amélie*, 2001), to co-produce *Ricky.* After auditioning a few actresses, Ozon knew Lamy was right for the part. But given Fidélité's frigid reaction, which ended his fourteen-year partnership with them, Ozon did not dare suggest Lamy to Ossard. He instead showed Ossard all the screen tests he had done with various actresses, asking for the producer's opinion but hiding his preference. "The best one by far is that TV actress, Alexandra Lamy," Ossard responded unhesitatingly (Sotinel).

Lamy does deliver an impressive performance in *Ricky.* The authenticity with which she incarnates the "mother of a flying baby" convinces, indeed making her look like *any* mother. On a sunny day near the end, Ricky reappears to Katie with his wings fully grown and saves her from suicide. This moment somehow manages to be touching without being mawkish. As one critic points out, the film seduces because it describes "universal anguishes, those that turn maternal instinct into blind love, into an overly protective, if not castrating, reflex" (Douin). Of course, the main victim of Katie's postpartum castrating tendencies is Paco. The film intimates at various points that Paco's presence after the baby's birth is, if not superfluous, something of an inconvenience. Once home from the hospital, Paco picks up his screaming son, but Katie requests that the father "leave him alone, and instead cut the chicken." Paco later leaves Katie because of her false accusations, and as Lisa brings up the man's name, Katie retorts: "I've completely stopped thinking about him [Paco] since the arrival of Ricky's wings."

The character of Paco is particularly fascinating, especially when compared to other father figures in Ozon's filmography. Paco in *Ricky* is much more complex than Chester in "Moth." Chester is crass, unloving, and money-hungry. Paco, in contrast, is caring and sincere. Katie suspects that Paco is a monster when she implies that he has hit their child, anticipating the monstrosity of Ricky's appendages in the eyes of strangers. But we quickly learn that the accusations are unfounded and that Paco, who visits Lisa outside of school, wishes to stay in their lives. When he later suggests negotiating with the media and agrees to temporarily exhibit his son's unique attributes, it is with the sole purpose of improving the financial situation of the entire family. At the same time, Paco *is* depicted as an outsider throughout the narrative. In the first sequence, Katie mentions to the social worker that Paco is "a Spaniard," who "may have returned to his home country" after the couple's separation (Lisa does not tell Katie that she has seen Paco since he moved out). When Paco kindly offers his help with Lisa's homework after Ricky's birth, the young girl reluctantly agrees but points out the fact that Paco "won't understand it," as he doesn't "speak French very well." In the television news report covering the extraordinary story of the flying baby, we hear a neighbor describe Paco as "a foreign guy" who no longer lives with the family. Paco's difference is underscored in other ways. As they lie in bed together, Paco mentions to Katie that he finds himself to be too hairy and wishes he had a smooth chest. The woman replies that she enjoys his pilosity, finding it "animal-like."

Comparison with *Western* (Manuel Poirier, 1997), another film starring Barcelona-born actor Sergi López, is useful here. In this French-language road movie, López's character (also named Paco) roams around the back roads of Brittany after his car is stolen by a Russian-born hitchhiker. The film, like *Ricky*, plays with López's otherness, highlighting both the character's own conflicting identity as a Spaniard born in Catalonia—a Spanish region with strong desires for independence—and the narrow-mindedness, if not xenophobia, of people he meets on his journey through the French countryside. When Katie asks Paco about his past, he responds that he used to be "married in Spain, when [he] was young," possibly eliciting a continuity between *Western*'s Paco (also a divorcé) and *Ricky*'s Paco. In *Ricky* the perpetual iteration of Paco's outsider status matches that of Ricky himself, whom the doctors as well as the press view as an anomaly.

When I asked François Ozon about the supernatural elements in

Ricky, he responded that he did not approach the film as one belonging to the fantasy genre. Ozon indicated that the special effects were handled in a pragmatic manner and that he insisted on exhibiting in long-duration, uninterrupted shots the anatomy of Ricky's wings. For the director, this cinematically created anatomy had to appear realistic, not whimsical. *Ricky* thus repeatedly, almost "scientifically" exposes the unembellished attributes of the baby's feathered appendices. As a result, *Ricky* displays the risk of appalling spectators unaccustomed to such direct methods. This frankness, nevertheless, enables the film to unearth its more captivating attributes. By staging a conflicted dialogue between the protective mother and the invasive outside world represented by the authoritative figure of the doctor, *Ricky* sharply critiques the rejection by society of anything or anyone it considers anatomically (and by extension, psychologically) abnormal. When he first meets Katie, the doctor mentions "veterinarian" friends of his who are eager to examine the baby and later proposes to remove the wings the same way one would approach the surgical separation of conjoined twins. Although not explicitly mentioned in the film, this obsession with normalcy, with repairing what does not "look right," also recalls the gender reassignment surgeries performed on babies exhibiting signs of "ambiguous genitalia" (Rossiter and Diehl).

While the camera in *Ricky* remains dangerously close to the baby's wings, the concluding sequences distance themselves from the rest of the film's painstakingly fabricated fiction. We know that equivocal endings are one of Ozon's trademarks. With *Ricky,* the filmmaker does not disappoint. To put it plainly, *Ricky* has three endings. Rather, it closes with three successive sequences that *could* function as conclusions. The first one is Katie's interrupted suicide, which references Pete's successful suicide in "Moth." The scene takes place in the early hours of a bright Sunday morning. Ricky has disappeared a few days earlier, and Paco tries to convince the grieving Katie that their son has probably died. But as Katie hears seagulls outside her window, she resolves to walk to the lake in her white sleeping gown. The lake and surrounding trees take on a new complexion in the shining sun. At once beautiful and strangely melancholy, the sight of Katie immersed in nature (no buildings appear in the shot) recalls Alphonse de Lamartine's depiction of an alpine lake in his famous autobiographical poem, "Le Lac." The film aestheticizes

Katie's grief, as we now see her walking slowly toward the deepest part of the lake, an image this time reminiscent of Nicole Kidman/Virginia Woolf's suicide in Stephen Daldry's *The Hours* (2002). The landing of Ricky on the lakeshore halts Katie's descent, and she jumps out of the water to marvel at her baby's magnificent wings (fig. 26). After a monologue in which she shares her maternal pride and love with the toddler, Ricky disappears into the open skies.

If the film's sole intentions were to close on a more auspicious note than Tremain's short story, *Ricky* could easily end here. It does not, however, and instead offers two additional sequences. In the first one, Katie returns home in her wet sleeping gown and declares her love to Lisa and Paco as she embraces them (fig. 27). Again, the finality of the image has the potential to satisfy spectators and give them appropriate closure. But the film seems dissatisfied with this traditional representation of a happy ending and continues its journey. The following segment initially appears more mundane. We see Lisa and Paco on Katie's scooter outside the building and what appears to be a countershot of Katie gazing at them from the window above. She is framed from the chest up, and we realize that she is pregnant only after she lies down on the couch, smiles, and dozes off. We then cut to a close-up of Lisa, smiling with her eyes closed as she tightly holds on to Paco.

Figure 26. Ricky and Katie in *Ricky*. |

Figure 27. Katie, Lisa, and Paco in *Ricky*. |

It is unclear at what point in the narrative the latter developments occur. Like the flash-forward sequence at the social worker's office, this segment is isolated from the rest of the story. The indoor scene in the apartment advances the possibility of a third pregnancy for Katie. However, in light of the last two shots framing both Katie and Lisa in a "dozing" state, this conclusion also questions the reality of Ricky's existence by suggesting that the mother or the daughter could have imagined everything. Echoing in its function the film's humorous moments, these distancing effects separate the story of the flying baby from the social reality of the characters. But it does something else. By making us doubt the veracity of the story, this conclusion exacerbates the film's fantastic attributes.

In 1970 the philosopher Tzvetan Todorov defined the fantastic genre in literature as distinct from both supernatural fiction and fairy tales:

> The fantastic requires the fulfillment of three conditions. First, the text must oblige the reader to consider the world of the characters as a world of living persons and to hesitate between a natural or supernatural explanation of the events described. Second, this hesitation may also be experienced by a character; thus the reader's role is so to speak entrusted to a character, and at the same time the hesitation is represented, it becomes one of the themes of the work . . . Third, the reader must adopt a certain attitude with regard to the text: he will reject allegorical as well as "poetic" interpretations. (33)

By anchoring the story in the actuality of a working-class suburb, the film unambiguously places its characters in "a world of living persons" that is disrupted by the intrusion of a supernatural element (the winged infant). Nevertheless, until the two closing shots, *Ricky* does not quite correspond to Todorov's definition of the fantastic. As we have seen, all events, including those involving Ricky and his development, are presented in a straightforward mise-en-scène, which renders difficult any "hesitation" on the part of the spectator. But as Katie's and Lisa's eyes slowly close, all previous occurrences become uncertain. "Things will go back to normal," Katie once reassures Paco after an argument. "I hope so," Paco replies. Katie's words should appease those of us who choose not to believe in, or be touched by, what the narrator in "Moth" describes as the "true story" of the flying baby.

For the purposes of this study, *Ricky* provides a fitting conclusion. We already know that in comparison to other films by Ozon, *Ricky* is somewhat of a deviation, one that abruptly ended his long-term relationship with his producers. Upon closer look, however, we find that *Ricky* may initially look unfamiliar because it innovatively marries two heretofore distinct aesthetic aspects of the director's work. The dramatic recording of the baby's wings, the staging of his flights as fascinating spectacles to behold (for both characters and spectators) reproduces Ozon's theatrical trend most manifest in such "performance films" as *Gouttes d'eau* and *8 femmes*. We also recognize in the film the combination of raw reality and artifice that *Les amants criminels* separated into two realms (the city and the forest). At the same time, the naturalistic trend of his more solemn works (*Regarde la mer, Sous le sable, Le temps qui reste,* and, to an extent, *Swimming Pool*) emerges in the forthright and compassionate depiction of Katie and Paco's social struggles.

Beyond the film's aesthetics, most of Ozon's thematic preoccupations permeate *Ricky*'s narrative. As one commentator concludes, *Ricky* "touches upon most of François Ozon's obsessions: the relationship between mother and child (*Regarde la mer*), the disintegrating family (*Sitcom*), the refusal to accept an inevitable separation (*Sous le sable*), the minutely examined couple (*5x2*), the decision to follow a fanciful destiny (*Angel*)" (Douin). To those obsessions, we may add the ambivalent position of the father within the nuclear family, a theme previously explored most notably in *Sitcom* and *8 femmes*.

Comparing Ozon's latest, *Ricky*, with *Sitcom*, his feature début, is a particularly fascinating exercise. Released eleven years apart from each other, the two films essentially recount the same story: a foreign element (a rat, a flying baby) appears suddenly, disrupting the quietude of a family and revealing its "true nature." Katie hints at a connection between the two films when she warns the doctor that she will not let anyone turn her baby into a "laboratory rat," referencing *Sitcom*'s principal intruder. *Ricky* includes fewer main characters than Ozon's first film, and its primary focus is on the two parents. Their reactions to the intrusion of the magic baby are recorded and contrasted with those of the outside world. It would be slightly inaccurate to qualify Katie as "un-motherly" before Ricky's birth. Yet the scene in which seven-year-old Lisa "takes care" of her mother in the same way that Katie "should" take care of her daughter, or so the narrative implies, reveals certain shortcomings in her maternal role. Ricky's arrival initially transforms Katie into an overprotective mother. She eventually learns, however, to control her maternal instincts, as the ending reveals. First, she "lets go" of her son, knowing that he belongs in the sky. As the shot of the embracing trio near the film's close intimates, Katie also manages to find a satisfactory balance between her relationship with Paco and her maternal rapport with her daughter. Paco, too, undergoes a transformation. When we first meet Ricky's future father, Katie asks if he has any children. His offhand answer, "None that I know of," which he accompanies with a giggle, demonstrates that his preoccupations lie elsewhere. In the course of the film, Paco's paternal love toward both Ricky and Lisa becomes evident, despite Katie's rejections and accusations.

There is a crucial difference between Ricky's parents and *Sitcom*'s Hélène and Jean. The distinction lies in their opposed reaction to otherness. When Nicolas reveals his homosexuality to his family at the beginning of *Sitcom*, Jean shrugs off the statement, discusses the pederasty of the Greeks, and moves on with his life. The revelation, however, devastates Nicolas's mother. Despite encouraging statements of other family members aimed at deflating the stigmas of same-sexuality, Hélène remains inconsolable. As far as she is concerned, her son, Nicolas, is positioned so far outside the norm that he might as well have wings on his back. Although Hélène eventually comes around, thanks in part to the supernatural powers of the rat, the father never really does. He is mildly accepting, but ultimately indifferent. Conversely, both Katie's and Paco's response to their son's difference is characterized by quasi-immediate, unconditional acceptance. In sharp contrast to the inadequate Chester in "Moth," who fathered both Lisa and Ricky but takes care of neither, Paco's paternal instincts come through in his relationship with both Ricky and his stepdaughter. The last scene of *Ricky,* in which Lisa smiles with contentment as she embraces him, establishes Paco as a competent parent. Paco's new role mirrors that of Annie at the conclusion of "Moth," as he, like the woman, becomes a caring surrogate parent for Lisa.

These changes signal a drastic evolution in the ways Ozon's cinema portrays fatherhood. Unlike other paternal figures, who are all monstrous in one way or another, Paco is initially *believed* to be something of a monster (his excessive hairiness, the allegations of child abuse) but turns out quite differently. With *Ricky,* the prevailing unfeasibility of everlasting love present in Ozon's other films (notably, *Gouttes d'eau* and *5x2*) and the impossibility of building a family that includes the father (*Sitcom*) are overcome, giving way to a much more sanguine, if traditional, scenario. Thus, despite the fact that *Ricky* hesitates to roll the credits after the "picture perfect," cinegenic image of happiness rendered by the emotive reunion of the mother, father, and child, the final shot on Lisa's face is, although subtler, just as uplifting. Earlier in the film, Paco fears that Katie will never forgive him for organizing the press conference that leads to their son's disappearance and possible death and voices his concerns to the doctor. "She will be mad at me for the rest of her life," Paco laments. The doctor's simple answer may well be the film's principal message: "Not if the two of you stay together." Indeed, this doctor's order suggests a new direction in the cinema of François Ozon.

An Interview with François Ozon |

Paris, October 6, 2009

THIBAUT SCHILT: Is your latest film, *Le refuge* [*Hideaway,* 2009], the third part of a "trilogy on mourning" of which *Sous le sable* and *Le temps qui reste* are the first two installments?

FRANÇOIS OZON: I hadn't thought of that, but it is true that this is yet another story about mourning, though a bit special because it is the story of a young woman who is a drug addict, along with her boyfriend. One day they both overdose, and when she wakes up she learns that her boyfriend is dead and that she is pregnant with his child. She will keep the child as a way of mourning for her loved one, but without necessarily developing a maternal instinct. It's more of a palliative response to death and mourning than a desire to give life.

TS: So in making this film you didn't have *Sous le sable* and *Le temps qui reste* in mind?

FO: Not at all, but inevitably there are certain themes that come back on their own. But *Le refuge* is quite an unusual film that I made very instinctively. Three weeks before shooting I didn't really have a scenario. I didn't have an actress to play the lead role either. First I offered the role to Ludivine Sagnier, who had called me to announce that she was pregnant. I told her that I'd always wanted to make a film with a pregnant woman, but she said she didn't feel up to the task. Then my casting director told me that there were three pregnant actresses in Paris, including Isabelle Carré. I'd never worked with her, but I called to ask if she would accept the role, indicating that I had an idea of the story but strictly speaking no script. She said yes and we went from there. So there really wasn't time to say to myself, "I've already told several similar stories before this film." We shot the film very quickly—we had to—because she was about to give birth.

TS: To return to mourning, the theme is present in *Le temps qui reste, Sous le sable,* and *Le refuge,* but we can trace it back even further in your career. I am thinking most notably of *La petite mort* or even, in a more playful way, of *Victor.* I showed *Le temps qui reste* in a university course two weeks ago, and a student asked me, "Why is there this recurrence of mourning and death in Ozon's films?" She mainly wanted to know if this comes from a specific event in your life or in the life of people close to you. I know that in the case of *Sous le sable* you have mentioned that you saw a Dutch couple . . .

FO: Yes, *Sous le sable* actually came out of an event that I witnessed as a child; I was on the beach with my parents . . .

TS: . . . and this event left a mark on you?

FO: Yes, we had been seeing these people on a daily basis when all of a sudden the husband went swimming and didn't come back. And the wife just left with their things; any witness to this incident would have been shocked. It's true that this is something that would have left its mark; I've always wondered what that woman ended up doing (the couple was Dutch, on a beach in the Landes region). What will she do the next day? Will she find the body? A child's imagination can run wild. It was a story that was inside of me. This film was commissioned for a series from the producer Chantal Poupaud, who did "Tous les garçons et les filles de leur âge" [All Boys and Girls of Their Age] for the television channel Arte. After that she conceived a new series called "Toutes les femmes sont folles" [All Women Are Crazy]. The objective was to portray women, and the only requirement for the project was that the films include a scene with the woman facing a doctor. I spoke with her about *Sous le sable*, where there was a short scene with a doctor, though it wasn't a central part of the film.

TS: So this particular story of mourning comes from this Dutch couple. What about the other films?

FO: The other films come from personal experiences, life stories. I am also interested in exploring the particular path, seemingly crazy and twisted, that people take to deal with their reality, to deal with difficulty, with the loss of someone or the end of a relationship, or other such things. It's the idea of mourning in a general sense, not strictly death. *5x2*, after all, was also about mourning the breakup of a couple.

TS: Yes, I agree, and for me *Swimming Pool* is also a film about mourning. In it Rampling/Sarah Morton mourns the end of her personal and professional relationships with her editor; she mourns the end of her career as a successful novelist, as well as the fact that she never had any children. That's how I see it, at least.

FO: Yes, in my films there is always the idea that these are characters who are in the process of evolving, who will undergo some kind of transformation in the course of the film. They are often in a situation in which they aren't happy, or are unstable or still coming out of their shell, and by the end they find their way. The road they take is often winding, bizarre, quirky, but in the end they manage to find their place, their identity, and to discover who they are.

TS: In addition to mourning, parent-child relations (father-son, brother-sister, mother-daughter) are often addressed in your oeuvre. During the press conference for the San Sebastian film festival, where you presented *Le refuge* and where you were awarded a prize, a journalist brought up the connection between your previous film *Ricky* and *Le refuge,* notably because of the physical or expected presence of the baby. This presence is nothing new for you, and we can trace it back to *Regarde la mer.* How do these films differ in the way they address maternity?

FO: I would say that a film like *Regarde la mer* is extremely violent and sadistic; I was just starting my career as a filmmaker and was full of aggressiveness. I wanted to do a portrayal of two women who for me were in fact just one woman. On one hand there was the monstrous side, the ogress side, and on the other a side that is much softer, more maternal, a side we are used to seeing. And these two seemingly contradictory aspects are present in the two women in that story. A film like *Ricky* also talks, perhaps in a gentler fashion, about the relationship to a child, but also of the tendency that a mother can have to merge with her child; this type of bond doesn't leave space for the man, for the husband, for the father, and creates jealousy from her other child. All things considered, *Ricky* is more realistic in its description of maternity than *Regarde la mer,* which is realistic and extreme but is more concerned with crime and the *fait divers. Le refuge* doesn't speak about the relationship with the child, because we virtually don't see the child. What interested me was the pregnancy, the gestation period. So does the baby already exist when it's in the womb? This is a debate you have in the United States. What is interesting is that Isabelle Carré's character in this film considers that the child doesn't exist. She has something in her stomach, but it is more of an extension of the man she loved than a full-fledged person.

TS: Nevertheless there is this intense scene on the beach, the only scene I've seen from the film, where a middle-aged woman is trying to convince the young, pregnant woman of the importance of motherhood.

FO: Absolutely. I've often noticed that people want to touch pregnant women, they want to talk to them. There is some kind of fascination with pregnancy. In this scene I wanted to have this woman who comes in like a fury [the beach woman is played by Marie Rivière, facing Isabelle Carré, who plays the part of Mousse, the pregnant woman], who seems very kind at first but ends up giving her advice, telling her that she must suffer, that she must speak to the child. And Carré's character sends her away because the conversation brings her back to the situation of her pregnancy, which she essentially denies is happening to her. But this encounter allows the expectant mother to confide in someone and to understand her situation. Nevertheless she experiences the conversation with this woman as an act of aggression. The woman represents the outside world, which internalized a ready-made, standardized discourse on motherhood, a discourse into which Mousse doesn't see herself fitting at all.

TS: So you were speaking paradoxically of *Ricky* as a realistic film. Your creations have often flirted with the fantastic (the transformation of the father into a rat in *Sitcom,* the spectral presence of Jean in *Sous le sable,* the real or imagined happenings in *Swimming Pool,* et cetera) and with fairy tales (*Les amants criminels*), but *Ricky,* which is inspired by the English short story by Rose Tremain titled "Moth," seems to dive deeper into the supernatural than the others. Do you consider *Ricky* to belong to the fantasy genre?

FO: No, not at all. I didn't approach the film as such. For example, the special effects are handled in an extremely realistic manner, which posed a problem for the special effects crew, who are used to making action films, American films with a tremendous amount of shots and where everything is highly edited and therefore the spectator has the idea of special effects without truly having the time to see them. And I told them that I wanted the shots to last a minute so that the special effects were visible and the spectator would have time to see whether it was well done or not. As a result, the process became quite worrisome for the technicians. So that is how I tried to introduce special effects into a realistic context. And for me the baby [who starts to fly] had to be real; I intended to show its development in concrete terms. How do you dress a baby with wings? If he wants to fly, do you give him a helmet? It was very important for me to anchor these supernatural elements in reality.

TS: A journalist from *Libération* thinks that *Ricky* is part of a new hybrid genre, which he calls the "fantastico-social." But if for you *Ricky* is anchored in social reality, are the baby's wings merely a pretext to address difference, otherness?

FO: Yes, at the end of the day it isn't the flying baby that interests me. But spectators can interpret the film as they wish. According to your background, if you received a religious education, if you are a Marxist, you can find in it whatever you wish to find; I like the idea that the film doesn't only make sense in one way. It is possibly for this reason that people were highly critical of *Ricky*. Some spectators are out of the habit of thinking, and for them this film was too opaque, or on the contrary it had too many meanings. As a result they didn't know what I was trying to say. Perhaps I went a little too far in this film . . .

TS: There is also the second-to-last shot of the film, which suggests that the entire story might have been imagined either by the mother or by the young girl . . . But beyond the question of genre, your films are cinephilic, which is to say that they cite, pay tribute, and refer to a multitude of works from the history of cinema. What role does your knowledge of the history and conventions of cinema play in the creation of your projects?

FO: It is not possible for me to make a clean sweep of the films I've seen. I don't act as if cinema didn't exist before me. Inevitably, therefore, I am a cinephilic director. I've seen many films at a certain period of my life, though I have less time to see them these days; I am too busy. This cinema nourished me as much as life and experience did. At certain points I am faced with problems of mise-en-scène when I need to shoot a scene that I have written. Suddenly seeing a scene from Bergman, a film from Buñuel might help me out of certain tough spots. While in life I'm not prone to worship or admire people, in cinema I do feel like I have many artistic fathers. Thanks to cinema I found a sense of connection, of belonging to a lineage. I was fostered by these films.

TS: But it goes further than that. For example, you specifically ask your actors to watch certain films before shooting.

FO: Yes, I also see it as a cinephilic game. There is a ludic element. When I made *8 femmes* there were numerous references to American cinema, but the film was made with French actresses. The film also referenced French cinema. When you're young, you dress up and play Superman. I do the same in my work.

TS: But there is the idea of lineage, of placing oneself into the history of cinema.

FO: Yes, absolutely, but that comes quite naturally; it is neither planned nor theorized. I do it simply for pleasure. I also include the spectator in the film. What was amusing about *8 femmes* is that the film was interpreted very differently in France, the United States, and Italy. All of the viewers were not familiar with the filmographies of the actresses and didn't necessarily understand all of the references. But since it is a whodunit, one can take the film at face value as well. Incidentally, children also really liked the film, but that was not because Catherine Deneuve, who did *Peau d'âne* and [Luis Buñuel's] *Belle de jour* [1967], is in it. The film works on several levels.

TS: I read in an interview you gave that the process of writing is what you like the least in cinematic creation and that you prefer editing, a stage full of possibilities. Could you talk about your recurring collaboration in the writing of certain scripts with Marcia Romano and Marina de Van at the beginning of your career, followed later by Emmanuèle Bernheim? How exactly did that work, and what did these collaborations bring to the table?

FO: In general I come up with the initial idea and develop the project, and I often call someone in when I am stuck. My collaborations are more about script doctoring than about cowriting. Most often I have a story, a first script, a first draft, and I'm in need of a hand. These people help me focus better on what I want to do, which allows me to speed up the writing process, which can last a year, two years, or sometimes as little as a month, depending on the project.

TS: And that can also be done as you go along, as with *Sous le sable*, for example.

FO: Absolutely. So with *Sous le sable* I needed a female point of view. I was stuck on certain scenes and needed some help. For *8 femmes* I asked Marina de Van to write certain scenes, she made suggestions, and I rewrote according to her advice. Emmanuèle Bernheim helped me with the second part of *Sous le sable*. I had already written the first part and didn't really know which direction I was going in. Emmanuèle watched the first twenty minutes of the film. I had an initial script that was more like a crime investigation; Charlotte Rampling's character was trying to find out what happened to her husband. And Emmanuèle and I came to the realization that this wasn't what interested me. The important thing wasn't to discover something about the husband but rather to find out how this woman would live after this disappearance. So my collaborators are assistants who help me to advance further in my screenwriting project. However, sometimes I write alone as well, so it really depends on the project.

TS: *Le refuge* was your first time working with Mathieu Hippeau as cowriter and also the first time you've worked with a man in that capacity.

FO: Ah, yes, I hadn't thought of that, but it's true.

TS: How did it work with him?

FO: Mathieu Hippeau is a friend; I'd read screenplays he'd written. He had already worked a bit on *Angel*, cutting [Elizabeth Taylor's] novel into scenes. He was also quite familiar with the theme of maternity, and when I found out that Isabelle was ready to make the film, I said to myself, "I don't have a script yet; I must write it quickly." I asked Mathieu to write a number of scenes, especially certain ones that did not inspire me. For the filming, he was in Paris and I was in the provinces. I sent him some sequences and asked him to write the dialogues. So it was a little bit of a "work in progress." If I'd had more time before the shooting, I may not have worked with him, but he helped me a lot on that project.

TS: Beyond scriptwriting, you are very faithful to those you work with, and you have collaborated with the same artists for years: Sébastien Charles for choreography, Pascaline Chavanne for costumes, Philippe Rombi for the sound tracks, and of course actors (Poupaud) and especially actresses (Sagnier, Rampling, Bruni-Tedeschi, Marie Rivière, et cetera). I imagine that these close relationships allow you to save a considerable amount of time (you have directed eleven feature films in eleven years, an impressive number). What else do these relationships mean to you?

FO: For me it means that we still have things to do together. Indeed, there is the element of time savings; we know each other well. It isn't about fidelity for the sake of fidelity, since there are certain people I have not worked with again. I think that those with whom I've worked recurrently are those who are most qualified to accomplish what I want to accomplish. Also it's not necessarily a question of friendship as often it is simply a professional relationship. I don't feel indebted to them, but rather I think that in working with them I do what is best for the film.

TS: You recently told a journalist that you don't regret any of the films you've made in your career.

FO: That's true, because the failures and the setbacks have made me stronger. There are films that I have no desire to watch again, scenes that I find to have missed their mark, but I'm sure that some failures have allowed me to succeed elsewhere.

TS: Yes, that was what I was going to ask you. Like [Jean-Luc] Godard, you have spoken of your film projects as "attempts" [tentatives]. Are there any particular films that have allowed you to grow artistically or that have helped you advance more than others?

FO: Not really. As you know, cinema is a collective process. It is about more than just me. Other people can play key roles in these situations as well. Above all I think that actors and the way they inhabit a character can take the film in a different direction. I am not one to storyboard everything. I had to do it for *Ricky* because of the special effects, but I don't usually do it. What I expect is for an accidental event to transpire, something that makes things come to life differently than I had foreseen. I don't really imagine in advance how my films will be; I have ideas, intuitions, and if during the shooting we go in a different direction, it's often for the better.

TS: But wasn't there a point in your career where something clicked and you said to yourself, "That's it. I'm getting better at this"?

FO: No, there are things that I did well at the very beginning of my career and others that were unsuccessful recently. It all depends on the particular case. A film is truly something organic and fragile. There is a large element of chance. Certain films find an audience and a positive critical reception. If the recipe for success for masterpieces was known, everyone would follow it. But there is no such recipe. And the life of a film is long. A film that initially doesn't find an audience can find one three years later. And sometimes it is enough for someone you love to like a film, even if everyone else hated it.

TS: I have watched all of your films (short and long) that I could get my hands on for this book. However, some are impossible to find, particularly *Jospin s'éclaire,* which I believe is the only documentary of your career.

FO: In my opinion this film was not really a documentary but rather a reportage. It started from an idea by Mathieu Vadepied, a friend of mine who was head cameraman on some of my shorts and whose father was close with Lionel Jospin. At the period where Jospin was in the second round of the presidential elections, my friend suggested that we make a film on him. We started out from there. We knew nothing of the world of politics nor about the Socialist Party, and we were not really able to make the film we wanted to make. We did what we could, but it's not really a film that I'm particularly happy with. There was also the fact that Serge Moati was making an official film for the Socialist Party. Unlike him, we didn't have access to certain places. We would have liked to film Jospin when he was awaiting the results, his private side, but we couldn't. So we filmed some minor moments then tried to put something together. The result was a sort of reportage on the two rounds of the elections. We were able to capture some things, but the final result didn't correspond to our initial goal.

TS: Why the title *Jospin s'éclaire?*

FO: Because of his campaign slogan, Jospin, *c'est clair* [Jospin, It's Clear], as opposed to Jacques Chirac, who wasn't clear. So we did a play on words with the verb *s'éclairer* [to light up].

TS: And the 1991 films from Fémis, which were not in the DVD collection that came out in 2001? *Une goutte de sang, Peau contre peau, Le trou madame, Deux plus un.* Could you talk about them briefly?

FO: These films were school exercises. *Une goutte de sang* [A Drop of Blood] and *Peau contre peau* [Skin against Skin] were part of the same film, half documentary and half fiction. It was in the middle of the AIDS era, and it deals with a young man who goes to get tested for HIV. I filmed the day of his test, the documentary side, as well as the day he received his results. The title comes from the fact that in the interview for the film he recounts that he refuses to have sex with a condom, that he prefers "skin against skin," a strange point of view. After the documentary *Peau contre peau,* I fictionalized the same story with the young man's twin brother. The beginning is identical. In the fictional version he learns that he is HIV positive, and he puts a drop of blood in his twin brother's glass to infect him. Obviously, AIDS isn't contracted like that, but my idea came from reading Hervé Guibert, who talked about doing that in his book *A l'ami qui ne m'a pas sauvé la vie* [1990, in which Guibert reveals that he is HIV positive a short time before his death in 1991].

TS: And *Le trou madame?* [Madame's Hole]

FO: It was a sort of fictional documentary on the representation of female genitalia in art. Not a very interesting film, in my opinion . . .

TS: And *Thomas reconstitué?* [Thomas Reconstituted]

FO: This film is more interesting. It was originally conceived as a documentary, but I turned it into a fictional film. I was supposed to tell the story of a twenty-year-old man who was suffering from AIDS, but he dropped out at the last minute, refusing to do the film, in which I was supposed to film his friends, parents, et cetera. As an alternative, I created a fictional film based on his story. I had actors play the role of his family.

TS: Since the beginning of your career there has been an ongoing attraction to the "foreign," first of all through actresses (Lucia Sanchez, Sasha Hails, Rampling, Bruni-Tedeschi), but also through places (Germany, Sardinia, England, and the sea/the ocean, which can be seen as a metaphor for an "elsewhere") and also the authors and directors who inspire you (Fassbinder for *Gouttes d'eau,* Bergman for *5x2,* Elizabeth Taylor for *Angel,* Rose Tremain for *Ricky*—Montherlant for *Un lever de rideau* being an exception). How do you explain this tendency? Are you escaping from a French cinema that you perhaps find too limiting? Is it a fascination with the "other"?

FO: I don't really analyze it; I think it is just part of me, part of my tastes. There is the idea of adventure in cinema, an idea of discovery, and it's true that I wish to get away from my French quotidian. There is some kind of excitement in seeking out, in discovering, the other. Yes, it is a way to escape what I am already familiar with.

TS: In an interview you gave to the magazine *Positif* in 2004, for a special issue on sex and eroticism in cinema, you said that women and gay directors have contributed a great deal to the representation of desire on screen—female directors by portraying feminine desire in a more complex manner, gay directors by returning to an eroticization of the male body. This remark struck me greatly because in France female and gay directors generally reject such categories (of gender and of sexual preference) within the context of their work, because they find them reductive. Do you agree with this idea?

FO: Well, I feel that in the United States you are defined first as either gay or straight, then secondly as a film director. In France and in Europe in general, one is first of all defined as a director, and our sexuality is considered a secondary factor. Sexuality is not necessarily secondary, but that is how it generally tends to be seen.

TS: Do you think we can say that there is a link between someone's identity and the films that he or she directs?

FO: One should not make generalizations. I am simply noting that female directors, for example, show actors' bodies. And in France speech is very important to cinema, perhaps more important than the body. French (male) actors are not usually eroticized. Our actors are Depardieu, who has a distinctive face [*une gueule*], or Fernandel, or Bourvil. In the United States actors like Tom Cruise, Brad Pitt, James Dean, and Rock Hudson are eroticized. So there is a significant difference between the two cinematographic cultures. Indeed, women like Denis and Breillat are directors who work with sensation, who have a tendency to eroticize men, as do a string of gay directors of my own generation and of the previous generation, like Chéreau and Téchiné. It's just an observation; I don't think we can generalize. But if we take directors like Claude Sautet, Claude Zidi, or Godard, it cannot be said that they eroticized the male body. Then again, Godard did with Belmondo in *A bout de souffle* [*Breathless*, 1960].

TS: Do you personally have the impression that you present an image of sexuality and of relationships within couples, male/female, male/male, or female/female, that is more complex than that shown in other contemporary films, aside from those directed by the filmmakers you just mentioned?

FO: I don't ask myself these kinds of questions. I try to speak about the difficulty of being in a couple . . .

TS: I ask because there was a very good article by Emma Wilson on *Le temps qui reste* in *Film Quarterly*, in which the author writes that the representation of desire, and, above all, of human behavior, in your work is profoundly surprising and borders on the experimental. That is to say that the behavior of your characters is completely unpredictable. Wilson was referencing in particular the ménage-à-trois scene in *Le temps qui reste.*

FO: It's true that what interests me in cinema is to show behaviors that could seem deviant but for me aren't so; they are simply roads that swerve away from the norm, from what we may call the classic heterosexual couple. I don't know if you could call it "activism," but I try to show characters who display what could be judged strange behavior and to understand them. So as the film progresses one can understand why this young man [Poupaud/Romain] suddenly sleeps with a woman and a man. Within the framework of the story this behavior becomes comprehensible. And a heterosexual spectator, a bit on the conservative side, may perhaps, if he really gets into the film, come to understand this type of behavior. For example, I really like a film by Buñuel called *El* [1953]. It is the story of a man who is completely obsessional, possessive, and jealous; he constantly believes his wife is cheating on him. It was made during Buñuel's Mexican period, and like all his films it is very ironic. We follow this character who is behaving sadistically. What is fascinating is how we see ourselves in the story and then laugh at what we see. The man is jealous to the point of wanting to sew shut his wife's genitals, to the point of putting needles in keyholes to poke out the eyes of anyone who might look through them. It becomes a sort of madness; what is absolutely fantastic about Buñuel is that the films are very funny, and at the same time we see ourselves reflected in them. I like the idea that with cinema, people who are a priori against such and such a thing can recognize themselves in a behavior that they otherwise could or should condemn.

TS: Do you set out to change mentalities?

FO: No, I don't think that cinema is capable of changing mentalities, but it can help us share unexpected moments. For the length of a film we can live a human experience that we perhaps haven't had the opportunity to live in real life, and to understand something that we wouldn't necessarily accept in daily life. By the way, it is not always simply a matter of words; sometimes it can be an emotional or sensory experience.

TS: So do you always put yourself in the place of the viewer?

FO: Yes, I ask myself what the viewer will feel, whether it is rejection, distaste, pleasure. Sometimes I am mistaken; I think that he will be pleased and this doesn't turn out to be the case. Fortunately there is no such thing as a "typical" spectator. Some of them understand everything that I wanted to say, and in talking to others I may realize that they didn't see the same things at all. And the film gets away from you, so you could say that there are as many different versions of a film as there are spectators.

TS: The reception a film gets can also vary by culture, which is what you were saying earlier about 8 *femmes.*

FO: Absolutely, and knowing that allows me to keep things in perspective.

TS: To conclude, do you have an idea of what your next project will be?

FO: Yes, it's a film called *Potiche.* It is an adaptation of a play by [Pierre] Barillet and [Jean-Pierre] Grédy, the starring role of which was played in France by Jacqueline Maillan. In my film Catherine Deneuve will play this role. I start filming in three weeks. [According to the Internet Movie Database, the project was completed in April 2010 and scheduled for release in France in November 2010.]

TS: And it is a comedy? That is a departure from your latest films, in which your characters have primarily been withdrawn from the world and rather narcissistic. Does *Potiche* mark the end of this period?

FO: It is true that my latest films have been quite dramatic, quite dark. I am returning to comedy with *Potiche.* People who read the script have laughed a lot. I admit that I am happy to head in a lighter direction, even though it will be complicated; the cast is important and it will be a difficult film to direct. But I realize that this type of project is truly what people want. Many of my recent films have been hard to finance. And all of a sudden I do a comedy with a large, all-star cast and it is funded right away. People would like for me to make *8 femmes 2, 8 femmes 3*. At the same time, it is the success of *8 femmes* that allowed me to continue to make films. Likewise I hope that *Potiche* will allow me to do many other things later on.

Feature Films

Sitcom (1998)
France
Production: Fidélité Productions, Studio Canal
Producers: Olivier Delbosc, Marc Missonnier
Distribution: Mars Distribution
Direction: François Ozon
Screenplay: François Ozon
Cinematography: Yorick Le Saux
Editing: Dominique Petrot
Costume Design: Hervé Poeydemenge
Music: Eric Neveux
Cast: Évelyne Dandry (Hélène/mother), François Marthouret (Jean/father),
    Stéphane Rideau (David), Lucia Sanchez (Maria), Adrien de Van (Nicolas),
    Marina de Van (Sophie), Jules-Emmanuel Eyoum Deido (Abdu), Jean
    Douchet (psychotherapist), Sébastien Charles (man with the zucchini),
    Vincent Vizioz (man with red hair), Kiwani Cojo (pierced man), Gilles
    Frilay (man with mustache), Antoine Fischer (little boy)
Color
85 minutes

Les amants criminels (*Criminal Lovers*; 1999)
France
Production: Fidélité Productions, Studio Canal, Arte France Cinema, Euro
    Space
Producers: Olivier Delbosc, Marc Missonnier
Distribution: Mars Distribution
Direction: François Ozon
Screenplay: François Ozon, Marina de Van, Annabelle Perrichon, Marcia
    Romano
Cinematography: Pierre Stoeber

Editing: Claudine Bouché, Dominique Petrot
Costume Design: Pascaline Chavanne
Music: Philippe Rombi
Cast: Natacha Régnier (Alice), Jérémie Renier (Luc), Miki Manojlovic (the hermit), Salim Kechiouche (Saïd), Yasmine Belmadi (Karim), Bernard Maume (teacher), Jean-Louis Debard (security guard), Catherine Vierne (jeweler), Marielle Coubaillon (cashier), Olivier Papot (police officer), Gil de Murger (member of GIGN)
Color
96 minutes

Gouttes d'eau sur pierres brûlantes (*Water Drops on Burning Rocks*; 2000)
France
Production: Fidélité Productions, Les Films Alain Sarde, Euro Space
Producers: Olivier Delbosc, Marc Missonnier, Alain Sarde, Kenzô Horikoshi
Distribution: Haut et Court
Direction: François Ozon
Screenplay: François Ozon, based on the play *Tropfen auf heisse Steine* by Rainer Werner Fassbinder
Cinematography: Jeanne Lapoirie
Editing: Laurence Bawedin, Claudine Bouché
Costume Design: Pascaline Chavanne
Music: Günter Loose
Cast: Bernard Giraudeau (Léopold), Ludivine Sagnier (Anna), Anna Thomson (Véra), Malik Zidi (Franz)
Color
90 minutes

Sous le sable (*Under the Sand*; 2000)
France
Production: Fidélité Productions, Haut et Court, Euro Space, Arte France Cinéma
Producers: Olivier Delbosc, Marc Missonnier
Distribution: Haut et Court
Direction: François Ozon
Screenplay: François Ozon, Emmanuèle Bernheim, Marina de Van, Marcia Romano
Cinematography: Antoine Héberlé, Jeanne Lapoirie
Editing: Laurence Bawedin
Costume Design: Pascaline Chavanne
Music: Philippe Rombi
Cast: Charlotte Rampling (Marie Drillon), Bruno Cremer (Jean Drillon), Jacques Nolot (Vincent), Alexandra Stewart (Amanda), Pierre Vernier

(Gérard), Andrée Tainsy (Suzanne, Jean's mother), Maya Gaugler (German woman), Damien Abbou (chief lifeguard), David Portugais (young lifeguard), Pierre Soubestre (police officer), Agathe Teyssier (in charge of luxury store), Laurence Martin (apartment seller), Jean-François Lapalus (Paris doctor), Laurence Mercier (Paris doctor's secretary), Fabienne Luchetti (pharmacist), Jo Doumerg (taxi driver), Michel Cordes (superintendant), Maurice Antoni (Landes doctor), Patricia Couvillers (Evelyne), Patrick Grieco (José), Axelle Bossard (student), Charlotte Gerbault (nurse), Nicole Lartigue (morgue attendant)
Color
92 minutes

8 femmes (*8 Women*; 2002)
France, Italy
Production: Fidélité Productions, Mars Films, France 2 Cinéma, BIM, Canal Plus, Centre National de la Cinématographie (CNC), Local Films, Gimages 5
Producers: Olivier Delbosc, Marc Missonnier, Stéphane Célérier
Distribution: Mars Distribution
Direction: François Ozon
Screenplay: François Ozon, Marina de Van, based on the play *Huit femmes* by Robert Thomas
Cinematography: Jeanne Lapoirie
Editing: Laurence Bawedin
Costume Design: Pascaline Chavanne
Music: Krishna Levy
Cast: Danielle Darrieux (Mamy), Catherine Deneuve (Gaby), Isabelle Huppert (Augustine), Emmanuelle Béart (Louise), Fanny Ardant (Pierrette), Virginie Ledoyen (Suzon), Ludivine Sagnier (Catherine), Firmine Richard (Madame Chanel), Dominique Lamure (Marcel, the husband)
Color
111 minutes

Swimming Pool (2003)
France, United Kingdom
Production: Fidélité Productions, France 2 Cinéma, Gimages, Foz, Headforce Limited, Canal Plus
Producers: Olivier Delbosc, Marc Missonnier, Christine de Jekel, Timothy Burrill
Distribution: Mars Distribution
Direction: François Ozon
Screenplay: François Ozon, Emmanuèle Bernheim

Cinematography: Yorick Le Saux
Editing: Monica Coleman
Costume Design: Pascaline Chavanne
Music: Philippe Rombi
Cast: Charlotte Rampling (Sarah Morton), Ludivine Sagnier (Julie), Charles
    Dance (John Bosload), Jean-Marie Lamour (Franck), Marc Fayolle
    (Marcel), Mireille Mossé (Marcel's daughter), Michel Fau (first man),
    Jean-Claude Lecas (second man), Emilie Gavois Kahn (waitress at café),
    Erarde Forestali (old man), Lauren Farrow (Julia), Sebastian Harcombe
    (Terry Long), Frances Cuka (woman on the underground), Keith Yeates
    (Sarah's father), Tricia Aileen (John Bosload's secretary), Glen Davies (pub
    bartender)
Color
102 minutes

5x2 (*Five Times Two*; 2004)
France
Production: Fidélité Productions, France 2 Cinéma, Foz, Canal Plus
Producers: Olivier Delbosc, Marc Missonnier, Philippe Dugay
Distribution: Mars Distribution
Direction: François Ozon
Screenplay: François Ozon, Emmanuèle Bernheim
Cinematography: Yorick Le Saux
Editing: Monica Coleman
Costume Design: Pascaline Chavanne
Music: Philippe Rombi
Cast: Valeria Bruni-Tedeschi (Marion), Stéphane Freiss (Gilles), Françoise
    Fabian (Monique), Michael Lonsdale (Bernard), Géraldine Pailhas
    (Valérie), Antoine Chappey (Christophe), Marc Ruchmann (Mathieu),
    Jason Tavassoli (American man), Jean-Pol Brissart (judge), Ninon
    Brétécher (lawyer), Marie-Madeleine Fouquet (Gilles's mother), Pierre
    Chollet (Gilles's father), Carlo-Antonio Angloni (receptionist), Domenico
    Sannino (Italian emcee), Andrea Cesolari (guest officer)
Color
90 minutes

Le temps qui reste (*Time to Leave*; 2005)
France
Production: Fidélité Productions, France 2 Cinéma, Banque Populaire
    Images 5, CanalPlus, Studio Canal, TPS Star
Producers: Olivier Delbosc, Marc Missonnier
Distribution: Mars Distribution
Direction: François Ozon
Screenplay: François Ozon

Cinematography: Jeanne Lapoirie
Editing: Monica Coleman
Costume Design: Pascaline Chavanne
Music: Edouard Dubois, Philippe Escanecrabe, Pascal Vonhatten
Cast: Melvil Poupaud (Romain), Jeanne Moreau (Laura), Valeria Bruni-
 Tedeschi (Jany), Daniel Duval (Romain's father), Marie Rivière (Romain's
 mother), Christian Sengewald (Sasha), Louise-Anne Hippeau (Sophie),
 Walter Pagano (Bruno), Henri de Lorme (doctor), Violetta Sanchez
 (agent), Ugo Soussan Trabelsi (Romain as a child), Alba Gaïa Kraghede
 Bellugi (Sophie as a child), Victor Poulouin (Laurent), Laurence Ragon
 (solicitor), Thomas Gizolme (assistant photographer)
Color
81 minutes

Angel (2007)
France, United Kingdom, Belgium
Production: Fidélité Productions, Poisson Rouge, SCOPE Invest, Foz,
 Virtual Films, Wild Bunch, France 2 Cinéma, Celluloid Dreams,
 CanalPlus, TPS Star, Soficinéma 2, Soficinéma 3
Producers: Olivier Delbosc, Marc Missonnier, Christopher Granier-Deferre,
 Genevieve Lemal, Alexandre Lippens, Tanya Seghatchian, Bernadette
 Thomas
Distribution: Wild Bunch Distribution
Direction: François Ozon
Screenplay: François Ozon, Martin Crimp, based on the novel *The Real Life
 of Angel Deverell* by Elizabeth Taylor
Cinematography: Denis Lenoir
Editing: Muriel Breton
Costume Design: Pascaline Chavanne
Music: Philippe Rombi
Cast: Romola Garai (Angel Deverell), Sam Neill (Theo), Charlotte Rampling
 (Hermione), Michael Fassbender (Esme), Lucy Russell (Nora Howe-
 Nevinson), Jacqueline Tong (Mother Deverell), Jacqueline Duvitski (Aunt
 Lottie), Christopher Benjamin (Lord Norley), Jemma Powell (Angelica),
 Simon Woods (Clive Fennelly), Alison Pargeter (Edwina), Tom Georgeson
 (Marvell), Seymour Matthews (Norley doctor), Una Stubbs (Miss Dawson),
 Jo Perrin (publisher's secretary), Ruth England (neighbor), Rosanna
 Lavelle (Lady Irania), Geoffrey Streatfield (Sebastian), Roger Morlidge
 (journalist), Teresa Churcher (governess), John Rowe (Paradise doctor),
 Edward MacLiam (Angelica's husband), Oscar Redif (Esme's son), Alice
 Hubbal (Esme's friend), Simon Smith Shrimpton (bearded man at awards),
 Roland Javornik (party guest), CinSyla Key (young aristocrat)
Color
134 minutes

Ricky (2009)
France, Italy
Production: Eurowide, Foz, Teodora, BUF, France 2 Cinéma, Coficup 3,
    Backup Films, Uni Etoile 5, CinéCinéma, Canal Plus, Le Pacte
Producers: Claudie Ossard, Chris Bolzli, Vieri Razzini
Distribution: Le Pacte
Direction: François Ozon
Screenplay: François Ozon, Emmanuèle Bernheim, based on the short story
    "Moth" by Rose Tremain
Cinematography: Jeanne Lapoirie
Editing: Muriel Breton
Costume Design: Pascaline Chavanne
Music: Philippe Rombi
Cast: Alexandra Lamy (Katie), Sergi López (Paco), Mélusine Mayance (Lisa),
    Arthur Peyret (Ricky), André Wilms (hospital doctor), Jean-Claude Bolle-
    Reddat (journalist), Marilyne Even (Odile), Véronique Joly (social worker),
    Martine Vandeville (hospital nurse), Myriam Azencot (factory guard),
    Diego Tosi (waiter), François Lequesne (factory manager), Julien Haurant
    (librarian), Eric Forterre (butcher), Hakim Romatif (salesperson)
Color
90 minutes

Short Films and Documentaries

Photo de famille (1988)
France
Producer: François Ozon
Distribution: Paramount Home Entertainment (France)
Direction: François Ozon
Screenplay: François Ozon
Cinematography: François Ozon
Editing: François Ozon
Cast: Guillaume Ozon (the son), Anne-Marie Ozon (the mother), René Ozon
    (the father), Julie Ozon (the daughter)
Silent
Color
7 minutes

Les doigts dans le ventre (1988)
France
Producer: François Ozon
Distribution: Paramount Home Entertainment (France)
Direction: François Ozon

Screenplay: François Ozon
Cinematography: François Ozon
Editing: François Ozon
Cast: Judith Cahen (the girl), Hermine Valois (the friend), Jean-Marc Cahen (the brother), Françoise Cahen (the mother)
Silent
Color
12 minutes

Mes parents un jour d'été (1990)
France
Producer: François Ozon
Distribution: Paramount Home Entertainment (France)
Direction: François Ozon
Screenplay: François Ozon
Cinematography: François Ozon
Editing: François Ozon
Cast: Anne-Marie Ozon (the mother, as Anne-Marie Godard), René Ozon (the father)
Silent
Color
12 minutes

Victor (1993)
France
Production: Fémis
Distribution: Paramount Home Entertainment (France)
Direction: François Ozon
Screenplay: François Ozon, Nicolas Mercier
Cinematography: Sylvia Calle
Editing: Thierry Bordes
Costume Design: Juliette Cheneau
Cast: François Genty (Victor), Isabelle Journeau (the maid), Jean-Jacques Forbin (the gardener), Laurent Labasse (the maid's lover), Martine Erhel (the mother), Daniel Martinez (the father)
Color
14 minutes

Une rose entre nous (*A Rose between Us*; 1994)
France
Production: Fémis
Producer: Ingrid Gogny
Distribution: Warner Home Video (France)

Direction: François Ozon
Screenplay: François Ozon, Nicolas Mercier
Cinematography: Sylvia Calle
Editing: Sylvie Ballyot
Costume Design: Juliette Cheneau
Cast: Sasha Hails (Rose), Christophe Hémon (Paul), Rodolphe Lesage (Rémy), Jacques Disses (Robert), Francis Arnaud (Yves), Gilles Frilay (the boss), François Ozon (man in the nightclub's restroom)
Color
27 minutes

Action vérité (*Truth or Dare*; 1994)
France
Production: Fidélité Productions
Producers: Olivier Delbosc, Marc Missonnier
Distribution: Warner Home Video (France)
Direction: François Ozon
Screenplay: François Ozon
Cinematography: Yorick Le Saux
Editing: François Ozon
Cast: Farida Rahmatoullah (Hélène), Aylin Argun (Rose), Fabien Billet (Rémy), Adrien Pastor (Paul)
Color
4 minutes

La petite mort (*Little Death*; 1995)
France
Production: Fidélité Productions
Producers: Olivier Delbosc, Marc Missonnier
Distribution: Warner Home Video (France)
Direction: François Ozon
Screenplay: François Ozon, Didier Blasco
Cinematography: Yorick Le Saux
Editing: Frédéric Massiot
Cast: François Delaive (Paul), Camille Japy (Camille), Martial Jacques (Martial), Michel Beaujard (the father)
Color
26 minutes

Jospin s'éclaire (1995)
France
Production: Elma Productions
Producers: No known producers

Distribution: No known distributor
Direction: François Ozon
Cinematography: Mathieu Vadepied
Editing: François Ozon
Cast: Lionel Jospin (himself)
Color
52 minutes

Une robe d'été (*A Summer Dress*; 1996)
France
Production: Fidélité Productions
Producers: Olivier Delbosc, Marc Missonnier
Distribution: Warner Home Video (France)
Direction: François Ozon
Screenplay: François Ozon
Cinematography: Yorick Le Saux
Editing: Jeanne Moutard
Cast: Frédéric Mangenot (Luc), Sébastien Charles (Sébastien), Lucia
    Sanchez (Lucia)
Color
15 minutes

Regarde la mer (*See the Sea*; 1997)
France
Production: Fidélité Productions, Local Films
Producers: Olivier Delbosc, Marc Missonnier, Nicolas Brevière
Distribution: Warner Home Video (France)
Direction: François Ozon
Screenplay: François Ozon
Cinematography: Yorick Le Saux
Editing: Jeanne Moutard
Music: Éric Neveux
Cast: Sasha Hails (Sasha), Marina de Van (Tatiana), Samantha (Sioffra, Sasha's
    daughter), Paul Raoux (Sasha's husband), Nicolas Brevière (man in the
    woods)
Color
52 minutes

Scènes de lit (*Bed Scenes*; 1998)
France
Production: Local Films
Producer: Nicolas Brevière
Distribution: Warner Home Video (France)

Direction: François Ozon
Screenplay: François Ozon
Cinematography: Yorick Le Saux, Mathieu Vadepied
Editing: François Ozon
Cast: Valérie Druguet (the prostitute in "Black Hole"), François Delaive (the john in "Black Hole"), Camille Japy (the woman in "Mr. Clean"), Philippe Dajoux (the man in "Mr. Clean"), Evelyne Ker (the woman in "Madame"), Loïc Even (the nineteen-year-old in "Madame"), Lucia Sanchez (the woman in "Heads or Tails"), François Genty (the man in "Heads or Tails"), Pascale Arbillot (the blond woman in "Ideal Man"), Régine Mondion (the dark-haired woman in "Ideal Man"), Margot Abascal (Virginie in "Love in the Dark"), Bruno Slagmulder (Frank in "Love in the Dark"), Sébastien Charles (the gay lover in "The Virgins"), Jérémie Elkaïm (Paul in "The Virgins")
Color
25 minutes

X2000 (1998)
France
Production: Fidélité Productions, Canal Plus
Producers: Olivier Delbosc, Marc Missonnier
Distribution: Warner Home Video (France)
Direction: François Ozon
Screenplay: François Ozon
Cinematography: Pierre Stoeber
Editing: Dominique Petrot
Cast: Bruno Slagmulder (the man), Denise Aron-Schropfer (the blond woman), Lucia Sanchez (female lover), Flavien Coupeau (male lover), Lionel Le Guevellou (twin), Olivier Le Guevellou (twin)
Color
8 minutes

Un lever de rideau (*A Curtain Raiser*; 2006)
France
Production: Foz, Canal Plus, Centre National de la Cinématographie (CNC)
Producer: Cécile Vacheret
Distribution: Kino Video (USA)
Direction: François Ozon
Screenplay: François Ozon, based on the play *Un incompris* by Henri de Montherlant
Cinematography: Yorick Le Saux
Editing: Muriel Breton
Costume Design: Pascaline Chavanne, Louise Hamel, Samir N'Khili

Cast: Mathieu Amalric (Pierre), Louis Garrel (Bruno), Vahina Giocante (Rosette)
Color
30 minutes

Note: Ozon's shorts *Une goutte de sang, Le trou madame, Peau contre peau, Deux plus un* (all made in 1991), and *Thomas reconstitué* (1992) are Fémis-produced films that were never distributed.

Abeel, Erica. "François Ozon on *Swimming Pool:* Fantasy, Reality, Creation." *IndieWire.* SnagFilms LLC. 2 July 2003. http://www.indiewire.com/article/ francois_ozon_on_swimming_pool_fantasy_reality_creation.

Alion, Yves. "Entretien avec Marina de Van, coscénariste de *8 femmes.*" *L'avant-scène cinéma* 513 (June 2002): 91–93.

Asibong, Andrew. *François Ozon.* Manchester: Manchester University Press, 2008.

————. "Meat, Murder, Metamorphosis: The Transformational Ethics of François Ozon." *French Studies* 59.2 (2005): 203–15.

Barthes, Roland. *Camera Lucida: Reflections on Photography.* Trans. Richard Howard. New York: Hill and Wang, 1981.

Bégaudeau, François. "*Le temps qui reste* de François Ozon." *Cahiers du cinéma* 607 (Dec. 2005): 66–67.

Benshoff, Harry, and Sean Griffin. *Queer Cinema, the Film Reader.* London: Routledge, 2004.

Beugnet, Martine. *Cinema and Sensation: French Film and the Art of Transgression.* Carbondale: Southern Illinois University Press, 2007.

Bingham, Adam. "Identity and Love: The Not-So-Discreet Charm of François Ozon." *Kinoeye* 3.13 (2003): n. pag. 11 July 2010. http://www.kinoeye .org/03/13/bingham13.php.

Blouin, Patrick. "La place du mort." *Cahiers du cinéma* 554 (Feb. 2001): 76–78.

Bolton, Zoe. "Entertainment and Dystopia: Film Noir, Melodrama, and *Mildred Pierce.*" *Crimeculture* (2005). 10 July 2010. http://www.crimeculture.com/ Contents/Articles Spring05/Mildred%20Pierce.html.

Bonnaud, Frédéric. "François Ozon: Wannabe Auteur Makes Good." *Film Comment* 37.4 (2001): 52–55.

Boujut, Michel. "Femmes entre elles au bord de la crise de nerfs." *L'avant-scène cinéma* 513 (June 2002): 1–2.

Bourcier, Marie-Hélène, ed. *Q comme Queer.* Paris: Zoo, Les Cahiers Gay Kitsch Camp, 1998.

Brassart, Alain. *L'homosexualité dans le cinéma français*. Paris: Nouveau Monde, 2007.

Bruyn, Olivier de. *"Les amants criminels."* *Positif* 463 (Sept. 1999): 48.

———. *"Le temps qui reste."* *Positif* 533–34 (July/Aug. 2005): 105.

Bruzzi, Stella. *Undressing Cinema: Clothing and Identity in the Movies*. London: Routledge, 1997.

Burdeau, Emmanuel. *"Angel* de François Ozon." *Cahiers du cinéma* 621 (Mar. 2007): 33–34.

Butler, Judith. *Gender Trouble: Feminism and the Subversion of Identity*. London: Routledge, 1990.

Cardullo, Bert. "The Space of Time, the Sound of Silence." *Hudson Review* 55.3 (2002): 473–80.

Cavitch, Max. "Sex after Death: François Ozon's Libidinal Invasions." *Screen* 48.3 (2007): 313–26.

Charcossey, Laure. "Les magiciens d'Ozon." *Cahiers du cinéma* 556 (Apr. 2001): 44–45.

Chilcoat, Michelle. "Queering the Family in François Ozon's *Sitcom*." Griffiths, 23–33.

Ciment, Michel, and Yann Tobin. "Entretien, Charlotte Rampling: Vous me donnerez ce que vous avez derrière les yeux." *Positif* 507 (May 2003): 10–15.

Cixous, Hélène. "The Laugh of the Medusa." *Signs* 1.4 (1976): 875–93.

Darke, Chris. "The Young French Cinema: On French Film in the 1990s." *Light Readings: Film Criticism and Screen Arts*. London: Wallflower, 2000. 154–58.

Defoy, Stéphane. "La solitude apprivoisée." *Cinébulles* 24.3 (2006): 58–59.

Delabre, Anne, and Didier Roth-Bettoni. *Le cinéma français et l'homosexualité*. Paris: Danger public, 2008.

De Lauretis, Teresa. *Alice Doesn't: Feminism, Semiotics, Cinema*. Bloomington: Indiana University Press, 1984.

Delcroix, Olivier. "L'ange du bizarre de François Ozon." *Le Figaro* 11 Feb. 2009: 31.

Delmotte, Benjamin. "Entretien avec François Ozon." *L'avant-scène cinéma* 513 (June 2002): 87–90.

———. "François Ozon: Le même et l'autre." *L'avant-scène cinéma* 513 (June 2002): 83–85.

Douchet, Jean. "Dix sur dix." *Cahiers du cinéma* 602 (June 2005): 67.

Douin, Jean-Luc. "Chronique d'une mort annoncée." *Le Monde* 30 Nov. 2005: n. pag. 11 July 2010. http://www.lemonde.fr/cinema/article/2005/11/29/le-temps-qui-reste-chronique-d-une-mort-annoncee_715531_3476.html.

———. *"Ricky:* Et le bébé s'envola." *Le Monde* 10 Feb. 2009: n. pag. 28 July 2010. http://www.lemonde.fr/cinema/article/2009/02/10/ricky-et-le-bebe-s-envola_1153321_3476.html.

Ehrenstein, David. "They Sing, They Dance, They Kill." *Advocate* 873 (1 Oct. 2002): 60.

Elia, Maurice. "*Sitcom:* Jouissons en choeur." *Séquences* 199 (Nov.-Dec. 1998): 48.

Eng, David L., and David Kazanjian, eds. "Introduction: Mourning Remains." *Loss: The Politics of Mourning*. Berkeley: University of California Press, 2003. 1–25.

Enjolras, Laurence. "Étale visuelle, ressac textuel: *Regarde la mer* de François Ozon." *Contemporary French and Francophone Studies* 11.1 (2007): 47–57.

Falcon, Richard. "Reality Is Too Shocking." *Sight and Sound* 9.1 (1999): 10–13.

———. "*Water Drops on Burning Rocks*." *Sight and Sound* 10.11 (2000): 64.

Fassbinder, Rainer Werner. *Gouttes dans l'océan/Anarchie en Bavière*. Trans. Jean-François Poirier. Paris: L'Arche, 1987.

Forbes, Jill. *The Cinema in France: After the New Wave*. Bloomington: Indiana University Press, 1992.

Frodon, Jean-Michel. "Un séducteur expérimental." *Le Monde* 6 Feb. 2002: n. pag. 29 July 2008. http://www.lemonde.fr.

Gilbey, Ryan. "*Criminal Lovers*." *Sight and Sound* 13.7 (2003): 38–39.

———. "*Swimming Pool*." *Sight and Sound* 13.10 (2003): 64–66.

———. "*Time to Leave*." *British Film Institute*. May 2006: n. pag. 11 July 2010. http://bfi.org.uk/sightandsound/review/3229.

Gorin, François. "*Regarde la mer*." *Télérama* 6 Dec. 1997: n. pag. 8 Dec. 2008. http://www.telerama.fr.

———. "Vive le déguisement!" *Télérama* 15 Mar. 2000: n. pag. 14 July 2008. http://www.telerama.fr.

Goudet, Stéphane. "Le court métrage en France: François Ozon." *Positif* 432 (Feb. 1997): 93–95.

———. "*Regarde la mer*: Projections scandaleuses." *Positif* 442 (Dec. 1997): 58–59.

———. "*Swimming Pool*: Millefeuille." *Positif* 507 (May 2003): 16–17.

Griffiths, Robin, ed. *Queer Cinema in Europe*. Bristol: Intellect, 2008.

Guest, Katy. "*The Darkness of Wallis Simpson* by Rose Tremain: Modernist Fairy Tales of Motherless Children and Childless Mothers." *Independent* 14 Nov. 2005: n. pag. 11 July 2010. http://www.independent.co.uk/arts-entertainment/books/reviews/the-darkness-of-wallis-simpson-by-rose-tremain-515284.html.

Hain, Mark. "Explicit Ambiguity: Sexual Identity, Hitchcockian Criticism, and the Films of François Ozon." *Quarterly Review of Film and Video* 24.3 (2007): 277–88.

Handyside, Fiona. "Melodrama and Ethics in François Ozon's *Gouttes d'eau sur pierres brûlantes/Water Drops on Burning Rocks* (2000)." *Studies in French Cinema* 7.3 (2007): 207–18.

Hanson, Ellis. "Introduction: Out Takes." *Out Takes: Essays on Queer Theory and Film*. Durham, N.C.: Duke University Press, 1999. 1–19.

Higuinen, Erwan. "Avoir un projet d'avance." *Cahiers du cinéma* 544 (Mar. 2000): 39–41.

———. "*Gouttes d'eau sur pierres brûlantes.*" *Cahiers du cinéma* 544 (Mar. 2000): 40.

Icher, Bruno. "*Ricky:* Ozon bat de l'aile." *Libération* 11 Feb. 2009: n. pag. 11 July 2010. http://www.liberation.fr/cinema/0101318578-ricky-ozon-bat-de-l-aile.

Ince, Kate, ed. "François Ozon's Cinema of Desire." *Five Directors: Auteurism from Assayas to Ozon.* Manchester: Manchester University Press, 2008. 112–34.

———. "Queering the Family? Fantasy and the Performance of Sexuality and Gay Relations in French Cinema, 1995–2000." *Studies in French Cinema* 2.2 (2002): 90–97.

Jeancolas, Jean-Pierre. "Sitcom." *Positif* 448 (June 1998): 44.

Jeanne, Boris. "Filmographie." *Cinéastes* 2 (Jan.-Mar. 2000): 16–17.

Johnston, Cristina. "Representations of Homosexuality in 1990s Mainstream French Cinema." *Studies in French Cinema* 2.1 (2002): 23–31.

Johnston, Sheila. "Death Every Day." *Sight and Sound* 11.4 (2001): 12–13.

Jousse, Thierry. "Ozon!" *Cahiers du cinéma* 505 (Sept. 1996): 12.

———. "Sans toit ni loi." *Cahiers du cinéma* 519 (Dec. 1997): 66–67.

Knecht, Susan. "The Nightmare in the Fairy Tale: François Ozon's *Criminal Lovers.*" *Bright Lights Film Journal* 30 (Oct. 2000): n. pag. 11 July 2010. http://www.brightlightsfilm.com/30/criminallovers.html.

Lalanne, Jean-Marc. "Les actrices: *Huit femmes* de François Ozon." *Cahiers du cinéma* 565 (Feb. 2002): 82–83.

———. "La place du père et celle du rat." *Cahiers du cinéma* 524 (May 1998): 107–08.

Landrot, Marine. "Pour: Une farce corrosive et pétillante." *Télérama* 15 Mar. 2000: n. pag. 11 July 2010. http://www.telerama.fr/cinema/films/gouttes-d-eau-sur-pierres-brulantes,49197,critique.php.

Larcher, Jérôme. "*Les amants criminels.*" *Cahiers du cinéma* 538 (Sept. 1999): 75.

Le Floch, Olivier. "François Ozon accouche d'un bébé fantastique." *La tribune* 11 Feb. 2009: 30.

Le Pacte, distributor. Press kit for *Ricky.* Paris, 2009.

"L'humour trash." *Tout va bien.* Canal Plus. 14 Apr. 1998. Television.

Lim, Dennis. "Movie Director Exploring the Family, Not Killing It." *New York Times* 14 Dec. 2009: C1, C6.

Lorrain, François-Guillaume. "Ozon a osé." *Le point* 12 Feb. 2009: 135.

Malandrin, Stéphane. "Bang Bang à Pantin." *Cahiers du cinéma* 505 (Sept. 1996): 12–13.

Martin, Michael. "Ozon Layers: The Many Faces of Cinema's Most Terrible Enfant." *Out* 26 July 2010. http://www.out.com/detail.asp?id=27130.

Marvier, Marie. "François Ozon: 'Je voulais réaliser un film sur l'écriture.'" *Synopsis* 25 (May-June 2003): 14–21, 68–69.

Maslin, Janet. "*See the Sea* (1997): A Mother, Her Baby and a Disarming Guest." *New York Times* 31 Mar. 1998: n. pag. 11 July 2010. http://movies.nytimes .com/movie/review?res=9400E5DB103AF932A05750C0A96E958260.

———. "*Sitcom* (1998): Film Festival Review: Until the Erotic Encounter with the Rat, It Was Cool." *New York Times* 9 Apr. 1999: n. pag. 11 July 2010. http://movies.nytimes.com/movie/review?res=9F03E2DE1538F93AA3575 7C0A96F958260.

Masson, Alain. "*8 femmes:* Une comédie janséniste." *Positif* 492 (Feb. 2002): 16–18.

Mayne, Judith. *The Woman at the Keyhole: Feminism and Women's Cinema.* Bloomington: Indiana University Press, 1990.

Mellini, Claire. "Osons le Boulevard au cinéma!" *Synopsis* 18 (Mar.-Apr. 2002): 50–53.

Morice, Jacques. "J'ai pris goût au péché." *Télérama* 2524 (27 May 1998): 43.

Mulvey, Laura. "Notes on Sirk and the Melodrama." In *Home Is Where the Heart Is: Studies in Melodrama and the Women's Film.* Ed. Christine Gledhill. London: British Film Institute, 1987. 75–82.

———. "Visual Pleasure and Narrative Cinema." *Screen* 16.3 (1975): 6–18.

Murat, Pierre. "Contre: Une potache postpubère." *Télérama* 27 May 1998: n. pag. 28 Dec. 2008. http://www.telerama.fr.

———. "Faire les femmes égales aux hommes en cruauté est presque un acte féministe." *Télérama* 2982 (6 Mar. 2007): n. pag. 11 July 2010. http://www .telerama.fr/cinema/15332-faire_les_femmes_egales_aux_hommes_en_ cruaute_est_presque_un_acte_feministe.php.

———. "*Swimming Pool:* Film français de François Ozon," *Télérama* 17 May 2008: n. pag. 11 July 2010. http://www.telerama.fr/cinema/films/swimming-pool,123257,critique.php.

———. "*Le temps qui reste:* Portrait d'un jeune arrogant qui va bientôt mourir." *Télérama* 30 Nov. 2005: n. pag. July 2008. http://www.telerama.fr.

Nicouleaud, Cécile. "Toujours tu chériras la mer." *Cinéastes* 2 (Jan.-Mar. 2000): 10–11.

Ozon, François. *5x2.* Paris: L'arche, 2004.

———. *8 femmes.* Paris: La Martinière, 2002.

———. *8 femmes: Scénario.* Paris: La Martinière, 2002.

———. "Entretiens divers." *François Ozon: Le site officiel.* Foz, n.d. 21 July 2010. http://www.francois-ozon.com/francais/entretiens/ozon-divers.html.

———. "Entretiens à propos du film *5x2.*" *François Ozon: Le site officiel.* Foz, n.d. 12 July 2010. http://www.francois-ozon.com/fr/entretiens-5x2-cinq-fois-deux.

———. "Entretiens à propos du film *8 femmes.*" *François Ozon: Le site of-*

ficiel. Foz, n.d. 12 July 2010. http://www.francois-ozon.com/fr/entretiens-8-femmes.

———. "Entretiens à propos du film *Les amants criminels.*" *François Ozon: Le site officiel.* Foz, July-Aug. 1999. 10 July 2010. http://www.francois-ozon.com/fr/entretiens-les-amants-criminels.

———. "Entretiens à propos du film *Angel.*" *François Ozon: Le site officiel.* Foz, n.d. 10 July 2010. http://www.francois-ozon.com/fr/entretiens-angel.

———. "Entretiens à propos de la collection DVD." *François Ozon: Le site officiel.* Foz, Dec. 2001. 10 July 2010. http://www.francois-ozon.com/fr/entretiens-collection-dvd.

———. "Entretiens à propos des courts-métrages." *François Ozon: Le site officiel.* Foz, n.d. 10 July 2010. http://www.francois-ozon.com/fr/entretiens-les-courts-metrages.

———. "Entretiens à propos du film *Gouttes d'eau sur pierres brûlantes.*" *François Ozon: Le site officiel.* Foz, Jan. 2000. 10 July 2010. http://www.francois-ozon.com/fr/entretiens-gouttes-eau-sur-pierres-brulantes.

———. "Entretiens à propos du film *Un lever de rideau.*" *François Ozon: Le site officiel.* Foz. 10 July 2010. http://www.francois-ozon.com/fr/entretiens-un-lever-de-rideau.

———. "Entretiens à propos de *Regarde la mer.*" *François Ozon: Le site officiel.* Foz, n.d. 10 July 2010. http://www.francois-ozon.com/fr/entretiens-regarde-la-mer.

———. "Entretiens à propos du film *Ricky.*" *François Ozon: Le site officiel.* Foz, n.d. 12 July 2010. http://www.francois-ozon.com/fr/entretiens-ricky.

———. "Entretiens à propos de *Sitcom.*" *François Ozon: Le site officiel.* Foz, May 1998. 12 July 2010. http://www.francois-ozon.com/fr/entretiens-sitcom.

———. "Entretiens à propos de *Sous le sable.*" *François Ozon: Le site officiel.* Foz, n.d. 12 July 2010. http://www.francois-ozon.com/fr/entretiens-sous-le-sable.

———. "Entretiens à propos du film *Swimming Pool.*" *François Ozon: Le site officiel.* Foz, n.d. 12 July 2010. http://www.francois-ozon.com/fr/entretiens-swimming-pool.

———. "Entretiens à propos du film *Le temps qui reste.*" *François Ozon: Le site officiel.* Foz, n.d. 12 July 2010. http://www.francois-ozon.com/fr/entretiens-le-temps-qui-reste.

———. "Interviews about *5x2.*" *François Ozon: Le site officiel.* Foz, n.d. 12 July 2010. http://www.francois-ozon.com/en/interviews-5x2-five-times-two.

———. "Interviews about *Criminal Lovers.*" *François Ozon: Le Site officiel.* Foz, n.d. 12 July 2010. http://www.francois-ozon.com/en/interviews-criminal-lovers.

———. Interview with Laurent Ruquier. *On a tout essayé.* France 2. 12 Mar. 2007. Television.

———. *Sous le sable.* Paris: L'arche, 2001.

———. *Swimming Pool.* Paris: L'arche, 2003.

———, and Emmanuèle Bernheim, audio commentary. *Sous le sable.* Paramount Home Entertainment (France), 2001. DVD.

———, and Bernard Giraudeau. Interview by Alexandre Devoise. *Nulle part ailleurs.* Canal Plus. 13 Mar. 2000. Television.

———, and Melvil Poupaud. Interview by Thierry Ardisson. *Tout le monde en parle.* France 2. 19 Nov. 2005. Television.

———, and Charlotte Rampling. Interview by Bernard Pivot. *Bouillon de culture.* France 2. 2 Feb. 2001. Television.

———, and Ludivine Sagnier. Interview by Daphné Roulier. *L'hebdo cinéma.* Canal Plus. 10 Mar. 2007. Television.

———, Olivier Delbosc, and Yorick Le Saux, audio commentary. *Sitcom.* Paramount Home Entertainment (France), 2001. DVD.

———, Yorick Le Saux, and Marina de Van, audio commentary. *Regarde la mer.* Warner Home Video (France), 2001. DVD.

Peck, Agnès. "Charlotte Rampling: L'ange au visage trouble." *Positif* 507 (May 2003): 6–9.

Philbert, Bertrand. *L'homosexualité à l'écran.* Paris: Henri Veyrier, 1984.

Pinter, Harold. *Betrayal.* New York: Grove Press, 1978.

Powrie, Phil. *French Cinema in the 1980s: Nostalgia and the Crisis of Masculinity.* Oxford: Clarendon, 1997.

———, ed. *French Cinema in the 1990s: Continuity and Difference.* Oxford: Oxford University Press, 1999.

———. "The Haptic Moment: Sparring with Paolo Conte in Ozon's *5x2.*" *Paragraph* 31.2 (2008): 206–22.

Prédal, René. *Le jeune cinéma français.* Paris: Nathan, 2003.

Provencher, Denis M. *Queer French: Globalization, Language, and Sexual Citizenship in France.* Burlington, Vt.: Ashgate, 2007.

Quandt, James. "Flesh and Blood: Sex and Violence in Recent French Cinema." *Artforum* 42.6 (2004): 126–32.

Rebello, Stephen. "The Shallow End." *Advocate* 894 (22 July 2003): 57.

Reeser, Todd W. "Representing Gay Male Domesticity in French Film of the Late 1990s." Griffiths, *Queer Cinema,* 35–47.

Rees-Roberts, Nick. *French Queer Cinema.* Edinburgh: Edinburgh University Press, 2008.

Régnier, Natacha, and Jérémie Renier, interviews. *Les amants criminels.* Paramount Home Entertainment (France), 2001. DVD.

Rich, B. Ruby. "New Queer Cinema." In *New Queer Cinema: A Critical Reader,* ed. Michele Aaron. Brunswick, N.J.: Rutgers University Press, 2004. 15–22.

Romney, Jonathan. "Ozon Layer: Jonathan Romney on Sex and Death in Bavaria." *New Statesman* 129.4507 (9 Oct. 2000): 44–45.

———. "Sitcom." *Sight and Sound* 9.1 (1999): 56.

Rossiter, Katherine, and Shonna Diehl. "Gender Reassignment of Children: Ethical Conflicts in Surrogate Decision Making." *Pediatric Nursing* (Jan.-Feb. 1998): n. pag. 20 Aug. 2009. http://findarticles.com/p/articles/mi_m0FSZ/is_n1_v24/ai_n18607684.

Rouyer, Philippe. "5x2 (Cinq fois deux): Comme une chanson populaire." *Positif* 523 (Sept. 2000): 28–29.

———. "Entretien avec François Ozon: L'ironie et l'émotion." *Positif* 553 (Mar. 2007): 21–25.

———. "*Le temps qui reste:* Sur la plage au crépuscule." *Positif* 538 (Dec. 2005): 22–23.

———, and Claire Vassé. "François Ozon: La vérité des corps." *Positif* 521/522 (July-Aug. 2004): 41–45.

———, and Claire Vassé. "François Ozon: Se mettre en danger." *Positif* 492 (Feb. 2002): 19–24.

Roy, Jean. "Cinéma. Entretien. Avec *Sous le sable,* François Ozon réunit Charlotte Rampling, Bruno Cremer et Jacques Nolot autour d'un deuil impossible." *L'humanité* Feb. 2001. 7 Dec. 2008. http://www.humanite.fr/2001–02–07_Cultures_-Cinema-Entretien-Avec-Sous-le-sable-Francois-Ozon-reunit.

Russo, Vito. *The Celluloid Closet: Homosexuality in the Movies.* New York: Harper and Row, 1987.

Schiller, Britt-Marie. "A Memorial to Mourning: *Under the Sand.*" *Literature Film Quarterly* 33.3 (2005): 217–23.

Schilt, Thibaut. "François Ozon." *Senses of Cinema* (Mar. 2004): n. pag. 28 July 2010. http://archive.sensesofcinema.com/contents/directors/04/ozon.html.

Scott, A. O. "*Water Drops on Burning Rocks* (2000): Film Review: "Leopold & Franz & Anna & Vera in Berlin." *New York Times* 12 July 2000: n. pag. 12 July 2010. http://movies.nytimes.com/movie/review?res=9C0DE4DB1038F931A25754C0A9669C8B63.

———. "*Time to Leave* (2005): Film Review: *Time to Leave* Shows Loneliness, Generosity, and Selfishness at the End of Life." *New York Times* 14 July 2006: n. pag. 12 July 2010. http://movies.nytimes.com/2006/07/14/movies/14time.html.

Sedgwick, Eve K. *Epistemology of the Closet.* Berkeley: University of California Press, 1990.

Séguret, Olivier. "Le prolifique Ozon réussit l'adaptation d'une pièce de R. W. Fassbinder." *Libération* 15 Mar. 2000: 39.

Sontag, Susan. "Notes on 'Camp.'" *Against Interpretation and Other Essays.* New York: Farrar, Straus and Giroux, 1967. 275–92.

Sotinel, Thomas. "La mieux, c'est cette actrice de télé, Alexandra Lamy . . ." *Le Monde* 10 Feb. 2009: n. pag. 28 July 2010. http://www.lemonde.fr/cinema/article/2009/02/10/la-mieux-c-est-cette-actrice-de-tele-alexandra-lamy_1153322_3476.html.

Straayer, Chris. *Deviant Eyes, Deviant Bodies: Sexual Re-Orientations in Film and Video*. New York: Columbia University Press, 1996.

Tarr, Carrie. *Reframing Difference: Beur and Banlieue Filmmaking in France*. Manchester: Manchester University Press, 2005.

———, with Brigitte Rollet. *Cinema and the Second Sex: Women's Filmmaking in France in the 1980s and the 1990s*. New York: Continuum, 2001.

Tesson, Charles. "Eau plate." *Cahiers du cinéma* 579 (May 2003): 48–49.

Todorov, Tzvetan. *The Fantastic: A Structural Approach to a Literary Genre*. Trans. Richard Howard. Cleveland: Case Western Reserve University Press, 1973.

Tremain, Rose. "Moth." *The Darkness of Wallis Simpson and Other Stories*. London: Chatto and Windus, 2005. 167–78.

Truffaut, François. "Une certaine tendance du cinéma français." *Cahiers du cinéma* 31 (Jan. 1954): 15–29.

Tyler, Parker. *Screening the Sexes: Homosexuality in the Movies*. New York: Da Capo Press, 1993.

Vasse, David. *Le nouvel âge du cinéma d'auteur français*. Paris: Klincksieck, 2008.

Vigié, Thierry. "Ozon reconstitué." *Cinéastes* 2 (Jan.-Mar. 2000): 8–9.

Vincendeau, Ginette. "Ageing Cool." *Sight and Sound* 13.9 (2003): 27–28.

Wild Bunch, distributor. Press kit for *Angel*. Paris, 2007.

Wilson, Emma. *French Cinema since 1950: Personal Histories*. Lanham, Md.: Rowman and Littlefield, 1999.

———. "Time to Leave (*Le temps qui reste*)." *Film Quarterly* 60.2 (2006): 18–24.

Wisniewski, Chris. "Look at Me: François Ozon's *Time to Leave* (Take 3)." *Indiewire* 17 July 2006: n. pag. 12 July 2010. http://www.indiewire.com/article/look_at_me_francois_ozons_time_to_leave.

Woolf, Virginia. *The Waves*. New York: Harcourt, 1931.

and *Mes parents un jour d'été*, 15; and
Victor, 17
Pialat, Maurice, 12, 16, 17
Piscine, La, 96–97
Pivot, Bernard, 36
Placard, Le (The Closet), 35
Poirier, Jean-François, 118
Poirier, Manuel, 147
Polanski, Roman, 25
Polnareff, Michel, 120
Potiche, 167–68
Poupaud, Chantal, 156
Poupaud, Melvil, 105, 106, 109, 162, 166;
and *Conte d'été*, 113–14
Powrie, Phil, 30, 135
Promesse, La, 60

Quandt, James, 32
queer cinema, 30, 34–36; and *Les amants
criminels*, 53–54, 58; and *Sitcom*, 46

Rampling, Charlotte, ix, 31, 115, 162,
164; and *Angel*, 139; biography of, 85,
91, 100–102; film career, 36, 81, 90, 91;
and *Sous le sable*, 36, 63, 80, 82, 126;
and *Swimming Pool*, 93, 94, 101–2, 157
Rees-Roberts, Nick, 35, 53–54, 57, 58
Refuge, Le (Hideaway), x, 155–56,
157–58, 161
Regarde la mer (See the Sea), 23–25, 45,
115, 151; and loss, 79; and *Mes parents
un jour d'été*, 15; and motherhood,
157–58; readings by film critics, 28,
32–33, 43, 93; and *Une robe d'été*, 38
Régnier, Natacha, 51, 55, 60–61
Renier, Jérémie, 51, 60–61, 63
Renoir, Jean, 17, 40, 41, 121
Resnais, Alain, 10
Rich, B. Ruby, 34
Ricky, x, 28, 115–16, 138, 140–53; com-
parison with *Sitcom*, 152–53; and
Lamy, Alexandra, 142, 146; and Ló-
pez, Sergi, 143, 147; and parenthood,
142–43, 146, 148, 151, 152–53; special
effects in, 147–48, 158–59; and Todo-
rov, Tzvetan, 150–51. *See also* Tremain,
Rose
Rideau, Stéphane, 39, 40

Rivette, Jacques, 16, 29
Rivière, Marie, 105, 114, 158, 162
Robe d'été, Une (A Summer Dress), ix,
1, 2, 5–9, 20; and *8 femmes*, 68; and
Butler, Judith, 7–8; and cross-dressing,
8–9; and gay filmmaking, 8–9, 37; and
Gouttes d'eau sur pierres brûlantes,
125, 128; and *La petite mort*, 21; and
Les amants criminels, 59; and the mu-
sical, 5; and *Regarde la mer*, 24; and
Scènes de lit, 24; and *Une rose entre
nous*, 19
Roberts, Julia, 65
Rohmer, Eric, 16, 29, 31, 131; and *Conte
d'été*, 113–14
Rombi, Philippe, 31, 98, 135, 162
Romney, Jonathan, 41, 43
Ronet, Maurice, 97
Roseaux sauvages, Les (Wild Reeds), 39
*Rose entre nous, Une (A Rose between
Us)*, 17, 18–20, 24
Rossellini, Roberto, 10
Ryan, Meg, 65

Sagnier, Ludivine, ix, 31, 156, 162; and
8 femmes, 64, 67, 68, 77; and *Angel*,
28–29; and *Gouttes d'eau sur pierres
brûlantes*, 68, 117, 124, 126; and *Swim-
ming Pool*, 4, 93, 94, 95–96, 98
Sanchez, Lucia, 31, 115, 164; and *Scènes
de lit*, 25, 27; and *Sitcom*, 40; and *Une
robe d'été*, 2
Sarris, Andrew, 29
Sautet, Claude, 67, 165–66
*Scener ur ett äktenskap (Scenes from a
Marriage)*, 129–30
Scènes de lit (Bed Scenes), 20, 25–26,
27, 31
Schneider, Romy, 10, 67, 97
Scorsese, Martin, 17
Sedgwick, Eve K., 33, 121
Sheila, 5–6, 7, 9, 68
*Sirène du Mississippi, La (Mississippi
Mermaid)*, 54, 72
Sitcom, ix, 1, 13, 33–34, 38–51; and
Freudian psychoanalysis, 49; and ho-
mosexuality, 42, 46–49; opinions of film
critics, 42–44; and patriarchy, 38–39,

49–51; and television situation comedies, 39–40
Slagmulder, Bruno, 27
Sous le sable (Under the Sand), ix, 24–25, 29, 63, 79–93; and Bernheim, Emmanuèle, 82, 160–61; and Cremer, Bruno, 80, 81, 90; and *Les diaboliques*, 92; and mourning, 64, 76, 79, 84–85, 92–93; and Nolot, Jacques, 82, 88–90; opinions of film critics, 32–33; and Rampling, Charlotte, 36, 63, 80, 82, 126; and Tainsy, Andrée, 91
Straub, Jean-Marie, 17
Sue Lost in Manhattan, 119
Swimming Pool, ix, 3, 4, 24–25, 93–105; and *Angel*, 139–40; autobiographical elements in, 96–97; dance sequence in, 97, 102–3, 135; intertextuality in, 96–99, 101–2; and loss, 76, 79, 100, 157; and *Ophelia*, 98, 100; opinions of critics and spectators, 99, 103–4; and Rampling, Charlotte, 93, 94, 101–2, 157

Tainsy, Andrée, 91
Tarr, Carrie, 30, 36–37
Téchiné, André, 35, 165; and *Le lieu du crime*, 68; and *Les roseaux sauvages*, 39; and *Les voleurs*, 72
Temps qui reste, Le (Time to Leave), ix, 13, 79, 104–15, 131; autobiographical elements in, 104–7; and Barthes, Roland, 107–9; and Bruni-Tedeschi, Valeria, 105; and Cavitch, Max, 107–8; and *Conte d'été*, 113–14; and Moreau, Jeanne, 105, 110; and mourning, 105–6, 109, 155, 156, 166; opinions of film critics, 106–7, 111–12; and Poupaud, Melvil, 105–6, 109, 162, 166
Teorema (Theorem), 41
There's Always Tomorrow, 66
Thomas, Robert, 64–65, 69, 70, 73
Thomas reconstitué, 17, 25, 164
Thomson, Anna, 4, 117, 124, 126, 127–28; and *Sue Lost in Manhattan*, 119

Todorov, Tzvetan, 150–51
Tous les garçons et les filles de leur âge, 30, 156
Tremain, Rose, x, 28, 115, 158, 164; and *Ricky*, 140–42, 143–44, 149
Tropfen auf heisse Steine (play), 116, 118–19, 123, 127–28. *See also* Fassbinder, Rainer Werner
Trou madame, Le, 17, 164
Truffaut, François, 36; and *8 femmes*, 36, 54, 71–72, 88; and *La femme d'à côté*, 72; and *La nuit américaine*, 97; and *La sirène du Mississippi*, 54, 72; and *Le dernier métro*, 72; and *Les 400 coups*, 63; and the New Wave, 29, 31–32
Tsai, Ming-liang, 92
Two Friends, 130–31

Vadepied, Mathieu, 163
Varda, Agnès, 14
Veber, Francis, 35
Vecchiali, Paul, 35
Vérité sur Bébé Donge, La (The Truth about Bebe Donge), 54, 68
Victor, 17–18, 25; and *La petite mort*, 23; and mourning, 79, 156; and *Photo de famille*, 12, 79
Vidor, Charles, 75
Vie rêvée des anges, La (The Dreamlife of Angels), 61
Vincendeau, Ginette, 101–2
Visconti, Luchino, 36
Voleurs, Les (Thieves), 72

Western, 147
Wilson, Emma, 110–11, 112, 166
Women, The, 65, 66

X2000, 20, 25, 26–28, 116

Zidi, Claude, 165
Zidi, Malik, 116, 124, 126
Zoncka, Eric, 61

Books in the series Contemporary
Film Directors

Thibaut Schilt is an assistant professor of French in the
department of modern languages and literatures at the
College of the Holy Cross in Worcester, Massachusetts.

The University of Illinois Press
is a founding member of the
Association of American University Presses.

Designed by Paula Newcomb
Composed in 10/13 New Caledonia LT Std
with Helvetica Neue LT Std display
Composed by Barbara Evans
at the University of Illinois Press
Manufactured by Cushing-Malloy, Inc.

University of Illinois Press
1325 South Oak Street
Champaign, IL 61820-6903
www.press.uillinois.edu